VALUE AT RISK:
The New Benchmark for Controlling Market Risk

PHILIPPE JORION
University of California, Irvine

McGraw-Hill
New York San Francisco Washington, D.C. Auckland Bogotá
Caracas Lisbon London Madrid Mexico City Milan
Montreal New Delhi San Juan Singapore
Sydney Tokyo Toronto

McGraw-Hill

A Division of The McGraw·Hill Companies

Library of Congress Cataloging-in-Publication Data
Jorion, Philippe, 1955-
      Value at risk : the new benchmark for controlling market risk /
   Philippe Jorion.
         p.   cm.
      Includes index.
      ISBN 0-7863-0848-6
      1. Financial futures.   2. Risk management.   I. Title.
   HG6024.3.J683 1997
   658. 15'5—dc20   96–21381

Printed in the United States of America
   67890DO3210987

ABOUT THE AUTHOR

Philippe Jorion is a professor of finance at the University of California, Irvine. He holds an M.B.A. and a Ph.D. from the University of Chicago and a degree in engineering from the University of Brussels.

Professor Jorion has also taught at Columbia University, Northwestern University, the University of Chicago, and the University of British Columbia. He is the author of more than 50 publications directed to academics and practitioners in finance. He also co-authored *Financial Risk Management: Domestic and International Dimensions,* a graduate-level textbook on the global dimensions of risk management. His most recent book is *Big Bets Gone Bad: Derivatives and Bankruptcy in Orange County,* which provides a detailed account of the biggest municipal failure in history.

Professor Jorion's research focuses on international financial markets. He has consulted for various institutions on managing financial risks and has particular expertise in derivatives and in global portfolio investments.

Contents

Chapter 3.

Banking Regulatory Initiatives for VAR   41

Part Two.

BUILDING BLOCKS   61

Chapter 4.

Sources of Financial Risk   63

Chapter 5.

Measuring Value At Risk   85

Chapter 6.

Fixed-Income Toolkit   103

Chapter 12.

Structured Monte Carlo   231

Chapter 13.

Credit Risk   247

Chapter 16.

Conclusions   315

PREFACE

1 THE NEED FOR VAR

Orange County, Barings, Metallgesellschaft, Showa Shell, Daiwa. . . . Some of the world's largest financial entities have lost billions of dollars in financial markets. In most cases, senior management poorly monitored the exposure to market risks. To address this problem, the world's leading banks and financial firms are turning to value at risk (VAR), an easy-to-understand method for calculating and controlling market risks.

The recent debate on *derivatives* has also brought to the forefront the issue of financial risk management. Derivatives have been viewed as dangerous financial instruments that "caused" huge losses and should be curtailed. An opposite view is that, provided they are judiciously used, derivatives are inherently stabilizing because they allow better allocation of risk. Regulators have also stated that the devotion of "substantial resources to the development of more sophisticated risk management tools . . . have had favorable spill-over effects on institutions' abilities to manage their total portfolios, not just their derivative activities." In other words, derivatives have started the revolution in financial risk management that is now leading to the widespread use of VAR.

What is VAR? VAR is a method of assessing risk that uses standard statistical techniques routinely used in other technical fields. Formally, *VAR measures the worst expected loss over a given time interval under normal market conditions at a given confidence level.* Based on firm scientific foundations, VAR provides users with a summary measure of market risk. For instance, a bank might say that the daily VAR of it trading portfolio is $35 million at the 99 percent confidence level. In other words, there is only 1 chance in a 100, under normal market conditions, for a loss greater than $35 million to occur. This single number summarizes the bank's exposure to market risk as well as the probability of an adverse move. Equally important, it measures risk using the same units as the bank's bottom line—dollars. Shareholders and managers can then decide whether they feel comfortable with this level of risk. If the answer is no, the process that led to the computation of VAR can be used to decide where to trim the risk.

No doubt this is why regulators and industry groups are now advocating the use of VAR systems. In 1995, the International Swap and Derivatives Association (ISDA) stated that

> ISDA *believes that the measurement of market risk is meaningful to readers of financial statements. The measure thought to be appropriate by most of the leading practitioners is some form of Value-At-Risk.*

VAR serves a number of purposes:

■ **Information Reporting**   VAR can be used to apprise senior management of the risks run by trading and investment operations. VAR also communicates the financial risks of a corporation to its shareholders in nontechnical terms. Thus, VAR will help speed up the current trend toward better disclosure based on mark-to-market reporting.

■ **Resource Allocation**   VAR can be used to set position limits for traders and to decide where to allocate limited capital resources. The advantage of VAR is that it creates a common denominator with which to compare risky activities in diverse markets. The total risk of the firm can also be decomposed into "incremental" VARs that allow users to uncover positions contributing most to total risk.

■ **Performance Evaluation**   VAR can be used to adjust performance for risk. This is essential in a trading environment, where traders have a natural tendency to take on extra risk. Risk-capital charges based on VAR measures provide corrected incentives to traders.

VAR is being adopted "en masse" by financial institutions and end users worried about derivatives. It is also widely embraced by the regulatory community. Generally, VAR can benefit any institution with exposure to financial risk:

■ **Financial Institutions**   Dealers with large trading portfolios have been at the vanguard of risk management. Institutions that deal with numerous sources of financial risk and complicated instruments are now implementing centralized risk-management systems. Those that do not, expose themselves to expensive failures, like Barings and Daiwa.

■ **Regulators**   The prudential regulation of financial institutions requires the maintenance of minimum levels of capital as reserves against financial risk. The Basle Committee on Banking Supervision, the U.S. Federal Reserve Bank, and regulators in the European Union have converged on VAR as an acceptable risk measure. In December 1995, the Securities and Exchange Commission issued a proposal to enhance the disclosure of market risk; the proposal would require publicly traded U.S. corporations to disclose information about derivatives activity using a VAR measure as one of three possible methods.

■ **Nonfinancial Corporations**   Centralized risk management is useful to any corporation that has exposure to financial risk. Multinationals, for instance, have cash inflows and outflows denominated in many currencies and suffer from adverse currency swings. VAR also applies to firms that need to rely on a steady stream of revenues to fund research and development; cash-flow-at-risk analysis can be used to tell how likely a firm will be to face a critical shortfall of funds. VAR allows such corporations to uncover their exporsure to financial risk, which is the first step toward an informed hedging policy.

■ **Asset Managers**   Institutional investors are now turning to VAR to better control financial risks. The $12.5 billion pension fund for Chrysler, for instance, recently purchased a risk analysis system. The director of the fund stated that[1]

> *We can now view our total capital at risk on a portfolio basis, by asset class and by individual manager. Our main goal was to . . . have the means to evaluate our portfolio risk going forward.*

In the end, the greatest benefit of VAR probably lies in the imposition of a structured methodology for critically thinking about risk. Institutions that go through the process of computing their VAR are forced to confront their exposure to financial risk and set up an independent risk-management function supervising the front and back offices. Thus the process of getting to VAR may be as important as the number itself. Indeed, judicious use of VAR may have avoided many of the financial disasters experienced over the past years. There is no doubt that VAR is here to stay.

2 PURPOSE OF THE BOOK

The purpose of this book is to provide a step-by-step approach to value at risk. While some of the concepts behind VAR are not new, currently no single book provides a consistent treatment of the topic. This may be because interest in VAR has exploded in the last two years only, no doubt as a result of the derivatives debate and discussions of capital requirements by bank regulators. Also, the computation of VAR is now made possible with the increased computer power necessary to run complex simulations. This is why a uniform treatment of the topic is needed, starting from the ground up, with the single purpose of explaining how to compute VAR.

The target audience for this book is composed of professionals who are interested in a comprehensive analysis of VAR methods. This book can also serve as a text for advanced graduate seminars on risk management, which are now being created in many business schools.

---

1. *Risk* (October 1995).

To reap maximum benefit from this book, readers should have had the equivalent of an MBA-level investment class. In particular, readers should have some familiarity with concepts of probability distribution, statistical analysis, and portfolio risk; prior exposure to derivatives and the fixed-income market is also a plus. The book provides a brief review of these concepts, then extends the analysis in the direction of measuring aggregate financial risks.

The variety of these topics reflects the fundamental nature of risk management, which is *integration*. Risk managers must be thoroughly familiar with a variety of financial markets, with the intricacies of the trading process, and with financial and statistical modeling. Risk management integrates fixed-income markets, currency markets, equity and commodity markets. In each of these, financial instruments must be decomposed into fundamental building blocks, then reassembled for risk measurement purposes. All of this information coalesces into one single number, a firm's VAR.

The approach to this book reflects the trend and motivation to VAR. As VAR is based on firm scientific foundations, I have adopted a rigorous approach to the topic. Yet the presentation is kept short and entertaining. Whenever possible, important concepts are illustrated with examples. In particular, the recent string of financial disasters provides a wealth of situations that illustrate various facets of financial risks. My hope is that these can serve as powerful object lessons in the need for better risk management.

3 STRUCTURE OF THE BOOK

The book is broadly divided into four parts:

1. **Motivation.** Chapters 1 to 3 describe the evolving environment that is now leading to the widespread acceptance of VAR.
2. **Building Blocks.** Chapters 4 to 9 review statistical and financial concepts underlying risk measurement systems.
3. **Value-at-Risk Systems.** Chapters 10 to 13 compare and analyze in detail various approaches to VAR.
4. **Risk Management Systems.** Chapters 14 to 16 discuss the implementation of VAR systems, as well as common pitfalls in risk management.

Going into more detail concerning the structure of the book, Chapter 1 shows how the need for risk management led to the growth of the derivatives markets. The chapter describes the types of financial risks facing corporations and provides a brief introduction to VAR.

Chapter 2 draws lessons from recent financial disasters. It presents the stories of Barings, Metallgesellschaft, Orange County, and Daiwa. The only constant across these hapless cases is the absence of consistent risk-management policies. These losses have led to increasing regulatory activity as well as notable private-sector responses, such as J. P. Morgan's RiskMetrics[2] system and Bankers Trust's RAROC 2020[3] system.

Chapter 3 analyzes recent regulatory initiatives for using VAR. We discuss the Basle agreement and the Capital Adequacy Directive imposed by the European Union, both of which use VAR to determine minimum capital requirements for commercial banks. The regulation of other institutions, pension funds, insurance companies and securities firms is also briefly presented.

Chapter 4 explains how to characterize financial risks. We discuss risk and returns and the statistical concepts that underlie the measurement of VAR. Initially, only one source of financial risk is considered.

Chapter 5 turns to a formal definition of VAR. We show how VAR can be estimated from a normal distribution or from a completely general distribution. The chapter also discusses the effect of quantitative parameters such as the confidence level and target horizon.

The basic insight of finance theory is that securities can generally be broken down into elementary building blocks. As the next three chapters show, this decomposition is useful for pricing purposes and also to understand risk. Chapter 6 provides a fixed-income toolkit essential to understanding the risk of fixed-income instruments. We describe the term structure of interest rates and show how a fixed-income portfolio can be valued from a sequence of cash flows. These cash flows form the basis for a uniform risk-measurement system.

Chapter 7 describes derivatives, including forwards/futures, swaps, and options. We review the pricing of each instrument, and show how derivatives can be decomposed into VAR building blocks.

Chapter 8 turns to portfolio risk. We discuss variances, correlations, and contributions to portfolio risk. Given that the dimensions of VAR risk structures can quickly become cumbersome, we also discuss methods to simplify the covariance matrix used in VAR computations.

---

2. RiskMetrics is a trademark of J. P. Morgan.
3. RAROC and RAROC 2020 are trademarks of Bankers Trust.

Chapter 9 discusses the measurement of dynamic inputs. The chapter covers the latest developments in the modeling of volatility and correlations, including moving averages and GARCH. Particular attention is paid to the model used by RiskMetrics.

The next four chapters then turn to the measurement of VAR for complex portfolios. Chapter 10 first compares the different methods available to compute VAR. The first and easiest method is the *delta-normal* approach, which assumes that all instruments are linear combinations of primitive factors and relies on "delta" valuation. For nonlinear instruments, however, the linear approximation is inadequate. Instead, risk should be measured by a "full" valuation method, which includes the *historical-simulation* method, *stress-testing*, and *structured Monte Carlo* simulations. The chapter discusses the pros and cons of each method, as well as situations where some methods are more appropriate.

Chapter 11 develops applications of the delta-normal method, sometimes called *variance–covariance* method. We show how to decompose portfolios of bonds, derivatives, and equities into sets of payoffs on "primitive" factors for the purpose of computing VAR.

Chapter 12 discusses a different approach to VAR, structured Monte Carlo (SMC) analysis. SMC simulates future sources of uncertainty with random numbers, from which complex portfolios can be priced. Because of its flexibility, SMC is by far the most powerful method to compute value at risk. It can potentially account for a wide range of risks, including price risk, volatility risk, credit risk, and model risk. This flexibility, however, comes at a heavy cost in terms of intellectual and systems development.

Chapter 13 tackles an increasingly important topic, the quantitative measurement of credit risk. Credit risk encompasses both default risk and market risk. The potential loss on a derivatives contract, for instance, depends on both the value of the contract and the possibility of default. We show how to adapt SMC methods to account for the possibility of default.

Chapter 14 illustrates applications of VAR to financial risk management. We show how to use VAR as an information reporting tool, as a resource allocation tool, and as a performance evaluation tool. The chapter also discusses integration of front and back offices through a "middle" office devoted to centralized risk management. Although integration of these functions presents information technology challenges, such systems allow corporations to monitor risks closely, which decreases the possibility of fraud by rogue traders.

Chapter 15 presents risk management guidelines that should accompany the implementation of a VAR system. Guidelines such as those proposed by the Group of Thirty are essential protection for any corporation exposed to financial risk. The chapter also discusses pitfalls in the interpretation of value at risk and remaining risks, nonetheless important, that are not covered by VAR systems.

Finally, Chapter 16 offers some concluding thoughts. We describe the steps leading us to VAR. This provides an interesting reflection of the evolution of modern financial management and suggests future developments.

4 ACKNOWLEDGMENTS

This book has benefited from the comments of numerous market observers. In particular, I would like to thank James Overdahl, of the Office of the Comptroller and Currency, for his detailed analysis of an early version of the book. This project has also benefited from the help of Lester Seigel, who initiated a continuing education program in finance at the Treasury Group at the World Bank; I am thankful to seminar participants for their insightful feedback. Finally, I would like to acknowledge the help of Jacob Boudoukh, of New York University, and Eli Talmor, of UC–Irvine. Needless to say, the author is responsible for any remaining errors.

5 WHY THIS BOOK?

This book is an outgrowth of my experience as a taxpayer in Orange County. The Orange County Investment Pool, a portfolio of $7.5 billion belonging to municipal investors, including the county, cities, and schools, lost $1.64 billion in December 1994. This led to the largest municipal failure in history. As the financial disaster unfolded, the first question on everybody's lips was, How could this have happened? Later, many people asked, How could this have been avoided?

Although the details of the Orange County investment portfolio were available to the public on a regular basis, the market risks incurred by the county treasurer were not transparently explained to investors. It soon became clear to me that, had a value-at-risk system been in place, the Orange County crisis would possibly have been avoided. Regular publication of a VAR number would have effectively communicated market risks to nontechnical investors. This is why I decided to write this book.

My hope is that this book will help foster a safer environment in financial markets.

Philippe Jorion
Irvine, California

PART ONE

Motivation

CHAPTER 1

The Need for Risk Management

All of life is the management of risk, not its elimination.

Walter Wriston, former chairman of Citicorp

Corporations are in the business of managing risks. The most adept ones succeed, others fail. Whereas some firms passively accept financial risks, others attempt to create a competitive advantage by judicious exposure to financial risks. In both cases, however, these risks should be carefully monitored because of their potential for damage.

This chapter is motivated by the need for careful management of financial risks. Section 1 describes the types of risks facing corporations and argues that, since the breakdown of the fixed exchange rate system, financial risks have sharply increased. The derivatives markets have grown in response to the need to manage these risks, as described in Section 2. The main purpose of value at risk (VAR) systems is to address market risks. However, corporations are also subject to other types of financial risks, which are discussed in Section 3. Finally, Section 4 provides a brief introduction to VAR.

1 RISKS

What exactly is risk? *Risk* can be defined as the volatility of unexpected outcomes, generally the value of assets or liabilities of interest. Corporations are exposed to three types of risks: business, strategic, and financial risks.

Business risks are those that the corporation willingly assumes to create a competitive advantage and add value for shareholders. Business, or operating, risk pertains to the product market in which a firm operates, and includes technological innovations, product design, and marketing.

3

Operating leverage, involving the degree of fixed versus variable costs, is also largely a choice variable. Judicious exposure to business risk is a "core competency" of all business activity.

In contrast, *strategic risks* are those resulting from fundamental shifts in the economy or political environment. Such an example was the rapid disappearance of the threat of the Soviet Union in the late 1980s, which led to a gradual build-down of defense spending, directly affecting defense industries. Another example is the negative sentiment against derivatives that started to surface in 1992 and led to a reduction in business activity in which derivatives dealers were caught. Expropriation and nationalization also fall under the umbrella of strategic risks. These risks are difficult to hedge, except by diversifying across business lines and countries.

Financial risks relate to possible losses in financial markets. Movements in financial variables such as interest rates and exchange rates create risks for most corporations. Exposure to financial risks can be carefully optimized so that firms can concentrate on what they do best—manage exposure to business risks. In contrast to industrial corporations, the primary function of financial institutions is to manage financial risks actively; banks now realize that they must precisely measure sources of risk as a prelude to controlling and properly pricing risks. Understanding risk means that financial managers can consciously plan for the consequences of adverse outcomes and, by so doing, be better prepared for the inevitable uncertainty; thus they can offer better prices for managing risks than the competition. Risk management is the process by which various risk exposures are identified, measured, and controlled. In sum, financial risk management has become a tool essential to the survival of all business activity.

1.1 Change: The Only Constant

The single most important reason for the growth of the risk management industry is the volatility of financial variables.

Consider the following developments:

- The fixed exchange rate system broke down in 1971, leading to flexible and volatile exchange rates.
- The oil-price shocks, starting in 1973, were accompanied by high inflation and wild swings in interest rates.
- On Black Monday, October 19, 1987, U.S. stocks collapsed by 23 percent, wiping out $1 trillion in capital.

- The drive toward economic and monetary unification in Europe was stalled by the blow-up in the European Monetary System in September 1992.

- In the bond debacle of 1994, the Federal Reserve Bank, after having kept interest rates low for three years, started a series of six consecutive interest rate hikes that erased $1.5 trillion in global capital.

- Japanese stock prices fell, with the Nikkei index sliding from 39,000 at the end of 1989 to 17,000 three years later. A total of $2.7 trillion in capital was lost, leading to an unprecedented financial crisis in Japan.

The only constant across all these events is their unpredictability. Each time, market observers were aghast at the rapidity of these changes. These events have had profound effects on financial markets and on corporations, global and domestic alike. Financial risk management provides a partial protection against such sources of risk. To illustrate the forces of change in the last 30 years, Figures 1–1 to 1–4 display movements in the dollar, in interest rates, in oil prices, and in stock prices since 1962.

Figure 1–1 graphs movements in the U.S. dollar against the Deutsche mark (DM), the Japanese yen (JY), and the British pound (BP). In 30 years, the dollar has lost about two-thirds of its value against the yen and mark: the yen/$ rate has slid from 361 to less than 100, and the mark/$ rate has fallen from 4.2 to 1.5. The dollar, however, has appreciated by 75 percent against the pound over the same period. In between, the dollar has reached dizzying heights, just to fall to unprecedented lows, thereby creating wild swings in the competitive advantage of nations—and nightmares for unhedged firms.

Figure 1–2 also shows that bond yields have widely fluctuated in the 1980s, reflecting creeping inflationary pressures spreading throughout national economies. These were created in the 1960s by the United States, trying to finance the Vietnam War as well as a domestic government assistance program, and spread to other countries through the rigid mechanism of fixed exchange rates. Eventually, the persistently high U.S. inflation led to the breakdown of the fixed exchange rate system and a sharp fall in the value of the dollar. In October 1979, the Federal Reserve Bank forcefully attempted to squash inflation. Interest rates immediately shot up, became more volatile, and led to a sustained appreciation of the dollar. Bond yields increased from 4 percent in the early 1960s to 15 percent at the height of the monetarist squeeze on the money supply, thereby creating havoc for

FIGURE 1–1

Movements in the Dollar

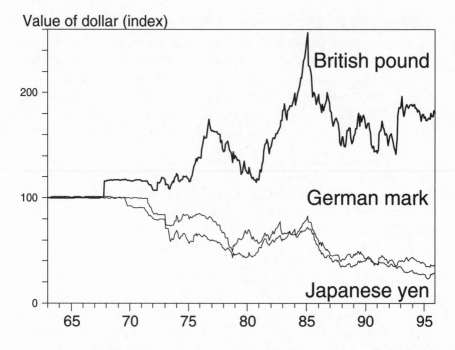

Value of dollar (index)

savings and loans that had made long-term loans, primarily for housing, using short-term funding.

Figure 1–3 shows that the sharp increases in the price of oil in the 1970s are correlated with increases in bond yields. These also had an impact on the value of national stock markets, displayed in Figure 1–4.[1] The great bear market of 1974–1975 was a global occurrence triggered by a threefold increase in the price of crude oil. This episode shows that it is difficult to understand financial risk without a good grasp of the links between interest rates, exchange rates, commodity prices, and stock markets.

In addition to this unleashed volatility, firms generally have become more sensitive to movements in financial variables. Before the 1970s, banks were either heavily regulated or comfortably cartelized in most industrial countries. Regulations such as ceilings on interest rate deposits effectively insulated bankers from movements in interest rates. Industrial

---

1. The graph displays Morgan Stanley stock market indexes in local currency with no dividends.

FIGURE 1–2

Movement in U.S. Interest Rates

10-Year yield

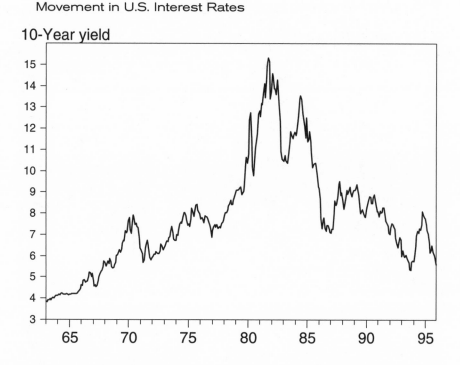

corporations, selling mainly in domestic markets, were not too concerned about exchange rates.

The call to reality came with deregulation and globalization. Deregulation forced financial institutions to pay more attention to the financial markets. Increased trade forced firms to recognize the truly global nature of competition. As a result, corporations cannot afford to ignore financial risks any more.

1.2 Risk Management

This unleashed volatility has created a new field of finance, *financial engineering*, which aims at providing creative ways to protect against, or speculate on, financial risks. Table 1–1 illustrates the expansion of risk-management tools since the early 1970s.

These *derivatives* provide a mechanism through which institutions can efficiently hedge themselves against financial risks. Hedging financial risks is similar to purchasing insurance; it provides insurance against the

FIGURE 1–3

Movement in Oil Prices

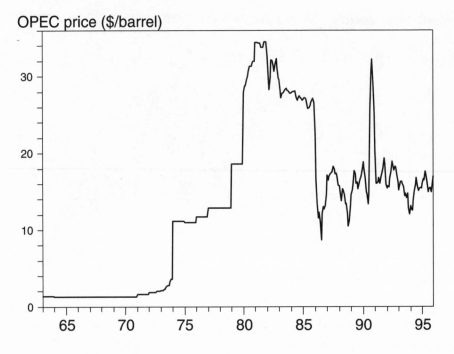

OPEC price ($/barrel)

adverse effect of variables over which businesses or countries have no control. The other side of hedging is that some of their counterparties might be speculators, who provide liquidity to the market in the hope of making profits on their transactions. Thus, risk has begotten derivatives.

2 DERIVATIVES

2.1 What Are Derivatives?

Many mistakes with derivatives stem from a misunderstanding of their basic functions. A derivatives contract can be generally defined as a "private contract deriving most of its value from some underlying asset, reference rate or index—such as a stock, bond, currency, or a commodity."[2]

---

2. For further descriptions of derivatives, see Culp and Overdahl (1996).

FIGURE 1–4

Movement in Stock Prices

MSCIP stock index

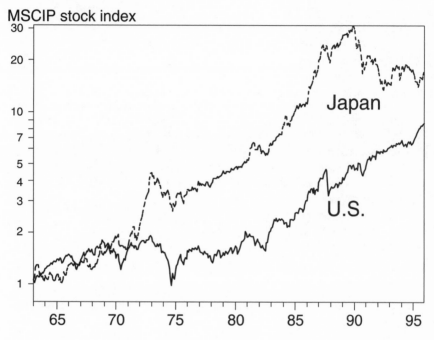

The simplest example of a derivative is a forward contract on a foreign currency, which is a promise to buy at a fixed price at some future date. Initially, the contract has a value of zero (if fairly priced), but will generate gains or losses as the exchange rate evolves over time. A cash position in the foreign currency can be perfectly replicated by a position in a short-term bill and a long position in this forward contract.

Derivatives therefore are strange animals. They separate ownership from market risks. A forward contract on an asset such as a stock involves no voting control nor dividends (until expiration), yet exposes the owner to market risks. As the initial investment can be very small, derivatives can be used to create leverage. Investors who are used to typical investments, with well-defined property rights, cannot apply their usual definitions to derivatives. Yet this forward contract is economically equivalent to holding the foreign currency (an asset) using a short position in a bill (a liability) to fund the purchase. Once this is recognized, the risk of derivatives

TABLE 1–1

The Evolution of Risk Management Tools

1972	Foreign currency futures
1973	Equity options
1975	T-bond futures
1981	Currency swaps
1982	Interest rate swaps; T-note futures; Eurodollar futures; Equity index futures; Options on T-bond futures; Exchange-listed currency options
1983	Options on equity index; Options on T-note futures; Options on currency futures; Options on equity index futures; Interest rate caps and floors
1985	Eurodollar options; Swaptions
1987	OTC compound options; OTC average options
1989	Futures on interest rate swaps; Quanto options
1990	Equity index swaps
1991	Differential swaps
1993	Captions; Exchange-listed FLEX options
1994	Credit default options

can be translated into risks of known quantities. This is one of the purposes of VAR.

2.2 The Derivatives Markets

In response to the need to manage financial risks, the derivatives markets have enjoyed explosive growth. Futures and option exchanges are now sprouting all over the world. Table 1–2 displays the growth of selected derivatives instruments from 1986 to 1994. The table shows the dollar value of *outstanding* (existing) positions in derivatives securities for which data are available, including exchange-listed derivatives and over-the-counter (OTC) swaps. From 1986 to 1994, the market for these derivatives has grown from $1,083 billion to $20,000 billion. That is, $20 trillion. A recent 1995 survey by the Bank of International Settlements (BIS) reveals that the total notional amount of OTC contracts, including forward and option contracts, amounted to $40,700 billion. Therefore, with exchange-listed contracts, these markets add up to about $50 trillion.

On the surface, these numbers are amazing. The annual gross national product of the entire United States is only about $7 trillion. The de-

TABLE 1–2

Global Markets for Selected Derivatives
Outstanding Contracts ($ billion)

	1986	1990	1993	1994
Exchange-Traded Instruments	583	2,292	7,839	8,838
Interest Rate Futures	370	1,454	4,960	5,757
Interest Rate Options	146	600	2,362	2,623
Currency Futures	10	16	30	33
Currency Options	39	56	81	55
Stock Index Futures	15	70	119	128
Stock Index Options	3	96	286	242
Selected OTC Instruments	500	3,450	7,777	11,200
Interest Rate Swaps	400	2,312	6,177	8,815
Currency Swaps	100	578	900	915
Caps, collars, floors and swaptions	-	561	700	1,470
Total	1,083	5,742	16,616	20,038

Source: Bank for International Settlements.

rivatives markets appear greater than the total value of global stocks and bonds, which is around $35 trillion. Among U.S. commercial banks only, off-balance-sheet derivatives amounted to $17.9 trillion in 1995, compared to total assets of $4.2 trillion and total equity of only $334 billion!

For risk management purposes, however, these numbers are highly misleading. The market risks of derivatives involve changes in contract market values, not notional amounts. If all these contracts were cancelled—an unlikely event—the BIS estimates that the replacement value for all OTC contracts would be only 4.3 percent of their notional amounts, which is $1.7 trillion. Value at risk precisely aims at capturing current and potential market values and provides a measure of risk that is far superior to notional amounts.

Still, the size of this market is astonishing, especially when one considers that financial derivatives have existed only for about 20 years. The first financial futures were launched in Chicago on May 16, 1972. This was a propitious time for currency futures, as exchange rates were just starting to float. Still, many observers were unconvinced of the need for derivatives. Most notably, Nobel Prize winner Paul Samuelson said the idea of currency futures would fall of its own weight, would tend to create volatility and add no net value.[3]

2.3 Why This Growth?

In general, the rationale for financial innovations follows two competing views.

One possible interpretation is that innovation is a response to changes in the *tax code* and *regulation*. For instance, zero-coupon bonds were initially created to take advantage of differences in tax rates. As the only return to "zeroes" is the capital appreciation, zeroes are beneficial if part of their return is taxed at a lower rate than regular coupon payments. In the early 1980s, zeroes were created from the "stripping" of bonds into their constituents payoffs. Since then, tax authorities have changed the tax code to bring zeroes and coupon-paying bonds into line.

Regulation can also be a powerful force for creativity. For example, the origins of swaps can be traced to parallel loans, which were created in response to British government restrictions on dollar financing by British firms. Parallel loans provided firms with the means to raise funds abroad in spite of capital controls.

The alternative view to innovations is that derivatives make markets more "complete" by increasing the opportunities for *risk sharing* among investors. Going back to the zero-coupon bond example, one could argue that this bond is a perfect hedge for an investor with a fixed liability at some future date. This explains why zeroes are still actively traded, even though their tax advantages have faded. Also, early regulations that gave the impetus for swaps have been abolished. Yet the swap market has continued to grow because swaps have evolved into remarkably flexible risk-management tools.

Therefore, it seems that derivatives are primarily risk management tools instead of regulatory avoidance tools. Indeed, in a study of recent innovations, Finnerty (1988) categorized risk reallocation as a primary factor

---

3. Powers (1992) writes a fascinating description of the introduction of currency futures by the Chicago Mercantile Exchange.

responsible for the product's introduction in a majority of cases; tax and regulatory reasons were a primary factor in a minority of cases only.

According to the risk-sharing viewpoint, three factors can be viewed as responsible for the growth of the derivatives markets:

- **Increased Volatility in a Global Economy**   The 1970s and 1980s were periods of high volatility, due to various factors, as explained previously. In addition, the globalization of financial and product markets has exposed firms to more sources of financial risks. This volatility has created a need for derivative products, which then took a permanent place in the panoply of financial instruments. Derivatives are sometimes blamed for creating volatility. As we will see, however, the most volatile period in bond markets was the early 1980s. Since most of the growth of derivatives has occurred in the 1990s, the causal relationship seems to be from volatility to market growth.

- **Technological Changes**   Technological changes have arisen from advances on two fronts: physical equipment and finance theory. On the one hand, the advent of cheaper communication and computing power has led to financial innovations, such as global 24-hour trading and on-line risk management systems. On the other hand, breakthroughs in modern finance theory have allowed institutions to create new instruments and better understand the dynamic management of financial risks. Such a model, for instance, is the celebrated Black-Scholes (1973) model, which is used to price and hedge options. The model provides a particularly elegant method to price options and by now is familiar to all derivatives traders. It has been hailed as "the most successful model in applied economics."

- **Political Developments**   Whereas governments were viewed as the principal vehicle for economic growth in the 1960s, widespread dissatisfaction with these policies led to major political changes in the 1970s. These created a worldwide movement to market-oriented policies and deregulation of financial markets. With the increased volatility of exchange rates and interest rates, financial institutions such as commercial banks and savings and loans became acutely aware of the need to address financial risks.

On the downside, the technology behind the creation of ever-more complex derivatives instruments seems at times to have advanced faster than our ability to control it. While the 1980s witnessed a rapid expansion in the types of derivatives, the 1990s should be an age of consolidation, leading to better control of financial instruments through formal risk management systems. We now turn to a more detailed description of financial risks facing corporations.

3 TYPES OF FINANCIAL RISKS

The focus of this book is on one aspect of financial risk, market risk. It should be recognized, however, that this is only one of the many sources of financial risk facing corporations. Generally, financial risks are classified into the broad categories of market risks, credit risks, liquidity risks, operational risks, and legal risks.[4]

Market Risks

Market risks arise from changes in the prices of financial assets and liabilities (or volatilities) and are measured by changes in the value of open positions or in earnings.

Market risks include *basis risk*, which occurs when relationships between products used to hedge each other change or break down, and *gamma risk*, due to nonlinear relationships. Holders of large positions in derivatives have been hurt by basis and gamma risk, even though they thought they were fully hedged.

Market risk can take two forms: *absolute risk*, measured by the loss potential in dollar terms, and *relative risk*, relative to a benchmark index. While the former focuses on the volatility of total returns, the latter measures risk in terms of *tracking error*, or deviation from the index. In addition to linear measures of risk, VAR can also capture basis risk, gamma risk, and can be extended easily to relative risks.

The primary purpose of VAR systems is to quantify market risk. Ideally, such systems should be structured to enable management to take prompt remedial action in case of losses or unusual exposures.

Credit Risks

Credit risk arises when counterparties are unwilling or unable to fulfill their contractual obligations. Its effect is measured by the cost of replacing cash flows if the other party defaults. More generally, credit risk can also lead to losses when debtors are downgraded by credit agencies, usually leading to a fall in the market value of their obligations.

---

4. For a good classification of financial risks, see the OCC *Banking Circular* (1993) on the risk management of financial derivatives.

Note that potential losses on derivatives if counterparties default are much lower than notional amounts (face value). Instead, the loss is the *change* in the value of the position, if positive when a default occurs. In contrast, corporate bonds and bank loans are exposed to the loss of the whole face value. In case of default, hapless investors can receive only cents on the dollar, sometimes after years of litigation.

Credit risk also includes *sovereign risk*. This occurs, for instance, when countries impose foreign-exchange controls that make it impossible for counterparties to honor their obligations. Whereas default risk is generally company specific, sovereign risk is country specific.

Credit risk takes the form of *presettlement risk,* described previously, and *settlement risk.* The latter refers to the possibility that a counterparty might default on a contract after one party has already made payment. This possibility is very real for foreign exchange transactions, where payments may be made in the morning in Europe against delivery in America later. Indeed, when Herstatt Bank went bankrupt in 1974, it had received payments from a number of counterparties but defaulted before payments were made on the other legs of the transaction, thus potentially destabilizing the global banking system. This bank failure was the impetus for the creation of the Basle Committee, which 20 years later promulgated capital adequacy requirements.[5]

Managing credit risk has both qualitative and quantitative aspects. Determining the creditworthiness of a counterpart is the qualitative component. Recent advances have led to quantitative assessment of credit risk. Although VAR methods best handle market risk, we will show that VAR simulations can also be used to gauge credit risk.

Liquidity Risks

Liquidity risk takes two forms: *market/product liquidity* and *cash flow/funding*. The first type of risk arises when a transaction cannot be conducted at prevailing market prices due to insufficient market activity. It is especially a problem for illiquid OTC contracts and when dynamic hedging is used. Liquidity risk, however, can be difficult to quantify and

---

5. Central bankers are growing increasingly worried about settlement risk, as curency payment volume has ballooned to $3 trillion. Settlement risk can be reduced through *bilateral netting systems,* which involve offsetting cash flows on the same value date and in the same currency between two counterparties, and *multilateral netting systems,* which allow each member bank to settle daily balances in each currency with a group of banks. An example of the latter is Multinet, which was established in 1994 as a clearinghouse for multilateral currency netting.

can vary across market conditions. Market/product liquidity risk can be managed by setting limits on certain markets or products and by means of diversification. Although liquidity risk cannot be formally included in VAR measures, orderly liquidation periods are quite relevant to the choice of the horizon for VAR measures.

The second type of risk refers to the inability to meet cash flow obligations, which may force early liquidation, thus transforming "paper" losses into realized losses. Funding risk can be controlled by proper planning of cash flow needs, which can be controlled by setting limits on cash flow gaps and diversification, as in the previous case.

Liquidity is also related to the holding horizon of the investor. Market conditions may prevent the immediate liquidation of a investment, say a collateralized mortgage obligation (CMO). Illiquidity translates into prices that are temporarily low for the CMO. If the condition is temporary, the investor could wait until market prices recover to levels close to theoretical, or model prices. In such a situation, illiquidity is a minor nuisance. However, for investors in a hurry, such as those who must sell because of the need to raise cash for collateral call payments, illiquidity can be fatal (as can be seen in Box 1–1).

Operational Risks

Operational risks refer to potential losses resulting from inadequate systems, management failure, faulty controls, fraud, or human error. This includes *execution risk*, which encompasses situations where trades "fail" to be executed, sometimes leading to costly delays or penalties, or more generally, any problem in back-office operations, which deal with the recording of transactions and reconciliation of individual trades with the firm's aggregate position.

Operational risk also includes *fraud,* situations where traders intentionally falsify information, and *technology risk,* which refers to the need to protect systems from unauthorized access and tampering. Other examples are systems failures, losses due to natural disasters, or accidents involving key individuals. The best protection against operational risks consists of redundancies of systems, clear separation of responsibilities with strong internal controls, and regular contingency planning.

Valuation issues also create potential operational problems. *Model risk* is the subtle danger that the model used to value positions is flawed. Traders using a conventional option pricing model, for instance, could be

B O X   1–1

DAVID ASKIN: A FAILED RISK-NEUTRAL STRATEGY

Some hedge funds lost heavily in the 1994 bond market debacle. David Askin was managing a $600 million fund invested in collateralized mortgage obligations. CMOs are securities obtained from splitting up mortgage-backed securities and have characteristics similar to derivatives but are quite complex to price. He touted his funds to investors as *market neutral,* in his words, "with no default risk, high triple-A bonds and zero correlation with other assets." David Askin used his proprietary valuation models to identify, purchase, and hedge underpriced securities, with an objective to return 15 percent and more to investors. The $600 million investment, however, was leveraged into a total of $2 billion, which was actually betting on low interest rates. From February to April 1994, as interest rates were being jacked up by the Fed, his funds had to meet increasingly large collateral call payments that in the end could not be met. After the brokers liquidated their holdings, all that was left of the $600 million hedge fund was $30 million— and a bunch of irate investors.

Investors claimed they were misled about the condition of the fund. In the 1994 turmoil, the market for CMOs had deteriorated to a point where CMOs were quoted with spreads of 10 percent, which is enormous. As one observer put it, "dealers may be obliged to make a quote, but not for fair economic value." Instead of using dealer quotes, Askin simply priced his funds according to his own valuation models. The use of model prices to value a portfolio is referred to by practitioners as *marking to model.*

Askin was initially reporting a 2 percent loss in February, but this was later revised to a 28 percent loss. One year later, he was sanctioned by the Securities and Exchange Commission for misrepresenting the value of his funds. He was also barred from the investment industry for a minimum of two years.

Askin's investors were victims of market, liquidity, and model risk.

---

exposed to model risk if the model is misspecified or if the model parameters are erroneous.

Unfortunately, model risk is insidious. Assessing this risk requires an intimate knowledge of the modeling process. To guard against model risk, models must be subjected to independent evaluation using market prices, when available, or objective out-of-sample evaluations.

BOX 1–2

CREDIT RISK AND LEGAL RISK

Investors who lose money on a transaction have the nasty habit of turning to courts to invalidate the transaction. One such approach is the *ultra vires* claim used by municipalities to invalidate losing transactions. The legal doctrine underlying this claim is that the investment activity was illegal because it went beyond the municipalities' powers.

The most extreme situation encountered so far is that of interest rate swaps entered by city councils in Britain. Municipalities had taken large positions in interest rate swaps, which turned out to produce large losses. The swaps were later ruled invalid by the British High Court. The court decreed that the city councils did not have the authority to enter these transactions and therefore that the cities were not responsible for the losses. As a result, their counterparties had to swallow losses amounting to about $800 million.

Legal Risks

Legal risks arise when a counterparty does not have the legal or regulatory authority to engage in a transaction. It can take the form of shareholder *lawsuits* against corporations that suffer large losses. After Procter and Gamble announced that it had lost $195 million on complex interest rate swaps entered with Bankers Trust, for example, a disgruntled shareholder filed suit against company executives. Legal risk is also directly related to credit risk, as shown in Box 1–2.

Legal risks also include *compliance* and *regulatory risks,* which concern activities that might breach government regulations, such as market manipulation, insider trading, and suitability restrictions. The regulatory framework, however, varies widely across countries and, even within a country, may be subject to changes and differences of interpretation. Imperfect understanding of regulations can lead to penalties. Regulatory risk manifests itself in enforcement actions, interpretation, and even "moral suasion."

After having described the panoply of financial risks, we now turn to a brief introduction of VAR as a method to control market risks.

4 IN BRIEF, WHAT IS VAR?

Every morning, Jim Garnett, the senior vice president in charge of global risk management at Chase Manhattan Bank, receives a neat 30-page report that summarizes the "value at risk" (VAR) of the bank.[6] The document is generated during the night by computers that quantify the risk of all the trading positions of the bank.

Today, many banks, brokerage firms, and mutual funds use similar methods to gauge their market exposure. Regulators can force implementation of this system, since they can set capital adequacy requirement based on banks' VAR. In the United States, rating agencies, such as Moody's and Standard and Poor's (S&P), the Financial Accounting Standards Board, and the Securities and Exchange Commission have all announced their support for VAR. But what is this VAR?

VAR

VAR summarizes the expected maximum loss (or worst loss) over a target horizon within a given confidence interval.

For instance, consider Figure 1–5, which plots monthly returns on medium-term bonds from 1953 to 1995.

Returns ranged from a low of −6.5 percent to a high of +12.0 percent. Now construct regularly spaced "buckets" going from the lowest to the highest numbers and count how many observations fall into each bucket. For instance, there is one observation below −5 percent, another observation between −5 percent, and −4.5 percent, and so on. By so doing, you will construct a "probability distribution" for the monthly returns, which counts how many occurrences have been observed in the past for a particular range. Such a distribution is represented in Figure 1–6.

For each return, you can then compute a probability of observing a lower return. Pick a confidence level, say $\alpha = 95$ percent. For this confidence level, you can find on the graph a point that is such that there is a 5 percent probability of finding a lower return. From Figure 1–6, this number is −1.7 percent. This is because all occurrences of returns less than −1.7 percent add up to 5 percent of the total number of months, or 26 out of 516 months.

---

6. *Institutional Investor* (February 1995).

FIGURE 1–5

Returns on Medium-Term Bonds

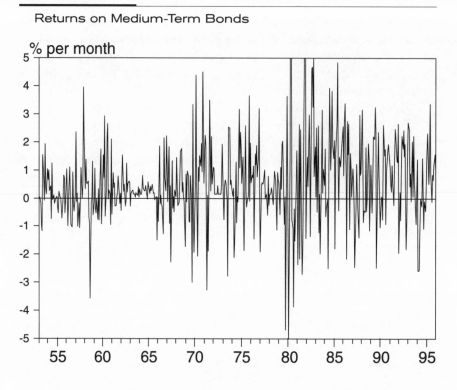

The choice of the 5 percent level is arbitrary. Commercial banks now report their VAR with various incompatible parameters. For instance, Bankers Trust uses a 99 percent level; Chemical and Chase, a 97.5 percent level; Citibank, a 95.4 percent level; Bank America and J.P. Morgan, a 95 percent level. Assuming a normal distribution, however, it is easy to convert all these disparate measures into a common number, as will be shown later.

The choice of the holding period, one month or one day, is also relatively subjective. For a bank trading portfolio invested in highly liquid currencies, a one-day holding period may be acceptable. For an investment manager with a quarterly rebalancing and reporting focus, a 90-day period may be more appropriate. Ideally, the holding period corresponds to the longest period needed for an orderly portfolio liquidation. This bank trading portfolio will be much easier to close out than a portfolio invested in stocks from emerging markets. In the former case, tens of millions of dol-

FIGURE 1–6

Measuring Value at Risk

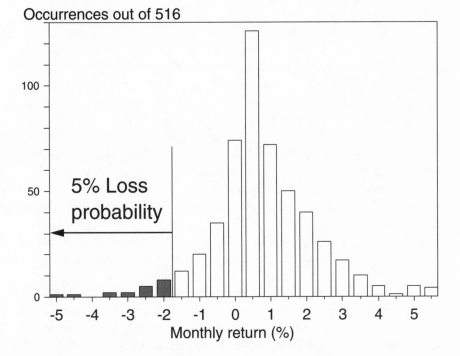

Occurrences out of 516

Monthly return (%)

lars can be transacted in an instant; in the latter case, the same amount may take days or weeks to find willing counterparts. From the viewpoint of a regulator, the horizon should reflect the trade-off between the costs of frequent monitoring and the benefits of early detection of potential problems.

Therefore, you are now ready to compute the VAR of a $100 million portfolio. There is only a 5 percent chance that the portfolio will fall by more than $100 million times −1.7 percent, or $1.7 million. The value at risk is $1.7 million. In other words, the market risk of this portfolio can be communicated effectively to a nontechnical audience with a statement such as this: *Under normal market conditions, the most the portfolio can lose over a month is $1.7 million.* Such statements would have gone a long way to avoid spectacular losses incurred by investors, who claimed they were not aware of the risk they were taking.

As we will show later, this number is directly related to the concept of duration, which measures exposure to one source of risk, interest rate risk. VAR combines the exposure to a source of risk with the probability of an adverse market movement.

The VAR approach, however, is more general, because it allows investors to include many assets such as foreign currencies, commodities, and equities, which are exposed to other sources of risk than interest rate movements. Thus, VAR is a giant step forward from conventional risk measures such as maturity, duration, or gap analysis.

This explains why VAR is fast gaining acceptance among institutions worried about financial risks. One bank has even volunteered information that greatly facilitates the computation of VAR. In October 1994, J.P. Morgan unveiled its "RiskMetrics" system. Available free on the Internet, RiskMetrics provides a datafeed for computing VAR. With the falling costs of computing power and widely available software, there simply is no excuse for not using a VAR system.

VAR is no panacea, however. VAR measures are useful only insofar as users grasp their limitations. As Till Guldimann, J.P. Morgan's head of global research, described his firm's system: "RiskMetrics isn't a substitute for good management, experience and judgment. It's a toolbox, not a black box." Thus, VAR is only an educated estimate of market risk. This does not lessen its value any more than other estimates do in other areas of science. Engineering is sometimes defined as "the art of the approximation." The same definition can be applied to risk management systems.

Finally, VAR should be viewed as a necessary but not sufficient procedure for controlling risk. It must be supplemented by limits and controls, in addition to an independent risk management function. If the widespread use of VAR leads to an increased focus on sound risk management practices, an important objective will have been met. As a market observer put it, "VAR's ultimate reward lies in advancing the risk debate about derivatives down a more constructive path."

CHAPTER 2

Lessons from Financial Disasters

Experience is a dear school.

Benjamin Franklin

Much like airplane disasters, derivatives have created much anxiety as news of spectacular losses have been splashed across headlines. These losses have spawned a flurry of legislative activity into the regulation of derivatives markets. Wall Streeter Felix Rohatyn has warned that "26-year-olds with computers are creating financial hydrogen bombs." Former House Banking Committee chairman, Henry Gonzalez, has claimed that derivatives are "a monstrous global electronic Ponzi scheme." Jim Leach, the new House Banking chairman, takes a more balanced approach, but still argues that "the sheer size of the market implies that it cannot be ignored."

Yet, disasters can occur without involvement in derivatives. Section 1 provides an overview of recent losses by corporations and in government funds, showing that derivatives losses are small in relation to the size of derivatives markets, to losses in cash markets, and to some other famous financial blunders. Section 2 goes over recent cases studies in risk, including Barings, Metallgesellschaft, Orange County, and Daiwa. These disasters are instructive, for they have one element in common, poor management of financial risks. The predictable reaction to these losses has been increased scrutiny of financial markets, in particular derivatives, by regulators and legislators. Faced with this "strategic risk," the private sector came up with a number of initiatives toward better risk management. Responses from the private sector and regulators are summarized in Sections 3 and 4. Regulations specific to financial institutions, because of their importance, are analyzed in the next chapter.

1 LESSONS FROM RECENT LOSSES

Indeed, losses attributed to derivatives have mushroomed in recent years. Figure 2–1 displays the sum of losses publicly attributed (rightly or wrongly) to derivatives since 1987. These market losses grew sharply in 1994 due to interest rate fluctuations, which created volatility in bond markets. From 1987 to 1995, these losses totaled $16.7 billion.

How significant are these losses? In relation to the size of a $50 trillion market, they represent only 0.03 percent of total notional amount, which is quite small in relative terms. On the other hand, the suddenness of losses makes derivatives look particularly dangerous. Much like airplane travel, which is actually safer than most other modes of transportation, derivatives make headlines.

As a result, a few managers, directors, and trustees have taken the extreme step of eliminating all derivatives from their portfolio. Ironically, these operations have in some instances increased their portfolio risk, as derivatives may be used to hedge risks. Further, the remaining portfolios may be producing noncompetitive returns or may be subject to higher borrowing costs, given that derivatives offer very low transaction costs. Some of these inconsistencies are apparent from the legislative backlash against derivatives at the state level: Several states have enacted bills that prohibit derivatives in local government investment portfolios yet actively use derivatives to lower their funding costs.

1.1 Corporate Losses Attributed to Derivatives

Since derivatives are particularly effective tools to hedge and speculate, they can lead to large losses if used inappropriately. Recent corporate losses involving derivatives are displayed in Table 2–1. Some foreign companies have been involved in losses above $1 billion, leading to bankruptcy in at least one case. The cases of Barings and Metallgesellschaft will be detailed in a future section.

Just focusing on these losses, however, may be misleading for three reasons. First, derivatives positions were taken in some, but certainly not all, situations as a hedge; that is, to offset other business risks. Thus, these

FIGURE 2-1

Cumulative Losses Attributed to Derivatives

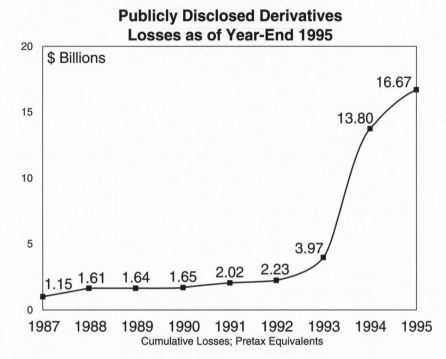

**Publicly Disclosed Derivatives
Losses as of Year-End 1995**

Source: © Capital Market Risk Advisors, Inc.

TABLE 2-1

Corporate Losses Attributed to Derivatives: 1993–1995

Corporation	Instrument	Loss ($ million)
Showa Shell Sekiyu, Japan	Currency forwards	1,580
Kashima Oil, Japan	Currency forwards	1,450
Metallgesellschaft, Germany	Oil futures	1,340
Barings, U.K.	Stock index futures	1,330
Codelco, Chile	Copper futures	200
Procter & Gamble, U.S.	Differential swaps	157

losses may be offset by operating profits. It has been argued, for instance, that the Metallgesellschaft derivatives losses were partially offset by increases in the value of oil contracts with customers. It is very important, therefore, to distinguish between losses due to outright speculation and losses due to a hedging program.

Second, the size of these losses is directly related to recent large movements in financial markets. In 1994 alone, movements in interest rates created losses for holders of U.S. Treasury bonds of about $230 billion. That is, just by buying and holding "safe" bonds, investors lost a quarter of a trillion dollars. Viewed in this context, these derivatives losses do not seem abnormally high.

Third, we should note the other side of the coin. Derivatives contracts are arrangements between two parties. Because derivative contracts are zero-sum games, any loss to one party is a gain to the other. Of course, the gainer usually complains less than the loser.

1.2 Other Recent Losses

Lest the reader think that disasters can occur only with derivatives, it is useful to point out other notable financial catastrophes in recent years:

- Bank Negara, Malaysia's central bank, lost more than $3 billion in 1992 and $2 billion in 1993 after bad bets on exchange rates. The bank had speculated that the British pound would stay in the European Monetary System (EMS). Instead, the Bank of England, under heavy attack by speculators, let sterling drop out of the EMS in September 1992. Sterling's defense has cost billions to British taxpayers. Some of the winners were hedge funds, one of which (George Soros's) is reported to have made profits of $2 billion.

- In December 1993, the Bank of Spain took control of Banesto, Spain's fifth biggest bank. Banesto had a "black hole" of $4.7 billion in hidden losses, out of a balance sheet of $43 billion; its bad loans and doubtful industrial investments were aggravated by Spain's economic slump. The bank went bust and was subsequently bought by Banco Santander.

- French taxpayers paid for the biggest-ever bailout of an individual institution in 1994. Crédit Lyonnais, the country's biggest state-owned bank, was kept afloat only with a $10 billion subsidy from the government. The bank's problems stemmed from unfet-

tered expansion and poor management. Notable among its difficulties was its large exposure to French real estate, which suffered huge losses during the 1992–1993 recession. But the bank
also suffered from investments in loss-making state-owned companies and even a troubled U.S. film studio.

- These losses pale in comparison to the cost of the savings and
  loans (S&Ls) industry in the United States, which are now estimated at $150 billion. In the 1980s, S&Ls were making long-term
  loans in residential housing that were funded by short-term deposits. As short-term interest rates zoomed up in the early 1980s,
  S&Ls were squeezed in a "duration gap." Their costs went up
  more than their revenues, and they started to bleed badly. In a be-
  lated and misconceived attempt to repair the damage, Congress
  deregulated the industry, which then strayed from housing finance
  into risky investments in commercial real estate and junk bonds.
  Eventually, a large number of S&Ls became insolvent.

- All this red ink is dwarfed by the looming financial crisis
  in Japan, where financial institutions are sitting on a total of
  $500 billion in "nonperforming" (bad) loans. Particularly trou-
  bled are housing-loan corporations, which lent heavily during
  the real estate bubble and collapsed after 1990. The Japanese financial deflation also hit the stock market, and with it, the reserves of the banking system.

In the same month that Barings failed, Crédit Lyonnais, once the
world's 12th largest bank, effectively went bankrupt, proving that derivatives do not have a monopoly on financial disasters.

1.3 Losses in Government Funds

More worrisome for the taxpayer is that many state and local government
funds have also suffered large losses in recent years. In the case of private
corporations, the shareholder is ultimately responsible for financial gains and
losses through his or her equity stake. In the case of public funds, who bears
the ultimate loss is not so clear. Should taxes be raised? Should services be
cut? Should the municipality default and lay the loss on debtholders?

The string of spectacular public fund losses in 1994 can generally be
traced to aggressive investment strategies. In recent years, municipalities
have been squeezed between ever-growing demands for services and

limited revenues. The revolt against taxes has even led to tax cuts, such as Proposition 13 in California, which created pressure on local governments to increase revenues through better management of cash reserves.

Another contributing factor was the historically low level of interest rates in 1993, when rates fell to only 3 percent. Municipalities, used to 5–7 percent annual returns, then tried various means of pumping up their portfolio returns, taking large interest rate bets or investing in derivatives and mortgages, perhaps without full understanding of the risks involved. These strategies started to unravel in February 1994, when the Federal Reserve (Fed) started the first of six sharp increases in interest rates in less than a year. Many public funds lost heavily. Table 2–2 reports recent losses (realized or not) in public funds.

With nearly 80,000 state and local government agencies having billions in public money to invest, these losses have led to renewed calls for stricter oversight of municipal funds. A recent survey by the Government Finance Officers Association has revealed that only 4 percent of its members said they were knowledgeable about derivatives and 76 percent said they had only some or no knowledge of derivatives.

There are two possible approaches to address problems in government funds: either regulate risk out of existence or allow funds to monitor their risk better. The simplistic approach is to eliminate derivatives; but then all of their benefits are lost, too.

In the wake of Orange County's fiasco, several bills were proposed in the California Senate to severely limit the range of allowed investments

TABLE 2–2

Losses in U.S. Public Funds

Public Entity	Loss ($ million)	Assets ($ million)	Percent Loss
Orange County, CA	1,640	7,400	22
San Diego, CA	357	3,300	11
West Virginia	279	1,200	23
Florida State Treasury	200	8,000	3
Cuyahoga County, Ohio	137	1,800	8
Texas State	55	3,700	1
City Colleges of Chicago	48	96	50
Placer County, CA	26	378	7

for local investment funds, including a complete ban on any derivatives. In effect, funds would have been restricted to short-term Treasury bills. Perhaps this explains why these bills were opposed by the California Association of County Treasurers, the California Society of Municipal Finance Officers, the California State Association of Counties, and many others—not a bunch of fiscal maniacs, to be sure. They argued that the additional restrictions imposed by these bills would cause an estimated loss of income of $265 million per year (to the taxpayer, of course).

2 CASE STUDIES IN RISK

2.1 Barings's Fall: A Lesson in Risk

On February 26, 1995, the Queen of Great Britain woke up to the news that Barings PLC, a venerable 233-year-old bank, had gone bankrupt. Apparently, the downfall of the bank was due to a single trader, 28-year-old Nicholas Leeson, who lost $1.3 billion from derivatives trading. This loss wiped out the firm's entire equity capital.[1]

The loss was caused by a large exposure to the Japanese stock market, which was achieved through the futures market. Leeson, the chief trader for Barings Futures in Singapore, had been accumulating positions in stock index futures on the Nikkei 225, a portfolio of Japanese stocks. Barings's notional positions on the Singapore and Osaka exchanges added up to a staggering $7 billion. As the market fell more than 15 percent in the first two months of 1995, Barings Futures suffered huge losses. These losses were made worse by the sale of options, which implied a bet on a stable market. As losses mounted, Leeson increased the size of the position, in a stubborn belief he was right. Then, unable to make the cash payments required by the exchanges, he simply walked away on February 23. Later, he sent a fax to his superiors, offering "sincere apologies for the predicament that I have left you in."

Because Barings was viewed as a conservative bank, the bankruptcy served as a wake-up call for financial institutions all over the world. The disaster has revealed an amazing lack of controls at Barings: Leeson had control over both the trading desk and the "back office." The function of the back office is to confirm trades and check that all trading activity is within guidelines. In any serious bank, traders have a limited amount of

---

1. Rawnsley (1995) wrote a detailed account of Barings's fall.

capital they can deal with and are subject to closely supervised "position limits." To avoid conflicts of interest, the trading and back-office functions are clearly delineated. In addition, most banks have a separate risk-management unit that provides another check on traders.

The Singapore and Osaka exchanges also drew some attention for their failure to notice the size of positions. On the Osaka exchange, Barings Futures had accumulated 20,000 contracts each worth $200,000. This was eight times the next largest position of 2,500 contracts. Officials at U.S. futures exchanges have stated that such positions would have attracted their attention much sooner had they been in the United States.

One of the reasons Leeson was so unsupervised was his great track record. In 1994, Leeson is thought to have made $20 million for Barings, or about one-fifth of the firm's total profits. These translated into fat bonuses for Leeson and his superiors. In 1994, Leeson drew a $150,000 salary with a $1 million bonus. At some point, the head of Barings Securities, Christopher Heath, was Britain's highest paid executive. The problem was also blamed on the "matrix" structure implemented by Barings. As Leeson's unit reported along both geographical and functional lines, the decentralization inherent in this structure led to poor supervision.

There were also allegations that senior bank executives were aware of the risks involved, and had approved cash transfers of $1 billion to help Leeson make margin calls. An internal audit drawn up in 1994 had also been apparently ignored by Barings's top management. The auditor warned of "excessive concentration of power in Leeson's hands."

The moral of this affair is summarized in a February 27, 1995, *Wall Street Journal* article:

> Bank of England officials said they did not regard the problem in this case as one peculiar to derivatives. . . In a case where a trader is taking unauthorized positions, they said, the real question is the strength of an investment houses' internal controls and the external monitoring done by exchanges and regulators.

Barings's shareholders bore the full cost of the losses. The price of Barings's shares went to zero, wiping out about $1 billion of market capitalization. Bondholders received five cents on the dollar. Some of the additional losses were borne by the Dutch financial-services group Internationale Nederlanden Group (ING), which offered to acquire Barings for the grand total of one British pound (about $1.50). Leeson was later extradited to Singapore, where he was sentenced to six-and-a-half years in prison.

2.2 Metallgesellschaft

The story of Metallgesellschaft (MG) is that of a hedge that went bad to the tune of $1.3 billion. The conglomerate, Germany's 14th-largest industrial group with 58,000 employees, nearly went bankrupt following losses incurred by its American subsidiary, MG Refining & Marketing (MGRM), in the futures market.

MGRM's problems stemmed from its idea of offering long-term contracts for oil products. The marketing of these contracts was successful because customers could lock-in fixed prices over long periods. By 1993, MGRM had entered into contracts to supply customers with 180 million barrels of oil products over a period of 10 years.

These commitments were quite large, equivalent to 85 days of Kuwait's oil output, and exceeded many times MGRM's refining capacity. To hedge against the possibility of price increases, the company ideally should have entered long-term forward contracts on oil, matching the maturity of the contracts and of the commitments. In the absence of a viable market for long-term contracts, however, MGRM turned to the short-term futures market and implemented a *rolling hedge*, where the long-term exposure is hedged through a series of short-term contracts, with maturities around three months, which are rolled over into the next contract as they expire.

As the three-month contract eventually will be rolled over into a contract that expires 10 years from now, the profits generated by the rolling hedge should converge (in 10 years) to the profits generated by buying and holding a 10-year forward contract.

In the meantime, the company was exposed to *basis risk*, which is the risk that short-term oil prices temporarily deviate from long-term prices. Over 1993, cash prices fell from $20 to $15, leading to about a billion dollars of margin calls that had to be met in cash.

Some of these losses may have been offset by gains on the long-term contracts with its customers, as the company now could sell oil at locked-in higher prices. But, apparently, the German parent did not expect to have to put up such large amounts of cash. Senior executives at the U.S. subsidiary were pushed out and a new management team flown in

from Europe. The new team immediately proceeded to liquidate the remaining contracts, which led to a reported loss of $1.3 billion. Since then,
the liquidation has been severely criticized, on the grounds that the liquidation effectively realized losses that would have decreased over time.[2]
The auditors' report, in contrast, stated that the losses were caused by the
size of the trading exposures.

In any event, the loss, the largest German postwar corporate disaster,
nearly brought the conglomerate to its knees. Creditors, led by Deutsche
Bank, stepped in with a $2.4 billion rescue package. They were asked to
write down some of their loans in exchange for equity warrants. Eventually, the stock price plummeted from 64 marks to 24 marks, wiping out
more than half of MG's market capitalization.

2.3 Orange County

The Orange County affair represents perhaps the most extreme form of un-
controlled market risk in a local government fund. Bob Citron, the county
treasurer, was entrusted with an $7.5 billion portfolio belonging to county
schools, cities, special districts, and the county itself. To get a bigger bang
for these billions, he effectively borrowed about $12.5 billion, through re-
verse repurchase agreements, for a total of $20 billion that was invested in
agency notes with an average maturity of about four years. In an environment where short-term funding costs were lower than medium-term
yields, the highly leveraged strategy worked exceedingly well, especially
as interest rates were falling.[3]

Unfortunately, the interest rate hikes that started in February 1994
unraveled the strategy. All through the year, paper losses on the fund led to
margin calls from Wall Street brokers that had provided short-term financing. In December, as news of the loss spread, investors tried to pull out
their money. Finally, as the fund defaulted on collateral payments, brokers
started to liquidate their collateral and Orange County declared bankruptcy. The following month, the remaining securities in the portfolio
were liquidated, leading to a realized loss of $1.64 billion.

County officials blamed Citron for undertaking risky investments
and not being forthcoming about his strategies. But they conveniently for-
got they were applauding Citron's track record all along. In his years in of-

---

2. This line of argument is advanced by Culp and Miller (1995).
3. Jorion (1995b) provides a detailed account of the Orange County story.

fice, he returned about \$750 million in free money to the county (over and above the state pool). These higher returns simply reflected higher risks.

The circumstances leading to the county's loss offer a striking parallel with the Barings disaster. Barings also went bankrupt because of big bets gone bad. But the main culprit was the lack of supervision of traders: Bob Citron for Orange County and Nick Leeson for Barings. In both cases, the traders had a great track record which made the life of their superiors easy. A few months before disaster struck, Barings executives sent Leeson \$850 million to cover a supposedly hedged position; in summer of 1994, the county supervisors approved a \$600 million bond issue to provide a cash infusion for Citron. In both cases, as their strategy started to turn sour, the traders shifted losses to separate accounts. One difference, though, is that Leeson reported zero risk to the bank whereas the risks of the Orange County pool were perfectly clear. The monthly statements to pool investors listed the \$20 billion position in bonds and the reverse repos. In spring of 1994, John Moorlach, running for county treasurer, had warned that the strategy was too risky and that the fund was probably down by \$1 billion. Unfortunately, Moorlach's arguments appeared to have been ignored, and he lost the election.

Citron's mistake was to report his portfolio at cost. He claimed that there was no risk in the portfolio because he was holding to maturity. As government accounting standards do not require municipal investment pools to record "paper" gains or losses, Citron did not report the market value of the portfolio. This explains why losses were allowed to grow to \$1.7 billion and why investors claim they were misled about the condition of the pool.

But regular, detailed disclosure might have saved Citron even from himself. If his holdings had been made public every month, for example, and measured at current market values, the treasurer might have recognized just how risky his investments actually were. Investors, in touch with monthly fluctuations in values, might also have refrained from the "run on the bank" that happened in December 1994. It is fair to say that, had the VAR of the portfolio been made public, investors would probably have been more careful with their funds.

2.4 Daiwa's Lost Billion

Daiwa's case provides a striking counterpart to the Barings disaster. On September 26, 1995, the bank announced that a 44-year-old trader in New

York, Toshihide Igushi, had allegedly accumulated losses estimated at $1.1 billion. The losses were of a similar magnitude as those that befell Barings, but Daiwa, the 12th-largest bank in Japan, managed to withstand the blow. The loss absorbed "only" one-seventh of the firm's capital.

Apparently, Igushi had concealed more than 30,000 trades over 11 years, starting in 1984, in U.S. Treasury bonds. As the losses grew, the bank said, the trader exceeded his position limits to make up for the losses. He eventually started selling, in the name of Daiwa, securities deposited by clients at the New York branch. The bank claims that none of these trades were reported to Daiwa and that Igushi falsified listings of securities held at the bank's custodian, Bankers Trust. Apparently, the bank failed to cross-check daily trades with monthly portfolio summaries.

As in the case of Barings, the problem arose because at some point Igushi had control of both the front and back offices. Unlike other Japanese workers who were rotated regularly, he had been hired locally. In their home market, Japanese banks rely on a group spirit that acts as an internal safety mechanism; in overseas operations, such an approach can be fatal.

This loss highlighted the poor risk-management policies of Japanese banks, which already pay a premium rate, up to an extra 0.25 percent, reflecting the nervousness over property losses in Japanese financial institutions. In many ways, the Daiwa case is more worrisome than Barings, because the losses were allowed to accumulate over 11 years, not just a few months.

The disclosure of the losses was a delayed reaction to increased supervision of foreign banks in the wake of the Bank of Credit and Commerce International's (BCCI) collapse. The Federal Reserve Board had inspected Daiwa's offices in November 1992 and November 1993. In both instances, the regulators had warned the bank about the risks in its management structure. Daiwa, however, failed to implement major changes and even reported that it deliberately hid records and temporarily removed bond traders in order to pass the 1992 inspection. Under pressure from regulators, Daiwa relegated Igushi to a back-office function. Even so, he continued to transact, hiding behind other traders. But, as bank auditors were scrutinizing the New York operation, increased oversight was making it very difficult for him to continue hiding the losses. Igushi confessed his actions in a July 1995 letter to top management.

In response to the loss, Daiwa Bank closed its New York office and top management announced in October 1995 it would be stepping down. The bank came under the wrath of U.S. regulators, who ordered the bank to close its U.S. operations, an unprecedented move. Regulators accused Daiwa of a "pattern of unsafe and unsound banking practices and violations of the law." Officials at the Japanese ministry of finance stated that, "Clearly, more disclosure is the way to go."

2.5 Lessons from the Case Studies

All of the disasters studied here involve losses in excess of $1 billion. As shown in Table 2–3, these losses were attributed to various causes: primarily rogue traders for Barings and Daiwa, market risks for Metallgesellschaft and Orange County. The only common thread across these hapless cases is the absence of enforced risk management policies.

Granted, there is no foolproof protection against outright fraud. The checks and balances provided by an additional risk management system, as well as uniform treatment of front- and back-office information, should provide a shield against rogue traders. With a good risk management system, they should be caught in a matter of days if not hours. This is why risk management systems are so invaluable in financial markets.

3 PRIVATE-SECTOR RESPONSES

The string of losses attributed to derivatives, as well as the exponential growth of the market, have attracted the scrutiny of regulators. A warning shot was fired on January 1992 by Gerald Corrigan, president of the New

TABLE 2–3

Risk Factors in Losses

	Market	Operational	Funding	Lack of controls
Barings	Yes, Japanese stocks	Yes, rogue trader		Yes
MGRM	Yes, oil		Yes, recapitalization	Yes
O.C.	Yes, interest rates		Yes, default	Yes
Daiwa	Yes	Yes, rogue trader		Yes

York Fed: "High-tech banking and finance has its place, but it's not all it's cracked up to be. I hope this sounds like a warning, because it is." These comments and the increased flurry of legislative and regulatory activity have led the private sector to come up with its own proposals.

In 1993, the Group of Thirty (G-30), a consultative group of top bankers, financiers, and academics from leading industrial nations issued a landmark report on derivatives. The report concludes that derivatives activity "makes a contribution to the overall economy that may be difficult to quantify, but is nevertheless both favorable and substantial." The general view of the G-30 is that derivatives do not introduce risks on a greater scale than those "already present in financial markets." The G-30 report also recommends guidelines for managing derivatives, which are described in more detail in Chapter 15. These sound practice principles, however, are equally valid for any portfolio, whether with or without derivatives.

A major G-30 recommendation is to value positions at market and assess financial risks using a value-at-risk system. Similar recommendations have been put forth by the rating agencies, Moody's and Standard and Poor's, and a trade group, the International Swap and Derivatives Association (ISDA).[4] The Derivatives Policy Group (DPG), formed in August 1994 to address public policy issues related to over-the-counter (OTC) derivatives, has also proposed that internal risk measures be used to establish capital guidelines for the derivative activities of unregulated affiliates of U.S. broker–dealers.[5]

Perhaps the most notable of private-sector initiatives is that of J.P. Morgan, which in October 1994 with great fanfare unveiled a new system, called RiskMetrics. The system initially made available risk measures for 300 financial instruments across 14 countries and has been greatly expanded since. Essentially, the data represent an elaborate variance/covariance matrix of risk and correlation measures that evolve through time. To produce their own VAR, users need computer software to integrate the RiskMetrics system with their own positions.

Although the system is available for free, this move is not totally disinterested. RiskMetrics is motivated by a desire to

---

4. The ISDA is an association that represents more than 150 leading financial institutions that deal in privately negotiated OTC derivatives transactions.

5. The DPG "Framework for Voluntary Oversight" for OTC derivatives (1995) also provides common standards for comparing market risk across firms. It advocates using a 99 percent VAR figure measured over a two week horizon. For further details, see Bair and Milligan (1996).

- Promote greater transparency of market risks.
- Make available sophisticated risk management tools to other potential users, especially those that cannot muster the resources to develop such systems from scratch.
- Establish J.P. Morgan methodology as an industry standard.

Also, helping financial institutions to better measure and disclose their risks may forestall heavy-handed regulatory restrictions on financial markets. Indeed, RiskMetrics has spawned an army of system developers and encouraged rival banks to develop new generations of risk management systems.

Other systems are quickly coming to the market. In contrast with RiskMetrics, which is basically a datafeed, Bankers Trust has now made available a system, called RAROC 2020, which is based on its internal risk-management experience. The RAROC system integrates the risk management calculation with volatility forecasts to produce value-at-risk measures. The system is quite sophisticated in that it can incorporate assets not normally distributed or with nonlinear payoffs, such as options and collateralized mortgage obligations (CMOs).[6]

4 THE VIEW OF REGULATORS

The explosive growth of the derivatives markets and well-publicized losses have created much concern for legislators and regulators. In 1993 and 1994, there has been a flurry of activity assessing the risks of derivatives, especially in the unregulated OTC swap markets. Since then, the unmistakable trend is toward more transparent reporting of financial risk, notably by the generalized use of VAR measures.

In May 1994, the General Accounting Office (GAO)[7] issued a widely watched report on derivatives after more than two years of study. The report states "derivatives serve an important function," but that they require careful management. Among many recommendations, the report advises financial regulators to perform regular evaluations of dealers' risk-man-

---

6. For a more detailed description, see *Risk* (October 1995).
7. The General Accounting Office is the investigative arm of the U.S. Congress, charged with examining all matters relating to the receipt and disbursement of public funds. The GAO performs a variety of services, the most prominent of which are audits and evaluations of government programs and activities.

agement systems and to provide expanded disclosure requirements for de-rivative products.

Indeed, the Office of the Comptroller of the Currency (OCC), which regulates America's national banks, has issued guidelines for the risk man-agement of financial derivatives.[8] The OCC expects national banks to fol-low this set of prudent practices.

The Financial Accounting Standards Board (FASB)[9] has issued sev-eral rules that address the disclosure and accounting treatment of deriva-tives. FAS 105, "Disclosure of Information about Financial Instruments with Off-Balance-Sheet Risks and Financial Instruments with Concentra-tion of Credit Risk," and FAS 107, "Disclosure about Fair Value of Finan-cial Instruments," were released in 1990 and 1991 and require disclosure of off-balance-sheet positions at fair market values.

FAS 115, issued in 1994, classifies equity and debt securities into three categories:

- *Held to maturity* issues, to be reported at amortized cost.
- *Trading security* issues, to be reported at market value, with un-realized gains and losses included in earnings.
- *Available for sale* issues, to be reported at market value, with un-realized gains and losses flowing to an equity account.

Later in 1994, the FASB announced FAS 119, "Disclosure about Deriva-tive Financial Instruments and Fair Value of Financial Instruments," which extends this classification to derivatives and takes effect for the fis-cal years ending after December 15, 1994. In the case of hedging transac-tions, FAS 119 also requires disclosure of the nature of the transaction being hedged. FAS 119 also encourages, but does not require, the disclo-sure of quantitative information that would help users understand the ob-jectives and risks of using these instruments—such as value at risk.

In September 1994, central bankers from the Group of Ten (G-10) countries issued a report on the public disclosure of market and credit risks by financial intermediaries (this is the same group that issued the capital adequacy requirements discussed in the next chapter.) This report, called the "Fisher Report," concluded that

---

8. OCC banking circular BC-277.
9. The FASB is an independent agency responsible for developing generally accepted accounting principles. Its legal authority to do so has been delegated by the SEC. The SEC, however, does prescribe the form of financial statement submitted to it.

Financial markets function most efficiently when market participants have sufficient information about risks and returns to make informed investment and trading decisions. . . During episodes of market stress, this lack of transparency can contribute to an environment in which rumours alone can cause a firm's market access and funding to be impaired.

The view is that public disclosure of risk can reduce systemic risks and help to stabilize the financial system. The report concludes that disclosure is highly desirable and likely to evolve to a framework that relies on VAR. Most recently, in December 1995, the Securities and Exchange Commission (SEC)[10] issued a proposal that would require companies to disclose information about derivatives activity in financial reports filed with the SEC. Registrants will be able to choose among three possible disclosure alternatives:

- A tabular presentation of expected cash flows and contract terms summarized by risk category.
- A sensitivity analysis expressing possible losses for hypothetical changes in market prices.
- Value-at-risk measures for the current reporting period, which are to be compared to actual changes in market values.

This quantitative information must be complemented by a discussion of qualitative information about market risk, including the company's primary market-risk exposure and the management of these exposures, including objectives and instruments used.

The rationale behind the SEC's approach is the general feeling by security analysts and accountants that "users are confused." Existing reporting guidelines provide insufficient detail on the scope of involvement in financial instruments and the potential effect of derivatives activity on corporate profits.

The unifying theme behind these reports and regulations is an increasing emphasis on risk management. In fact, one could argue that better control of market risk through VAR systems is a direct outgrowth of the derivatives markets. By providing tools to control market risk, derivatives will have fulfilled an important social function.

---

10. The SEC is a federal agency that has wide authority to oversee the nation's security markets. Among other things, it regulates the financial reporting practices of public corporations.

CHAPTER 3

Banking Regulatory Initiatives for VAR

The Committee investigated the possible use of banks' proprietary in-house models for the calculation of market risk capital as an alternative to a standardised measurement framework. The results of this study were sufficiently reassuring for it to envisage the use of internal models to measure market risks.

Basle Committee on Banking Supervision, April 1995

In addition to these financial disasters, the impetus behind value at risk also came from bank regulators. In their quest for a safe and sound financial system, regulators have grown increasingly worried about the potentially destabilizing effect of expanding trading activities of financial institutions. These worries stem from the increased involvement of banks in the derivatives markets, which are becoming global, more complex, and therefore are thought to run the risk of cascading defaults. To make things worse, these instruments do not show up on balance sheets.

The landmark Basle accord of 1988 provided the first step toward tighter risk management. The Basle accord sets minimum capital requirements that must be met by commercial banks to guard against credit risk. This agreement led to a still-evolving framework to impose capital adequacy requirements against market risks. In their latest proposals, dated April 1995, central bankers implicitly recognized that risk management models in use by major banks are far more advanced than anything they could propose. Banks now have the option to use their own VAR risk management model as the basis for required capital ratios. Thus VAR is being officially promoted as sound risk management practice.

Indeed banks have long recognized that managing financial risks is the natural business of financial institutions. Better risk-management systems allow them to deploy their capital more efficiently and provide a source of comparative advantage. But this extends beyond the realm of commercial banks. Securities houses are also in the business of managing financial risks. Here the trend is also, inexorably, to VAR.

This chapter presents regulatory initiatives for VAR. Section 1 discusses the rationale behind regulation of the financial sector. The 1988 Basle accord is summarized in Section 2, which is followed by the latest proposals on market risks in Section 3. These include the Basle-imposed standard model, the banks' own internal models, and the precommitment approach. Next, Section 4 describes the European Union's Capital Adequacy Directive, which is coming into force in 1996. Finally, Section 5 concludes with the regulation of nonbank financial intermediaries.

1 WHY REGULATION?

One could ask at the outset why regulations are necessary. After all, the owners of a financial institution should be free to define the risk parameters in which their company should evolve. Shareholders are putting their own capital at risk and suffer the direct consequences of failure to control market risk. Essentially, this is what happened to Barings, where complacent shareholders failed to monitor the firm's management. Poor control over traders led to increasingly risky activities and bankruptcy.

The Bank of England is reported to have agonized over the decision of whether it should bail out Barings. In the end, it let the bank fail. Many observers said this was the correct decision. In freely functioning capital markets, badly managed institutions should be allowed to fail. This failure also serves as a powerful object lesson in risk management.

Nevertheless, regulation is generally viewed as necessary when free markets appear to be unable to allocate resources efficiently. For financial institutions, this is said to be the case for two situations, externalities and deposit insurance.

Externalities arise when an institution's failure affects other firms. Here the fear is that of systemic risk. *Systemic risk* arises when default by one institution has a cascading effect on other firms, thus posing a threat to the stability of the entire financial system. Systemic risk is rather difficult to evaluate since it involves situations of extreme instability, thus happening infrequently. In recent years, however, two large firms, Drexel and Barings, failed without creating other defaults.

Deposit insurance also provides a rationale for regulation. By nature, bank deposits are destabilizing. Depositors are promised to be repaid the full face value of their investment on demand. They may then rationally cause a "run on the bank" if they fear that a bank's assets have fallen behind its liabilities. Given that bank assets can be invested in illiquid securities or real estate investments, the run will force liquidation at great costs.

One solution to this problem are government guarantees for bank deposits, which eliminate the rationale for bank runs. These guarantees are also viewed as necessary to protect small depositors, who cannot efficiently monitor their bank. Such monitoring is complex, expensive, and time-consuming for the thousands of small depositors who entrusted their funds to the bank.

One could argue that deposit insurance could be provided by the private sector instead of the government. But, realistically, private financial systems may not be able to provide guarantees to investors if large macroeconomic shocks such as the depression of the 1930s occur. Assuming such coverage is desirable, governments can provide this coverage by forcing other sectors of the economy to provide backup capital through taxation.

This government guarantee is no panacea, for it creates a host of other problems, generally described under the rubric of *moral hazard*. Given government guarantees, there is even less incentive for depositors to monitor their banks, but rather to flock to institutions offering high deposit rates. Bank owners are now offered what is the equivalent of a "put" option. If they take risks and prosper, they partake in the benefits. If they lose, the government steps in and pays back the depositors. As long as the cost of deposit insurance is not related to the riskiness of activities, there will be perverse incentives to take on additional risk. These incentives no doubt played a part in the great savings and loans debacle, where total losses are now estimated at $150 billion, most of which was paid for by U.S. taxpayers. The national commission set up to consider the lessons of this fiasco called deposit insurance the "necessary condition" without which this debacle would not have occurred.

The moral hazard problem due to deposit insurance explains why regulators attempt to control risk-taking activities. This is achieved by forcing banks to carry minimum levels of capital, thus providing a cushion to protect the insurance fund. Capital adequacy requirements can also serve as a deterrent to unusual risk taking if the amount of capital to set aside is tied to the amount of risk undertaken.

Still, a remaining issue is the appropriate level of capital required to ensure a "safe and sound" financial system. Historically, regulators have been tempted to set high capital-adequacy levels, just to be safe. Perhaps the best warning against imposing capital standards that are too high was articulated by Alan Greenspan, chairman of the Federal Reserve, in May 1994. He pointed out that

- Bank shareholders must earn a competitive rate of return on capital at risk and that returns are adversely affected by high capital requirements.
- In times of stress, banks can take steps to reduce their exposure to market risks.
- "When market forces . . . break loose of economic fundamentals, . . . sound policy actions, and not just bank capital, are necessary to preserve financial stability."

A more radical approach to the deposit insurance/moral hazard dilemma is to rely on market discipline only. The central bank of New Zealand, for instance, has recently abolished deposit insurance. Thus, the Reserve Bank will not bail out failing banks, although it is still responsible for protecting the overall banking system. As a result, depositors must now rely on information provided by commercial banks and ratings agencies to decide whether their funds will be safe. This system puts an increased responsibility on bank directors to ensure that their institution is sound, as failure may lead to creditor lawsuits.

The New Zealand experiment will surely be watched intensely by bank regulators all over the world. In the meantime, the alternative regulatory path is evolving toward a system where capital requirements are explicitly linked to the risk of activities undertaken by commercial banks.

2 THE 1988 BASLE ACCORD

In the central banker quest for financial stability, a landmark financial agreement was reached by the Basle accord, concluded on July 15, 1988, by the central bankers from the Group of Ten (G-10) countries.[1] The bankers announced the accord would result in the "international conver-

---

1. The Basle Committee's members are senior officials from the G-10, Belgium, Canada, France, Germany, Italy, Japan, the Netherlands, Sweden, United Kingdom, and the United States plus Luxembourg and Switzerland, who meet four times a year, usually in Basle under the aegis of the Bank for International Settlements.

gence of supervisory regulations governing the capital adequacy of international banks." The main purpose of the Basle agreement was to provide a level playing field for commercial banks by providing a minimum standard of capital requirements that applies across member countries.

The 1988 agreement defined a common measure of solvency (the Cooke ratio) which only covers *credit risks* and thus deals solely with the identity of banks' debtors. The new ratios were fully implemented in 1993, covering all insured banks of signatory countries.

2.1 The Cooke Ratio

The Basle accord requires capital to be equal to at least 8 percent of the total risk-weighted assets of the bank. Capital, however, is interpreted more broadly than the usual definition of equity, since its goal is to protect deposits. It consists of two components:

- *Tier 1* capital, or "core" capital. This includes stock issues and disclosed reserves. General loan loss reserves constitute capital that has been earmarked to absorb future losses; when these losses occur, they are charged against the reserve account rather than to earnings, which helps to smooth out income over time.

- *Tier 2* capital, or "supplementary" capital. This includes perpetual securities, undisclosed reserves, subordinated debt with maturity greater than five years, and shares redeemable at the option of the issuer. Since long-term debt has a junior status relative to deposits, debt acts as a buffer to protect depositors (and the deposit insurer).

Of the 8 percent *capital charge,* at least 50 percent must be covered by tier 1 capital. Risk capital weights were set according to asset classes, as described in Table 3–1. For instance, U.S. Treasuries, being obligations of an Organization for Economic Cooperation and Development (OECD) government, are assigned a weight of zero. So is cash and gold held by banks. As the perceived credit risk increases, so does the risk weight. At the other end of the scale, claims on corporations, including loans, bonds, and equities, receive a 100 percent weight, which means that they must effectively be covered by 8 percent capital.

Signatories to the Basle accord are free to impose higher capital requirements in their own countries. Accordingly, shortly after the Basle accord, U.S. legislators passed the Federal Deposit Insurance Corporation

TABLE 3-1

Risk Capital Weights by Asset Class

Weights	Asset Type
0%	U.S. Treasury and obligations of OECD central governments
	Cash held
	Gold bullion held
20%	Cash to be received
	Claims on OECD banks
	U.S. government agency securities
	Agency CMOs
	Municipal general obligation bonds
50%	Municipal revenue bonds
100%	Corporate bonds
	Less developed country (LDC) debt
	Claims on non-OECD banks above 1 year
	Equity
	Real estate
	Plant and equipment
	Mortgage strips and residuals

Improvement Act (FDICIA) of 1991, aimed at promoting the safety and soundness of American financial institutions. Among the newly established bank capital requirements, U.S. regulators[2] have added the restriction that tier 1 capital must be no less than 3 percent of total assets; this ratio can be set higher for banks deemed to be weaker.

In addition, the current risk-based capital guidelines include capital requirements on the credit exposure of derivatives contracts. The computation of the required capital charges will be detailed in the chapter on credit risk.

2.2 Activity Restrictions

In addition to capital adequacy requirements, the Basle accords set limits on "excessive risk takings." These are restrictions on *large risks,* defined as positions that exceed 10 percent of a bank's capital. Large risks must be

---

2. Which include the Federal Reserve Board, the Office of the Comptroller of the Currency, and the Federal Deposit Insurance Corporation.

BOX 3-1

BARINGS'S LARGE RISK

Barings went bankrupt because of positions on the Singapore Monetary Exchange (SIMEX) and the Osaka Securities Exchange (OSE) that were quite large in relation to the firm's capital. At the time, it was not clear whether Barings's exposure to these exchanges could be classified as "quasi-sovereign" risk or corporate risk. This was an important issue to resolve, since the "large-risk" limit does not apply to sovereign risk.

Barings formally requested from the Bank of England (BoE) a clarification as to the status of its exposure to exchanges. The BoE took two years to answer. On February 1, 1995, it said that this exposure could not be considered as sovereign and that the 25 percent limit applied. On that day, Barings's exposure to SIMEX was 40 percent of its capital base and to OSE, 73 percent. Eventually, this exposure led to Barings's downfall. Later, a report on the bankruptcy stated that the "delay was unacceptable; the Bank was not entitled to assume that the delay would be inconsequential."

---

reported to regulatory authorities. Positions that exceed 25 percent of a firm's capital are not allowed, and the total of large risks must not exceed 800 percent of capital. In practice, however, the rules behind these ratios have not always been formally defined and sometimes need clarification from regulatory authorities. As the example in Box 3–1 shows, clarification came too late to save Barings.

2.3 Criticisms of the 1988 Approach

The 1988 Basle regulations have been criticized on several fronts. First, they do not account for the *portfolio risk* of the bank. Correlations between components of the portfolio may significantly alter total portfolio risk. Credit risk can be offset by diversification across issuers, industries, and geographical locations. The 1988 regulations actually raise the capital requirements from hedging operations.

Second, these regulations do not account for *netting*. If a bank matches lenders and borrowers, its net exposure may be small. If a counterparty fails, the loss may be small if the amount lent is matched by the amount borrowed. Actually, netting was an important driving force behind the creation of swaps. Swaps are derivatives contracts that involve a series of exchange of payments and are written with explicit offset provisions. In case of default, banks are exposed to only the net exposure, not the notional amount.

Finally, and maybe most important, these regulations poorly account for *market risk,* such as interest rate risk. Assets are recorded at book values, which may substantially differ from their current market values. As a result, accounting lags may create a situation where an apparently healthy balance sheet with acceptable capital hides losses in market values. This omission is particularly glaring for the trading portfolio of banks with positions in derivatives. In recognition of this drawback, the Basle Committee has moved toward measuring market risk with the value-at-risk approach.

3 THE BASLE PROPOSALS ON MARKET RISKS

Aware of the shortcoming of the previous agreement, which focused mainly on credit risk, the Basle Committee produced a series of consultative proposals on market risks. Eventually, these proposals will be combined with the 1988 credit risk requirements and implemented at the end of 1997.

3.1 The April 1993 Proposals: The Standard Model

The first set of proposals, issued in April 1993, is based on a building block approach. VAR is first computed for portfolios exposed to interest rate risk, exchange rate risk, equity risk, and commodity risk, using specific guidelines. The bank's total VAR is then obtained from the summation of VARs across the four categories. Because the construction of VAR follows a highly structured and standardized process, this approach is sometimes called the *standard model.*

For interest rate risk, the proposals define a set of maturity bands, within which net positions are identified across all on- and off-balance-sheet items. A duration weight is then assigned to each of the 13 bands, varying from 0.20 percent for positions under three months to 12.50 percent for positions over 20 years. The sum of all weighted net positions then yields an overall interest-rate-risk indicator. Note that the netting of positions within a band and aggregation across bands essentially assumes perfect correlations across debt instruments.

For currency and equity risk, the market-risk capital charge is essentially 8 percent of the net position; while for commodities, the charge is

15 percent.[3] All of these capital charges apply to the trading books of commercial banks, except for currency risks, which apply to both trading and banking books.

Although this approach aims at identifying banks with unusual exposure, it is still beset by problems. The *duration* of some instruments cannot be easily identified. Mortgages, for instance, contain prepayment options that allow the homeowner to refinance the loan if interest rates fall. Conversely, homeowners will make payments over a longer period if interest rates increase. The effective duration of mortgages thus changes with the level of interest rates and the past history of prepayments for a mortgage pool. Assigning a duration band to one of these instruments becomes highly questionable. More generally, the risk classification is arbitrary. The capital charges of 8 percent are applied uniformly to equities and currencies (and gold) without regard for their actual return volatilities.

Another issue is that the 1993 proposals do not account for *diversification across risks*. Low correlations imply that the risk of a portfolio can be much less than the sum of individual component risks. This diversification effect applies across market risks or across different types of financial risks.

Diversification across market risks is the easiest to measure. Historical data reveal that correlations across sources of risk are not perfect. Investing across global fixed-income markets, for instance, is less risky than investing in a single market. These diversification benefits are not recognized by simply aggregating across markets. Similarly, exchange-rate movements are not perfectly correlated nor are movements between interest rates and exchange rates. Assuming perfect correlations across various types of risks overestimates portfolio risk and leads to capital adequacy requirements that are too high.

Correlations across different types of risks are more difficult to deal with. Most notably, default risk may be related to interest rate risk. This is true for most floating-rate instruments (such as adjustable rate mortgages), where borrowers may default should interest rates increase to insufferable amounts.

At times, even credit rating agencies have overlooked the effect of market risk on the possibility of default. A prime example is the Orange County bankruptcy in December 1994. At that time, S&P's and Moody's

---

3. For precise rules, the reader is referred to the Basle Committee proposals. In addition to the market-risk charge, interest rate and equity positions carry a "specific" risk capital-charge, which is intended to cover changes in market values due, for instance, to changes in credit quality.

long-term credit ratings for the county were close to the highest possible: AA and Aa1, respectively, in spite of more than $1 billion in unrealized losses in the investment pool. The agencies claimed to have conducted a thorough examination of the county's finances, yet they remained unaware of the impending cash crisis. This is because the agencies focused on only credit risk; that is, the possibility that a borrower could fail to repay. The rating agencies failed to recognize that market risk can lead to credit risk (as shown in Box 3–2).

3.2 The April 1995 Revision: The Internal Model

In April 1995, the Basle Committee came forth with a major extension of market risk models.[4] For the first time, it would allow banks the option of using their own risk measurement models to determine their capital charge. This decision stemmed from a recognition that many banks have developed sophisticated risk management systems, in many cases far more complex than can be dictated by regulators. As for institutions lagging behind the times, this proposal provides a further impetus to create sound risk management systems.

To use this approach, banks have to satisfy various qualitative requirements, including regular review by various management levels within the bank and by regulators. The latest "internal model" proposal is based on the following approach:

1. The computation of VAR shall be based on a set of uniform quantitative inputs:
   a. A horizon of 10 trading days, or two calendar weeks
   b. A 99 percent confidence interval
   c. An observation period based on at least a year of historical data and updated at least once a quarter.
2. Correlations can be recognized in broad categories (such as fixed income) as well as across categories (e.g., between fixed income and currencies). As discussed before, this is an improvement over previous proposals.
3. The capital charge shall be set at the higher of the previous day's VAR or the average VAR over the last 60 business days, times a "multiplicative" factor (sometimes called a *hysteria* factor). The

---

4. See the Basle Committee proposals (1995a, 1995b).

BOX 3–2

TELESCOPING OF CREDIT AND INTEREST RATE RISKS

As an example of a similar telescoping of market and credit risk, consider the overseas debt crisis of the 1980s. American (and other) commercial banks had been eager to lend to developing countries like Brazil and Mexico, but they hoped to escape exposure to currency, interest, and credit risk.

An instrument known as the *syndicated Eurodollar loan* seemed to provide the perfect answer. It was denominated in dollars (no currency risk), was payable on a floating-rate basis (no interest risk), and was made to governments (which were unlikely to go out of business). But, after U.S. interest rates skyrocketed in the early 1980s, countries like Mexico and Brazil went into default: They were unable to make the (floating) interest payments on their loans. In short, market risk had turned into credit risk, and on a huge scale.

---

exact value of this factor is to be determined by local regulators, subject to an absolute floor of 3. This factor is intended to provide additional protection against environments that are much less stable than historical data would lead to believe.

4. A penalty component shall be added to the multiplicative factor if back-testing reveals that the bank's internal model incorrectly forecasts risks. The purpose of this factor is to give incentives to banks to improve the predictive accuracy of their models and to avoid overly optimistic projections of profits and losses due to model fitting. Tommasso Padoa-Schioppa, chairman of the Basle Committee, describes this problem as "driving by using the rear-view mirror." As the penalty factor may depend on the quality of internal controls at the bank, this system is designed to reward truthful internal monitoring, as well as develop sound risk-management systems.

To summarize, the general market-risk charge on any day t is

$$\text{MRC}_t = \text{Max}(k\, \frac{1}{60} \sum_{i=1}^{60} \text{VAR}_{t-i},\ \text{VAR}_{t-1}), \qquad (3.1)$$

where k is the supervisory-determined multiplicative factor, which can be set higher than its minimum of 3 if the supervisor is not satisfied with the bank's internal risk model.

To obtain total capital-adequacy requirements, banks will add their credit-risk charge to their market-risk charge applied to trading operations.

In exchange for having to allocate additional capital, banks will be allowed to use a new class of capital, tier 3 capital, which consists of short-term subordinated debt. The amount of tier 3 capital (tier 2 or both) is limited to 250 percent of tier 1 capital allocated to support market risks.

This proposal has been severely criticized by the International Swap and Derivatives Association (ISDA). In particular, the multiplicative factor of 3 is viewed as too large. The ISDA showed that a factor of 1 would have provided enough capital to cover periods of global turmoil, such as the 1987 stock market crash, the 1990 Gulf War, and the 1992 European Monetary System (EMS) crisis. An even more serious criticism is that the proposed method based on an internal VAR creates a capital requirement that is generally higher than the "standard model" proposed by the Basle Committee. Hence, the current proposal provides a negative incentive to the development of internal risk models. How the Basle Committee will respond to these criticisms is an open question.

3.3 The Precommitment Model

The debate around the appropriate risk measurement system took another turn as the Federal Reserve Board (1995) proposed a "precommitment" approach to bank regulation. Under this third alternative, the bank would precommit to a maximum trading loss over a designated horizon. This loss would become the capital charge for market risk. The supervisor would then observe, say, after a quarterly reporting period, whether trading losses exceed the limit. If so, the bank would suffer a penalty, which may include a fine, regulatory discipline, or higher future capital charges. Violations of the limits would also bring public scrutiny to the bank, which provides a further feedback mechanism for good management.

The main advantage of this "incentive-compatible" approach is that the bank itself chooses its capital requirement. As Kupiec and O'Brien (1995) have shown, this choice is made optimally in response to regulatory penalties for violations. Regulators can then choose the penalty that will induce appropriate behavior.

This proposal has been welcomed by the ISDA, which argued that this approach explicitly recognizes the links between risk-management practices and firm-selected deployment of capital. Critics, in contrast, point out that quarterly verification is very slow in comparison to the real-time daily capital requirements of the Basle proposals. Others worry that dynamic portfolio adjustments to avoid exceeding the maximum loss could exacerbate market movements, in the same way that portfolio insurance supposedly caused the crash of 1987.

3.4 Comparison of Approaches

At this point, it is useful to compare the pros and cons of each method. The first, standard-model method is generally viewed as least adequate because of the following factors.

- *Portfolio considerations*   The model ignores diversification effects across sources of risk.
- *Arbitrary capital charges*   The capital charges are only loosely related to the actual volatility of each asset category. This can distort portfolio choices, as banks move away from assets for which the capital charge is abnormally high.
- *Compliance costs*   Given that many banks already run sophisticated risk measurement systems, the standard model imposes a significant additional reporting burden.

The second, internal model method addresses all of these issues. It relies on the self-interest of banks to develop accurate risk-management systems. Internal VAR systems measure the total portfolio risk of the bank, account for differences in asset volatilities, and impose only small additional costs. In addition, regulatory requirements will automatically evolve at the same speed as risk measurement techniques, as new developments will be automatically incorporated into internal VARs.

Unfortunately, from the viewpoint of regulators, the internal model still has some drawbacks.

- *Performance verification*   Supervisors are supposed to monitor whether internal VARs indeed provide good estimates of future profits and losses in trading portfolios. As capital charges are based on VARs, there may be an incentive to artificially lower the VAR figure to lower capital requirements; thus verification by regulators is important. The problem is that, even with a well-calibrated model, there will be instances when losses will exceed the VAR just by chance (e.g., 5 percent of the time using a 95 percent confidence level). Unfortunately, long periods may be needed to distinguish between chance and model inaccuracies as shown in Chapter 5. This issue makes verification difficult.

- *Endogeneity of positions*   Banks' internal VARs typically measure risk over a short interval, such as a day. Extending these numbers to a 10-day trading period ignores the fact that positions will change, especially in response to losses or unexpectedly high volatility.[5] Therefore, measures of long-horizon exposure ignore efficient risk management procedures and controls. Perhaps this is why the ISDA has found that the current proposal appears too conservative.

Note that these problems do not detract from the usefulness of VAR models for corporate risk management. From the viewpoint of regulators, however, the precommitment approach has much to recommend, since it automatically accounts for changing positions. In addition, the risk coverage level is endogenously chosen by the bank, in response to the penalty for failure, which creates fewer distortions in capital markets.

Unfortunately, all models suffer from a performance verification problem. The regulator can compare only "ex post," or realized performance, to "ex ante" estimates of risk or maximum loss. Unless the maximum loss is set extremely high, there always will be instances where a loss will exceed the limit even with the correct model. The key then for regulators is to separate good intentions and bad luck from reckless behavior.

4 THE EU CAPITAL ADEQUACY DIRECTIVE

The history of capital adequacy requirements in Europe must be put in the perspective of plodding movements toward economic and political integration in Europe. The Single European Act of 1985 committed member countries to achieving a free market in goods, services, capital, and labor. To this end, the European Union's Investment Services Directive (ISD), which came into effect on January 1, 1996, sweeps away restrictions against nonlocal financial services. Up to then, a securities firm that wanted to do business in another European Union (EU) country had to abide by local rules; for instance, having to establish separately capitalized

---

5. A typical management response is to cut positions as losses accumulate. This pattern of trading can be compared to portfolio insurance, which attempts to replicate a put option. Therefore, attempts by management to control losses will create a pattern of payoffs over long horizons that will be asymmetrical, like options. The problem is that traditional VAR measures are inadequate with highly nonlinear payoffs.

subsidiaries (and expensive offices) in foreign countries. In effect, this raised the cost of doing business abroad and made Europe's internal market less efficient than might otherwise be.

Under new regulations, firms based in one EU country will be authorized to carry out business in any other EU country. This will lead to the general consolidation of office networks. For instance, Deutsche Bank has announced that its global investment-banking activities would be centralized in London.[6] Also, the centralization of risk management will provide for better control of financial risks. In addition to efficiency gains, more competition should drive down transaction costs and increase the liquidity of European financial markets.

To avoid firms setting up shop in the country with the lowest level of regulations, however, the EU has adopted Europe-wide capital requirements known as the Capital Adequacy Directive (CAD). The CAD, published in March 1993, lays down minimum levels of capital to be adopted for EU banks and securities houses by January 1996.

In many ways, the CAD parallels the Basle guidelines. It extends the 1989 Solvency Ratio and Own Funds Directives, which were similar to the 1988 Basle accord. The 1993 requirements are very similar and, in some cases, identical to those laid out in the 1993 Basle proposal. The latest version of the CAD also allows institutions to run their own VAR model for daily calculation.

There are some differences, however. First, the Basle guidelines were aimed only at banks, not securities houses. Regulation of securities houses is concerned mainly with orderly liquidation, while bank regulators aim at preventing outright failure. Second, the CAD guidelines will be put in effect in 1996, while the Basle rules will apply only in 1998, which leaves a period during which European firms have to comply with a separate set of guidelines.

5 REGULATION OF NONBANKS

In many ways, the regulation of nonbank financial intermediaries parallels that of banks. Each of these institutions must learn to deal effectively with similar sources of financial risks. Also, there is a tendency for lines of

---

6. *The Economist* (November 5, 1994).

business to become increasingly blurred. Commercial banks now move into trading of securities and provide some underwriting and insurance functions. The trading portfolio of banks contains assets, liabilities, and derivatives that are no different from those of securities houses. Therefore, trading portfolios are measured at market values, while traditional banking items are still reported at book value. With the trend toward securitization, however, more and more assets (such as bank loans) have become liquid and tradeable.

Table 3–2 compares the structure of balance sheets for financial intermediaries. These are now discussed in more detail.

5.1 Pension Funds

While pension funds are not subject to capital adequacy requirements, a number of similar restrictions govern *defined-benefit* plans. The current U.S. regulatory framework was defined by the Employee Retirement Income Security Act (ERISA) promulgated in 1974. Under ERISA, companies are required to make contributions that are sufficient to provide coverage for pension payments. In effect, the minimum capital is the present value of future pension liabilities. The obligation to make up for unfunded liabilities parallels the obligation to maintain some minimal capital ratio. Also, asset-risk weights are replaced by a looser provision of diversification and of not taking excessive risks, as defined under the "prudent man rule."

TABLE 3–2

Balance Sheets of Financial Intermediaries

Type	Assets	Liabilities
Banks (banking books)	Loans, securities at book values	Deposits, CDs, subordinated debt
Pension funds	Market value of assets	Present value of defined-benefit pensions
Insurance companies	Market value of assets	Actuarial value of insurance payments
Securities firms	Securities (long)	Securities (short)

As in the case of banking regulation, federal guarantees are provided to pensioners. The Pension Benefit Guarantee Corporation (PBGC), like the Federal Deposit Insurance Corporation (FDIC), charges an insurance premium and promises to cover default by corporations. Other countries have similar systems, although most other countries rely much more heavily on public *pay-as-you-go* schemes, where contributions from current employees directly fund current retirees. The United States, Britain, and the Netherlands are far more advanced in their reliance on private pension funds. Public systems in countries afflicted by large government deficits can ill-afford generous benefits to an increasingly aging population. As a result, private pension funds are likely to take on increasing importance all over the world. With those will come the need for prudential regulation.

5.2 Insurance Companies

Regulation for insurance companies is less centralized than for other financial institutions in the United States, where insurance is regulated at the state level. As in the case of FDIC protection, insurance contracts are ultimately covered by a state guaranty association. State insurance regulators set nationwide standards through the National Association of Insurance Commissioners (NAIC).

In December 1992, the NAIC announced new capital adequacy requirements for insurers. As in the case of the early 1988 Basle accord, the new rules emphasize credit risk. For instance, no capital is needed to cover holdings of government bonds and just 0.5 percent for mortgages. But 30 percent of the value of equities must be covered.[7] This ratio is much higher than the 8 percent ratio required for banks, which some insurers claim puts them at a competitive disadvantage vis-à-vis other financial institutions that are increasingly branching out into insurance products.

In the EU, insurance regulation parallels that of banks, with capital requirements, portfolio restrictions, and regulator intervention in cases of violation. For life-insurance companies, capital must exceed 4 percent of *mathematical reserves,* computed as the present values of future premiums minus future death liabilities. For non-life-insurance companies, capital must exceed the highest of about 17 percent of premiums charged for the

---

7. *The Economist* (May 15, 1993).

current year and about 24 percent of annual settlements over the last three years.

5.3 Securities Firms

The regulation of securities firms is still evolving. Securities firms hold securities on the asset and liability sides (usually called long and short) of their balance sheet. Regulators generally agree that some prudent reserve should be available to cover financial risks. There is no agreement, however, as to whether securities firms should hold capital to cover their *net* positions, consisting of assets minus liabilities, or their *gross* positions, consisting of the sum of all long plus short positions.

The United States and Japan use the gross position approach, the United Kingdom uses the net position, and the Basle Committee and the European Union consider a variant of both approaches. The EU, for instance, requires firms to have equity equal to 2 percent of their gross positions plus 8 percent of their net positions as of 1996.

Dimson and Marsh (1995) compare the effectiveness of these approaches for a sample of detailed holdings of British market makers. Comparing the riskiness of the portfolio to various capital requirements, they show that the net position approach as required by the United Kingdom dominates the EU and U.S. approaches, as it best approximates the actual portfolio risk. The net position approach comes closest to what portfolio theory would suggest.

Although there are differences in the regulations of banks and securities firms, capital requirements are likely to converge as banks and securities firms increasingly compete in the same markets. Currently, the same accounting rules apply to the *trading book* activities of banks and the trading activities of securities firms. In the United States, the 1933 *Glass-Steagall Act,* which separates the commercial and investment bank functions, is slowly being chipped away. The 1933 act is widely viewed as obsolete, overly restrictive, especially in comparison with the universal banking system prevalent in Europe. Cracks in the Glass-Steagall wall started to appear in 1989, when commercial banks were allowed to underwrite stocks and bonds on a limited basis (although no more than 10 percent of their revenues can come from underwriting). Banks have also been expanding into insurance products, such as annuities, although further expansion is being fiercely resisted by U.S. insurance companies.

More recently, VAR has been gaining prominence for the regulation of securities firms. The Securities and Exchange Commission, the Commodity Futures Trading Commission, and six major Wall Street securities houses have entered an agreement to base capital requirements in VAR methodology. As for the commercial banking system, VAR is bound to become a universally accepted benchmark.

PART TWO

Building Blocks

CHAPTER 4

Sources of Financial Risk

The stock market will fluctuate.

J. P. Morgan, when asked what the market was going to do.

Although in modern parlance the term *risk* has come to mean "danger of loss," finance theory defines *risk* as the dispersion of unexpected outcomes due to movements in financial variables. Thus, both positive and negative deviations should be viewed as sources of risk. Countless investors have missed this point as they failed to realize that the superior performance of traders, such as Nick Leeson and Bob Citron, really reflected greater risks. Extraordinary performance, both good and bad, should raise red flags.

In practice, to measure risk formally, one has to define first the variable of interest, which could be portfolio value, earnings, capital, or a particular cash flow. Financial risks are created by the effects of financial factors on this variable.

As risk needs to be rigorously defined, this chapter lays the statistical foundation of portfolio theory that is behind the use of value at risk. Readers who are thoroughly familiar with these concepts could skip directly to the next chapter, which formally introduces VAR. Section 1 first discusses various sources of financial risk. The concepts of risk and return are formally defined in Section 2, which shows how to use the normal distribution to find the probability of a loss. This section also introduces Bankers Trust's RAROC measure of risk-adjusted capital. As the target horizon for measuring VAR is not necessarily equal to that over which risk is measured, Section 3 explains how to adjust risk measures for different horizons.

1 FINANCIAL RISK

Broadly, there are four different types of financial risks: interest rate risk, exchange rate risk, equity risk, and commodity risk. Basic analytical tools apply to all these markets. Risk is measured by the standard deviation of unexpected outcomes, or "sigma" (σ), also called *volatility*.

Losses can occur through a combination of two factors: the volatility in the underlying financial variable and the exposure to this source of risk. Whereas corporations have no control on the volatility of financial variables, they can adjust their exposure to these risks; for instance, through derivatives. Value at risk captures the combined effect of underlying volatility and exposure to financial risks.

Measurements of linear exposure to movements in underlying risk variables appear everywhere under different guises. In the fixed-income market, exposure to movements in interest rates is called *duration*. In the stock market, this exposure is called *systematic risk,* or beta (β). In derivatives markets, the exposure to movements in the value of the underlying asset is called *delta* (δ). Second derivatives are called *convexity* and *gamma* (γ) in the fixed-income and derivatives markets, respectively. Convexity measures the change in duration as the interest rate changes; likewise, gamma measures the change in delta as the underlying price changes. Both terms measure the second-order, or quadratic, exposure to a financial variable.

Chapter 1 has argued that the increased interest in risk management was partly driven by the increase in volatility in financial variables, which was described in Figures 1–1 to 1–4. These graphs, however, plot movements in the level of financial variables and therefore give only an indirect view of risk.

Risk can be more precisely measured by short-term volatility. Figures 4–1 to 4–4 present the standard deviation of trailing 12-month relative price changes, expressed in percent per annum. Figure 4–1 confirms that the volatility of the DM/$ rate has increased sharply after 1973. The demise of the system of fixed exchange rates has added to financial risks. Note that this volatility, on the order of 10–15 percent per annum, is large enough to wipe out typical profit margins for firms with international operations, given that profit margins are also often around 10–15 percent.

The measure of risk seems to fluctuate over time, with peaks in 1974 and 1994 and troughs in 1977 and 1991. This begs the question of whether risk is truly unstable over time or whether these patterns are due to our estimation method and just reflect "noise" in the data. This is an important question to which a whole chapter will be devoted later.

FIGURE 4–1

Volatility in the German Mark/Dollar Rate

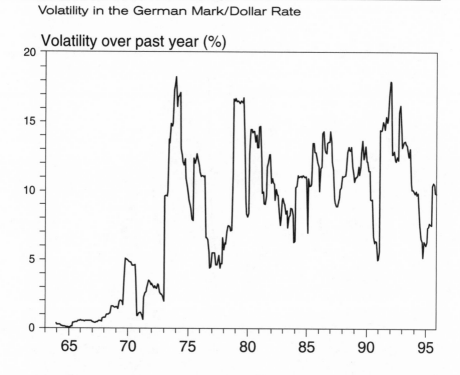

The volatility in U.S. bond prices is presented in Figure 4–2. Here, the typical volatility was about 5 percent per annum before 1980. In the 1980s, however, it shot up to 20 percent per annum, only to subside in the 1990s. Figure 4–3 displays the volatility of oil prices. Before 1970, the volatility was very low, as oil was a regulated market. Since then, oil price risk has sharply increased, notably during the OPEC price hikes of 1974 and 1979.

Last, Figure 4–4 measures risk in the U.S. stock market. Volatility appears to be more stable, on the order of 10–20 percent per annum. Risk is more consistent in this market, reflecting residual claims on corporations subject to business risks in a mature stock market. Notable peaks in volatility occurred in October 1974, when U.S. stocks went up by 17 percent, after three large consecutive drops, and during the October 1987 crash, when U.S. equities lost 20 percent of their value. Volatility therefore occurs because of large unexpected price changes, whether positive

FIGURE 4–2

Volatility in Interest Rates

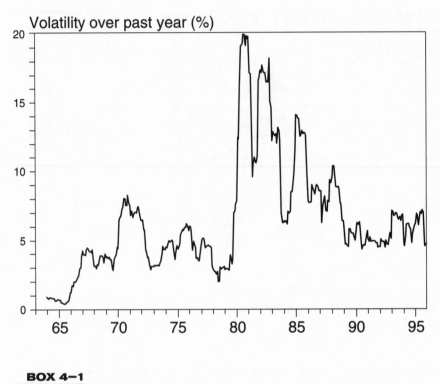

RISK

The origins of the word *risk* can be traced to Latin, through the French *risque* and Italian *risco*. The original sense of *risco* is cut off like a rock, from the latin *re-,* back, and *secare,* to cut. Hence, the sense of peril to sailors who had to navigate around dangerous, sharp rocks.

or negative. This symmetric treatment is logical since players in these markets can be long or short, domestic or foreign, consumers or producers. Overall, the volatility of financial markets creates risks (see Box 4–1) and opportunities, which must be measured and controlled.

FIGURE 4–3

Volatility in Oil Prices

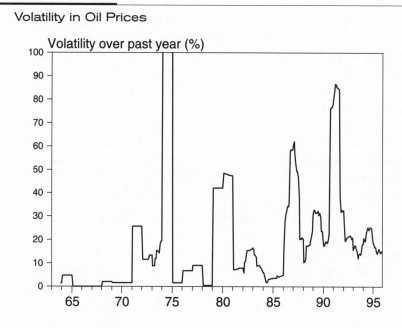

FIGURE 4–4

Volatility in Stock Prices

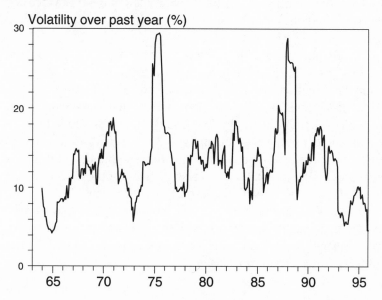

2 RISK AND RETURN

Risk can be generally defined as the uncertainty of outcomes. It is best explained in terms of probability, which traces its roots to problems of fair distribution. In fact, in the Middle Ages the word *probability* meant an "opinion certified by authority." The question of justice led to notions of equivalence between expectations. And work on expectations set the stage for probability theory.

Probability traces its roots to the work of Girolamo Cardano, an Italian who was also an inveterate gambler. In 1565 Cardano published a treatise on gambling, *Liber de Ludo Alae*, which was the first serious effort at developing the principles of probability.

2.1 A Gambler's Experiment

Probability theory took another leap when a French nobleman posed a gambling problem to Blaise Pascal in 1654. He wanted to know how to allocate equitably profits in a game that was interrupted. In the course of developing answers to this problem, Pascal laid out the foundations for probability theory.

Cardano and Pascal defined *probability distributions*, which describe the number of times a particular value can occur in an imaginary experiment. Consider for instance a gambler with a pair of dice. The dice are fair, in the sense that each side has equal probability, or one chance in six, to happen.

We tabulate all possible outcomes; for example, the combination of (1,1), or a total of 2, can happen once; a total of 3 can happen twice through combinations of (1,2) and (2,1); and so on. Figure 4–5 displays the total distribution for all possible values, which range from 2 to 12.

Table 4–1 summarizes the *frequency distribution* of the total points. The total number of dice combinations is 36. This first result is not so obvious, for Cardano had to explain to his readers that the total number of possibilities is 36, not 12. Cardano also defined for the first time the conventional format for probabilities expressed as fractions.

Define X as the random variable of interest, the total number of points from rolling the dice. It takes 11 possible values x_i, each with associated frequency n_i. Rescaling the frequencies so that they add up to unity, we obtain the associated probability p_i.

FIGURE 4–5

Distribution of Payoff

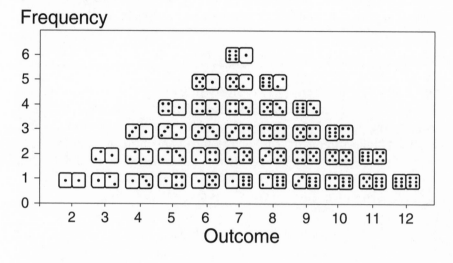

TABLE 4–1

Computing Expected Value and Standard Deviation

Value (x_i)	2	3	4	5	6	7	8	9	10	11	12	Total
Frequency of Occurrence (n_i)	1	2	3	4	5	6	5	4	3	2	1	36
Probability of Occurrence (p_i)	$\frac{1}{36}$	$\frac{2}{36}$	$\frac{3}{36}$	$\frac{4}{36}$	$\frac{5}{36}$	$\frac{6}{36}$	$\frac{5}{36}$	$\frac{4}{36}$	$\frac{3}{36}$	$\frac{2}{36}$	$\frac{1}{36}$	1
Computing $E(X)$: $p_i x_i$	$\frac{2}{36}$	$\frac{6}{36}$	$\frac{12}{36}$	$\frac{20}{36}$	$\frac{30}{36}$	$\frac{42}{36}$	$\frac{40}{36}$	$\frac{36}{36}$	$\frac{30}{36}$	$\frac{22}{36}$	$\frac{12}{36}$	$\frac{252}{36}$
Computing $V(X)$: $p_i[x_i\text{-}E(X)]^2$	$\frac{25}{36}$	$\frac{32}{36}$	$\frac{27}{36}$	$\frac{16}{36}$	$\frac{5}{36}$	$\frac{0}{36}$	$\frac{5}{36}$	$\frac{16}{36}$	$\frac{27}{36}$	$\frac{32}{36}$	$\frac{25}{36}$	$\frac{210}{36}$

These probabilities define a *probability distribution function* (pdf) that by construction must sum to unity:

$$\sum_{i=1}^{11} p_i = 1. \tag{4.1}$$

The distribution can be usefully characterized by two variables: its mean and spread.

The expected value $E(X)$, or *mean* can be estimated as the weighted sum of all possible values, each weighted by its probability of occurrence.

$$E(X) = \sum_{i=1}^{11} p_i x_{i.} \tag{4.2}$$

To shorten the notation, $E(X)$ is also written as μ. In our example, the summation yields 252/36, which is also 7. Therefore, the expected value from throwing the dice is 7. The figure also shows that this is the value with the highest frequency, defined as the *mode* of the distribution.

Next, we would like to characterize the dispersion around $E(X)$ with a single measure. This is done first by computing the *variance*, defined as the weighted sum of squared deviations around the mean.[1]

$$V(X) = \sum_{i=1}^{11} P_i [x_i - E(X)]^2. \tag{4.3}$$

Note that, because deviations from the mean are squared, positive and negative deviations are treated symmetrically. In the dice example, the term that corresponds to the outcome $x_1 = 2$ is $(1/36)$ $[2-7]^2 = 25/36$. The table shows that all of these add up to $V(X) = 210/36$.

The variance is measured in units of x squared and thus is not directly comparable to the mean. The *standard deviation*, or volatility, is then defined as the square root of the variance,

$$SD(X) = \sqrt{V(X)}. \tag{4.4}$$

Again to shorten notation, $SD(X)$ is written as σ. In our example, the standard deviation of future outcomes is $\sqrt{(210/36)} = 2.415$. This number is particularly useful because it indicates a typical range of values around the mean.

2.2 Properties of Expectations

Our gambler's experiment involved a discrete set of outcomes, characterized by a discrete *pdf*. For many variables, such as the rate of return on an investment, the range of outcomes is continuous. We therefore redefine the

---

1. The term variance was first introduced by the statistician R. A. Fisher in 1918, in the context of a paper on genetics.

pdf as $f(x)$. As in (4.1), it must sum, or integrate, to unity over all possible values, going from $-\infty$ to ∞:

$$\int_{-\infty}^{+\infty} f(x)dx = 1. \tag{4.5}$$

The expectation and variance are then, by extension of (4.2) and (4.3)

$$E(X) = \int_{-\infty}^{+\infty} xf(x)dx, \tag{4.6}$$

$$V(X) = \int_{-\infty}^{+\infty} [x - E(X)]^2 f(x)dx. \tag{4.7}$$

In what follows, we will make extensive use of transformation and combinations of random variables. How do these affect expectations and variances?

First, let us define a new random variable as $Y = a + bX$, a linear transformation of the original X. The parameters a and b are fixed. We have, after insertion into (4.6) and (4.7),

$$\begin{aligned} E(a+bX) &= \int (a+bx)f(x)dx \\ &= a\int f(x)dx + b\int xf(x)dx \\ &= a + bE(X), \end{aligned} \tag{4.8}$$

by (4.5), and

$$\begin{aligned} V(a+bX) &= \int [a+bx - E(a+bX)]^2 f(x)dx \\ &= \int [a+bx - a - bE(X)]^2 f(x)dx \\ &= \int b^2 [x - E(X)]^2 f(x)dx = b^2 V(X). \end{aligned} \tag{4.9}$$

Therefore, the volatility of Y is $\sigma(a+bX) = b\sigma(X)$.

Let us now turn to linear combinations of random variables, such as $Y = X_1 + X_2$, such as the payoff on a portfolio of two stocks. Here, the uncertainty is described by a pdf of two variables, $f(x_1, x_2)$. If we abstract from the other variable, the distribution for one variable is known as the *marginal distribution*,

$$\int_2 f(x_1, x_2)\, dx_2 = f(x_1). \tag{4.10}$$

The expectation is, by extension of (4.6) and (4.10),

$$\begin{aligned} E(X_1 + X_2) &= \int_1 \int_2 (x_1 + x_2) f(x_1, x_2)\, dx_1 dx_2 \\ &= \int_1 \int_2 x_1 f(x_1, x_2) dx_1 dx_2 + \int_1 \int_2 x_2 f(x_1, x_2)\, dx_1 dx_2 \end{aligned}$$

$$= \int_1 x_1 \left[\int_2 f(x_1, x_2) \, dx_2 \right] dx_1 + \int_2 x_2 \left[\int_1 f(x_1, x_2) \, dx_1 \right] dx_2$$

$$= \int_1 x_1 f(x_1) \, dx_1 + \int_2 x_2 f(x_2) dx_2 = E(X_1) + E(X_2). \tag{4.11}$$

This is remarkably simple: The expectation is a linear operator. The expectation of a sum is the sum of expectations.

Developing the variance, however, is more involved. We have

$$V(X_1 + X_2) = \int_1 \int_2 \{x_1 + x_2 - E(X_1 + X_2)\}^2 f(x_1, x_2) \, dx_1 dx_2$$

$$= \int_1 \int_2 \{[x_1 - E(X_1)]^2 + [x_2 - E(X_2)]^2 + 2[x_1 - E(X_1)]$$
$$[x_2 - E(X_2)]\} \, f(x_1, x_2) dx_1 dx_2$$

$$= \int_1 [x_1 - E(X_1)]^2 f(x_1) dx_1 + \int_2 [x_2 - E(X_2)]^2 f(x_2) dx_2$$

$$+ 2 \int_1 \int_2 [x_1 - E(X_1)][x_2 - E(X_2)] f(x_1, x_2) dx_1 dx_2$$

$$= V(X_1) + V(X_2) + 2\text{Cov}(X_1, X_2), \tag{4.12}$$

where the last term is defined as the *covariance* between X_1 and X_2.

The variance turns out to be a nonlinear operator: In general, the variance of a sum of random variables is not equal to the sum of variances. It involves a cross-product term that is very important because it drives the diversification properties of portfolios.

However, in the special case where the two variables are independent, which can be formally written as $f(x_1, x_2) = f(x_1) \times f(x_2)$, the last integral reduces to

$$\int_1 \int_2 [x_1 - E(X_1)] \, [x_2 - E(X_2)][f(x_1) \times f(x_2)] \, dx_1 dx_2$$

$$= \int_1 [x_1 - E(X_1)] f(x_1) dx_1 \times \int_2 [x_2 - E(X_2)] f(x_2) dx_2$$

$$= 0, \tag{4.13}$$

since $\int x_1 f(x_1) dx_1 = E(X_1)$. The variance of a sum is equal to the sum of variances if the two variables are independent of each other: $V(X_1 + X_2) = V(X_1) + V(X_2)$.

2.3 Normal Distributions

Upon closer inspection, the distribution in Figure 4–5 resembles the ubiquitous "bell-shaped" curve, proposed two centuries ago by Karl F.

Gauss (1777–1855), who was studying the motion of celestial bodies (hence its name, Gaussian).[2] The "normal" distribution plays a central role in statistics because it describes adequately many existing populations. Furthermore, P. S. Laplace later proved the *central limit theorem,* which showed that the mean converges to a normal distribution as the number of observations increases. Also, as the number of independent draws increases (i.e., here increasing the number of dice from two to a large number), the distribution converges to a smooth normal distribution. This explains why the normal distribution has such a prominent place in statistics.

A direct application of these century-old observations is the evaluation of credit risk. Consider the problem of evaluating the capital at risk in a large portfolio containing many small consumer credits. Individually, each loan default can be modeled by a *binomial* distribution, with two realizations only, assuming no partial repayment. In the limit, however, the distribution of a sum of binomial variables converges to a normal distribution. Therefore, the portfolio can be modeled by a normal distribution as the number of credits increases. It should be noted that this result relies heavily on the independence of the defaults. If a severe recession hits the economy, it is likely that many defaults will occur at the same time, which invalidates the normal approximation.

A normal distribution has convenient properties. In particular, the entire distribution can be characterized by its first two moments, the mean and variance: $N(\mu, \sigma^2)$. The first parameter represents the location; the second, the dispersion. The distribution function has the following expression

$$f(x) = \Phi(x) = \frac{1}{\sqrt{2\pi\sigma^2}} e^{\left[-\frac{1}{2\sigma^2}(x-\mu)^2\right]}, \qquad (4.14)$$

where $e^{[y]}$ represents the exponential of y.

This function, which is also at the heart of the Black–Scholes option pricing model, could be tabulated for different values of μ and σ. However, this can be simplified considerably by using tables for a normal distribution with a mean of zero and variance unity, which is called a *standard normal distribution function.*

---

2. Galton first coined the term *normal,* which has become almost universal in English, although continental European writers prefer to use the term *Gaussian.*

Start from a *standard* normal variable ϵ such that $\epsilon \sim N(0,1)$. Define next X as

$$X = \mu + \epsilon\sigma. \tag{4.15}$$

Going back to (4.8) and (4.9), we can show that X has a mean $E(X)$ $= E(\epsilon)\sigma + \mu = \mu$, and $V(X) = V(\epsilon)\sigma^2 = \sigma^2$.

The standard normal distribution is plotted in Figure 4–6. As the function is perfectly symmetrical, its mean is the same as its mode (most likely point) and median (which has a 50 percent probability of occurrence).

About 95 percent of the distribution is contained between values of $\epsilon_1 = -2$ and $\epsilon_2 = +2$. And 66 percent of the distribution falls between values of $\epsilon_1 = -1$ and $\epsilon_2 = +1$. If we want to find 95 percent confidence limits for movements in an exchange rate, with mean 1 percent and volatility 12 percent, we have

$$X_{MIN} = 1\% - 2 \times 12\% = -23\%$$
$$X_{MAX} = 1\% + 2 \times 12\% = +25\%.$$

The $[-2, +2]$ confidence interval for ϵ thus translates into $[-23\%, +25\%]$ for the exchange rate movement X.

More precise cutoff points are given in Table 4–2. The table reports *quantiles*, which are points q such that the area to their right (or left) represents a given probability c

$$c = \text{Prob}(X \ge q) = \int_q^{+\infty} f(x)dx. \tag{4.16}$$

To find the number of standard deviations for a given confidence level c, choose a number in the first row. For instance, the goal might be to find the VAR at the one-tailed 95 percent confidence level. The table shows that this corresponds to 1.645 deviation below the mean.

2.4 Risk

Risk therefore is measured as the dispersion of possible outcomes. A flatter distribution indicates greater risk; and a tighter distribution, lower risk. Figure 4–7 displays the distribution of two exchange rates, the Deutsche mark (DM) and Canadian dollar (C\$) against the U.S. dollar. The graph shows the frequency of monthly returns over the period 1973 to 1994. As shown in the figure, the DM/\$ rate is riskier than the C\$/\$ rate because it has a greater range of values. Box 4–2 shows how to penalize positions with greater risks.

FIGURE 4–6

Normal Distribution

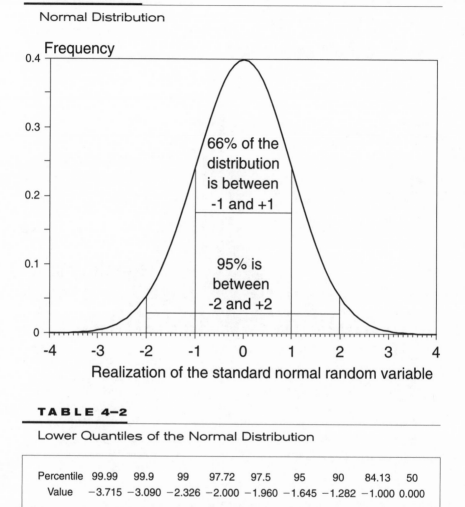

Realization of the standard normal random variable

TABLE 4–2

Lower Quantiles of the Normal Distribution

Percentile	99.99	99.9	99	97.72	97.5	95	90	84.13	50
Value	−3.715	−3.090	−2.326	−2.000	−1.960	−1.645	−1.282	−1.000	0.000

2.5 Asset Returns

In the context of the measurement of market risk, the random variable is taken as the rate of return on a financial asset (although gambling is sometimes an appropriate comparison). The range of possible payoffs on a security can also be described by its probability distribution function.

Define, for instance, the measurement horizon as a month. Returns are measured from the end of the previous month, denoted by the subscript

FIGURE 4–7

Comparison of Distributions

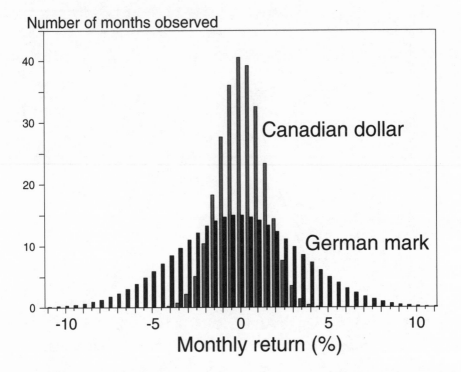

Number of months observed

Canadian dollar

German mark

Monthly return (%)

$t - 1$ to the end of the current month, denoted by t. The *arithmetic*, or *discrete*, rate of return is defined as the capital gain plus any interim payment such as dividend or coupon:

$$r_t = (P_t + D_t - P_{t-1})/P_{t-1}. \qquad (4.17)$$

Note that this definition implies that any income payment is reinvested only at the end of the month.

To focus on long-horizon returns, the practice is to focus on the *geometric* rate of return, which is defined in terms of the logarithm of the price ratio:

$$R_t = \ln[(P_t + D_t)/P_{t-1}]. \qquad (4.18)$$

For simplicity, we will assume that income payments D_t are zero in what follows. Alternatively, we could think of P as the value of a mutual fund that reinvests all dividends. Thus, no rebalancing takes place with geometric returns, while arithmetic means correspond to the case

BOX 4-2

RAROC: BANKERS TRUST'S RISK ADJUSTMENT

Bankers Trust has been a pioneer in risk management, introducing risk measurement through its risk adjusted return on capital (RAROC) system in the late 1970s. The system was inspired by the need to adjust trader profit for risk. Take, for instance, two traders, each of whom makes a profit of $10 million, one in short-term Treasuries, the other in foreign exchange. This raises a number of essential questions: which trader performed better? How should they be compensated for their profit? And, where should the firm devote more capital? RAROC adjusts profits for capital at risk, defined as the amount of capital needed to cover 99 percent of the maximum expected loss over a year. The same one-year horizon is used for all RAROC computations, irrespective of the actual holding period, to allow meaningful comparisons across asset classes.

To compute the RAROC for the foreign exchange position, assume that the face value of the contracts was $100 million. The volatility of the DM/$ rate is 12 percent per annum. The firm needs to hold enough capital to cover 99 percent of possible losses. As 1 percent of the normal distribution lies 2.33 standard deviations below the mean, the worst possible loss is $2.33 \times 0.12 \times \$100m = \$28m$, which is also the capital requirement to sustain this position. Therefore, the RAROC for the foreign exchange trader is $10/$28 = 36%. This measure is a reward-to-risk ratio.

Let us now turn to the bond trader. Assume that the gain was obtained with an average notional amount of $200 million and that the risk of these bonds is about 4 percent. The maximum loss is then $2.33 \times 0.04 \times \$200m = \$19m$. The RAROC for the bond trader is $10/$19 = 54%. When adjusted for the capital resources, the bond trader provided a bigger bang for the buck.

RAROC also provides limits on trading. For instance, a trader who loses 10 percent of his or her RAROC capital in a month must stop trading. Again, RAROC allows meaningful comparisons between different markets.

This adjustment yields a number of essential insights that have shaped the course of Bankers Trust's strategy over the last 10 years. By compensating traders based on their RAROC, risk adjustment permeates the culture of the bank. In the words of the company itself, risk management is practiced "with a holistic approach." Bankers Trust discovered that most of its loan lending was less profitable than other operations and strategically adjusted the direction of the bank into more profitable risk-management functions. This, of course, assumes that the volatility of returns captures all essential aspects of business risks.

of a fixed investment; that is, where gains are withdrawn and losses are added back.

The advantage of using geometric returns is twofold. First, they may be more economically meaningful than arithmetic returns. If geometric returns are distributed normally, then the distribution can never lead to a price that is negative. This is because the left tail of the distribution such as $\ln(P_t/ P_{t-1}) \to -\infty$ is achieved as $(P_t/P_{t-1}) \to 0$, or $P_t \to 0$.

In contrast, in the left tail of normally distributed arithmetic returns, $R_t = (P_t - P_{t-1}) / P_{t-1} \to -\infty$ is achieved as $(P_t/P_{t-1}) -1 < -1$, or $P_t < 0$. Economically, this is meaningless. Therefore, imposing a normal distribution on the arithmetic rate of return allows some aberrant behavior in prices.

For some series, using a geometric return may also be more consistent. For instance, exchange rates can be defined in two different base currencies. Using S($/BP) as the dollar price of the British pound, the random variable of interest is $x = \ln(S_t/S_{t-1})$. Now, taking the viewpoint of a British investor, who measures asset values in pounds, the variable is $y = \ln[(1/S_t)/(1/S_{t-1})] = -\ln(S_t/S_{t-1}) = -x$. The distributions of x and y therefore are consistent with each other, which is not the case if returns are defined in discrete terms.

Using the logarithm is also particularly convenient for converting returns or risk measures into other currencies. Assume a German investor wants to measure returns in Deutsche marks. This can be derived from dollar-based data, as $\ln[S(DM/BP)] = \ln[S(DM/\$)] + \ln[S(\$/BP)] = -\ln[S(\$/DM)] + \ln[S(\$/BP)]$. The DM-based return is equal to the difference between the dollar return on the pound and the dollar return on the mark, $z(DM/BP) = x(\$/BP) - x(\$/DM)$, from which variances and correlations immediately follow.

The second advantage of using geometric returns is that they easily allow extensions into multiple periods. For instance, consider the return over a two-month period. The geometric return can be decomposed as

$$R_{t,2} = \ln(P_t/P_{t-2}) = \ln(P_t/P_{t-1}) + \ln(P_{t-1}/P_{t-2}) = R_{t-1} + R_t. \quad (4.19)$$

This is particularly convenient since the two-month geometric return is simply the sum of the two monthly returns. With discrete returns, the decomposition is not so simple.

This said, it must be admitted that, in many situations, the differences between the two returns are small. Consider that $R_t = \ln(P_t/P_{t-1}) = \ln(1 + r_t)$. If r_t is small, R_t can be decomposed into a Taylor series as $R_t = r_t +$

$r_t^2 / 2 + r_t^3 / 3 + \ldots$, which simplifies to $R_t \approx r_t$ if r_t is small. Thus, in practice, as long as returns are small, there will be little difference between continuous and discrete returns. This may not be true, however, in markets with large moves, such as emerging markets, or when the interval horizon is measured in years.

2.6 Sample Estimates

In practice, the distribution of rates of return is usually estimated over a number of previous periods, assuming all observations are *identically* and *independently distributed* (iid). If T is the number of observations, the expected return, or first moment, $\mu = E(X)$ can be estimated by the sample mean,

$$\hat{\mu} = \frac{1}{T} \sum_{i=1}^{T} x_i, \qquad (4.20)$$

and the variance, or second moment, $\sigma^2 = E[(X - \mu)^2]$, can be estimated by the sample variance,

$$\hat{\sigma}^2 = \frac{1}{(T-1)} \sum_{i=1}^{T} (x_i - \hat{\mu})^2. \qquad (4.21)$$

The square root of σ^2 is the standard deviation of X, often referred to as the *volatility*. It measures the risk of a security as the dispersion of outcomes around its expected value.

Going back to the distribution of monthly exchange rate changes in Figure 4–7, we find that the mean of DM/$ changes was -0.21 percent and that the standard deviation was 3.51 percent. The C$/$ rate displayed a lower volatility of 1.3 percent.

Note that equation (4.21) can be developed as

$$\hat{\sigma}^2 = \frac{1}{(T-1)} \sum_{i=1}^{T} x_i^2 - \frac{T}{(T-1)} \hat{\mu}^2. \qquad (4.22)$$

This shows that the variance is composed of two terms, the first being an average of the squared returns and the second being the square of the average.

For most financial series sampled at daily intervals, the second term is negligible relative to the first. In the DM/$ example, the squared average return is $(-0.0021)^2 = 0.0000044$, versus a variance term on the order of $(0.0351)^2 = 0.00123$, which is much greater. Therefore, in such situations, we can ignore the mean in the estimation of daily risk measures.

For completeness, we should also mention two other moments. *Skewness* describes departures from symmetry. The skewness of a normal distribution is 0. It is measured as

$$\hat{\gamma} = \frac{1}{(T-1)} \sum_{i=1}^{T} (xx_i - \hat{\mu})^3 / \hat{\sigma}^{3/2}. \tag{4.23}$$

Kurtosis describes the degree of "flatness" of a distribution. It is measured as

$$\hat{\delta} = \frac{1}{(T-1)} \sum_{i=1}^{T} (x_i - \hat{\mu})^4 / \hat{\sigma}^4. \tag{4.24}$$

The kurtosis of a normal distribution is 3. These two measures can be used as a quick check on whether the sample distribution is close to normal. Large negative values of the skewness coefficient, or large values of the kurtosis coefficient, indicate that the left tail of the empirical distribution, which is used to compute value at risk, does not resemble a normal distribution.

3 TIME AGGREGATION

Computing VAR requires first the definition of a period over which to measure unfavorable outcomes. This period may be set in terms of hours, days, or weeks. For an investment manager, it may correspond to the regular reporting period, monthly or quarterly. For a bank manager, the horizon should be sufficiently long to catch traders taking positions in excess of their limits. Regulators are now leaning toward enforcing a horizon of two weeks, which is viewed as to the period necessary to force bank compliance.

To compare risk across horizons, we need a translation method—a problem known as *time aggregation* in econometrics. Suppose we observe daily data, from which we obtain a VAR measure. Using higher frequency data is generally more efficient because it uses more information.

The investment horizon, however, may be three months. So the distribution for daily data must be transformed into a distribution over a quarterly horizon. If returns are uncorrelated over time (or behave like a random walk), this transformation is straightforward.

The problem of time aggregation can be brought back to the problem of finding the expected return and variance of a sum of random variables. From (4.19), the two-period return (from $t - 2$ to t) $R_{t,2}$ is equal to R_{t-1} +

R_t, where the subscript 2 indicates that the time interval is two periods. A previous section has shown that $E(X_1 + X_2) = E(X_2)$ and that $V(X_1 + X_2) = V(X_1) + V(X_2) + 2\text{Cov}(X_1, X_2)$.

To aggregate over time, we now introduce an extremely important assumption: Returns are uncorrelated over successive time intervals. This assumption is consistent with *efficient markets*, where the current price includes all relevant information about a particular asset. If so, all price changes must be due to news that, by definition, cannot be anticipated and therefore must be uncorrelated over time: Prices follow a *random walk*. The cross-product term $\text{Cov}(X_1 \, X_2)$ must then be 0. In addition, we could reasonably assume that returns are identically distributed over time, which means that $E(R_{t-1}) = E(R_t) = E(R)$ and that $V(R_{t-1}) = V(R_t) = V(R)$.

Based on these two assumptions, the expected return over a two-period horizon is $E(R_{t,2}) = E(R_{t-1}) + E(R_t) = 2E(R)$. The variance is $V(R_{t,2}) = V(R_{t-1}) + V(R_t) = 2V(R)$. The expected return over two days is twice the expected return over one day; likewise for the variance. Both the expected return and the variance increase linearly with time. The volatility, in contrast, grows with the square root of time.

In summary, to go from daily, monthly, or quarterly data to annual data, we can write

$$\mu = \mu_{\text{annual}} \, T \tag{4.25}$$
$$\sigma = \sigma_{\text{annual}} \, \sqrt{T}, \tag{4.26}$$

where T is the number of years (e.g., 1/12 for monthly data or 1/252 for daily data if the number of trading days in a year is 252). Therefore, *adjustments of volatility to different horizons can be based on a square root of time factor when positions are constant.*

As an example, let us go back to the DM/$ rate data that we wish to convert to annual parameters. The mean of changes is -0.21% per month $\times$ 12 = -2.6% per annum. The risk is 3.51% per month $\times \sqrt{12} = 12.2\%$ per annum.

Table 4–3 compares the risk and average return for a number of financial series, measured in percent per annum over the period 1973–1994. Stocks are typically the most volatile of the lot (15 percent). Next come exchange rates against the dollar (12 percent), and U.S. bonds (9 percent). Some currencies, however, are relatively more stable. Such is the case for the French franc versus the Deutsche mark, which have been fixed to each other since March 1979.

TABLE 4–3

Risk and Return: 1973–1994 (% per annum)

| | Exchange Rate | | | | U.S. Stocks | U.S. Bonds |
	DM/$	FF/DM	C$/$	Yen/$		
Volatility	12.2	4.9	4.5	11.1	15.4	8.7
Average	−2.6	3.6	1.7	−4.4	11.1	8.6

Note that, since the volatility grows with the square root of time and the mean with time, the mean will dominate the volatility over long horizons. Over short horizons, such as a day, volatility dominates. This provides a rationale for focusing on measures of value at risk based on volatility only and ignoring expected returns.

To illustrate this point, consider an investment in U.S. stocks that, according to Table 4–3, returns an average of 11.1 percent per annum with a risk of 15.4 percent. Table 4–4 compares the risks and average returns of holding a position over successively shorter intervals, using equations (4.25) and (4.26). Going from annual to daily and even hourly data, the mean shrinks much faster than the volatility. Based on a 252-trading day year, the daily expected return is 0.04 percent, very small compared to the volatility of 0.97 percent.

Table 4–4 can be used to infer the probability of a loss over a given measurement interval. For annual data, this is the probability that the return, distributed $N(\mu = 11.1\%, \sigma^2 = 15.4\%^2)$ falls below 0. Transforming to a standard normal variable, this is the probability that $\epsilon = (R - 0.111)/0.154$ falls below 0, which is the area to the left of the standard normal variable $-0.111/0.154 = -0.7208$. From normal tables, we find that the area to the left of 0.7208 is 23.6 percent. Thus, the probability of losing money over a year is 23.6 percent, as shown in the last column of Table 4–4. In contrast, the probability of losing money over one day is 48.2 percent, which is much higher!

This observation is sometimes taken as support for the conventional wisdom that stocks are less risky in the long run than over a short horizon.

TABLE 4–4

Risk and Return over Various Horizons
U.S. Stocks, 1973–1994

Horizon	Years T	Mean m	Risk s	Ratio m/s	Probability of Loss (%)
Annual	1	11.1000	15.40	0.7208	23.6
Quarterly	0.25000	2.7750	7.70	0.3604	35.9
Monthly	0.08333	0.9250	4.45	0.2081	41.8
Weekly	0.01918	0.2129	2.13	0.0998	46.0
Daily	0.00397	0.0440	0.97	0.0454	48.2
Hourly	0.00050	0.0055	0.34	0.0161	49.4

Unfortunately, this is not necessarily correct, since the dollar amount of the loss also increases with time.[3]

By now, we have covered the statistical tools necessary to compute value at risk. This is the purpose of the next chapter.

---

3. Merton and Samuelson (1974) have written a number of articles denouncing this "fallacy." See also Harlow (1991).

CHAPTER 5

Measuring Value at Risk

The Daily Earnings at Risk (DEaR) estimate for our combined
trading activities averaged approximately $15 million . . .

J. P. Morgan 1994 annual report

Perhaps the greatest advantage of VAR is that it summarizes in a single
number, easy to understand, the total exposure of an institution to market
risk. No doubt this explains why VAR is fast becoming an essential tool
for conveying trading risks to senior management, directors, and shareholders. J. P. Morgan, for example, revealed in its 1994 annual report that
its daily trading VAR was an average of $15 million at the 95 percent level
over one day. Shareholders can then assess whether they are comfortable
with this level of risk. Before such figures were released, shareholders had
only a vague idea of the extent of trading activities assumed by the bank.

This chapter turns to a formal definition of value at risk. Section 1
shows how to derive VAR figures from probability distributions. This can
be done in two ways, either by considering the actual empirical distribution or by approximating the distribution by a normal curve, in which case
VAR is derived from the standard deviation.

Section 2 turns to techniques for verifying the accuracy of VAR models. These procedures, sometimes called *reality checks,* are important for
regulators, who want to ensure that a bank's internal VAR models are not
systematically biased one way or another. The Basle Committee recommends "back-testing" as a means to verify the accuracy of VAR figures.
Verification is also important for users, who need to check that their model
accurately forecasts how many times the VAR figure will be exceeded.
Verification was one of the recommendations of the landmark G–30 study.

In both cases, the key to verification is to understand the role of sampling variation, which makes verification more difficult and VAR estimates less precise. Accordingly, Section 2 provides a framework for analyzing normal sampling variation in VAR and discusses methods to improve the accuracy of VAR figures. Finally, Section 3 provides some concluding thoughts.

1 COMPUTING VAR

With all of the requisite tools in place, we can now formally define the VAR of a portfolio. As stated previously, *VAR summarizes the expected maximum loss (or worst loss) over a target horizon within a given confidence interval.*

1.1 Quantitative Factors

The first step toward measurement of VAR is the choice of two quantitative factors: the length of the holding horizon, and the confidence level. Both are somewhat arbitrary. As an example, the internal model approach of the Basle Committee defines a 99 percent confidence interval over 10 days. The resulting VAR is then multiplied by a safety factor of 3 to provide the minimum capital requirement for regulatory purposes.

Presumably, the Basle Committee chose a 10-day period because it reflects the trade-off between the costs of frequent monitoring and the benefits of early detection of potential problems. From the viewpoint of users, the horizon can be determined by the nature of the portfolio. Commercial banks currently report their trading VAR over a daily horizon because of the rapid turnover in their portfolios. In contrast, investment portfolios such as pension funds generally adjust their risk exposures only slowly, which is why a one-month horizon is generally chosen for investment purposes. As the holding period should correspond to the longest period needed for an orderly portfolio liquidation, the horizon should be related to the liquidity of the securities, defined in terms of length of time needed for normal transaction volumes.

Fewer guidelines are available for the choice of the confidence level. Presumably also, the Basle Committee chose a 99 percent level which reflects the trade-off between the desire of regulators to ensure a safe and sound financial system and the adverse effect of capital requirements on bank returns. Users set widely different confidence levels. For instance, Bankers

Trust uses a 99 percent level, Chemical and Chase use a 97.5 percent level, Citibank uses a 95.4 percent level, BankAmerica and J. P. Morgan use a 95 percent level. Higher confidence levels imply higher VAR figures.

Whether these differences are significant depends on their usage. If the resulting VARs are directly used for the choice of a capital cushion, then the choice of the confidence level is crucial. This choice should reflect the degree of risk aversion of the company and the cost of a loss of exceeding the VAR. Higher risk aversion, or greater cost, implies that a greater amount of capital should cover possible losses, thus leading to a higher confidence level.

In contrast, if the VAR numbers are used just to provide a company-wide yardstick to compare risks across different markets, then the choice of the confidence level is not too important. Assuming a normal distribution, this chapter will show that it is easy to convert all these disparate bank measures into a common number.

The choice of the confidence level, however, is important for *model validation.* The level of confidence should be chosen in preference to a higher level, which would give a loss measure that would rarely be exceeded. Take for instance a 95 percent level. We know that, just by chance, we expect a loss worse than the VAR figure in 1 month out of 20. If we had chosen a 99 percent level, we would have to wait on average 100 days to confirm that the model conforms to reality. Therefore, on average, it will take longer to tell whether we observe too many observations in excess of the VAR. It is important to choose a confidence level that allows users to check the estimates on a regular basis. This concept will be more formally developed in the next section.

1.2 VAR for General Distributions

To compute the VAR of a portfolio, define W_0 as the initial investment, and R as its rate of return. The portfolio value at the end of the target horizon is $W = W_0 (1 + R)$. As before, the expected return and volatility of R are μ and σ. Define now the lowest portfolio value at the given confidence level c as $W^* = W_0 (1 + R^*)$. VAR is defined as the dollar loss, relative to the mean,

$$\text{Value at risk (mean)} = E(W) - W^* = -W_0(R^* - \mu). \quad (5.1)$$

Sometimes VAR is defined as the *absolute* dollar loss; that is, relative to zero or without reference to the expected value,

$$\text{Value at risk (zero)} = W_0 - W^* = -W_0 R^*. \qquad (5.2)$$

In both cases, finding the VAR is equivalent to identifying the minimum value W^*, or the cutoff return R^*.

In its most general form, VAR can be derived from the probability distribution of the future portfolio value $f(w)$. At a given confidence level c, we wish to find the worst possible realization W^* such that the probability of exceeding this value is c:

$$c = \int_{W^*}^{\infty} f(w)\, dw, \qquad (5.3)$$

or such that the probability of a value lower than W^*, $p = P(w \le W^*)$, is $1 - c$:

$$1 - c = \int_{-\infty}^{W^*} f(w)\, dw = P(w \le W^*) = p. \qquad (5.4)$$

In other words, the area from $-\infty$ to W^* must sum to $p = 1 - c$, for instance 5 percent. The number W^* is called the sample *quantile* of the distribution. Note that we did not use the standard deviation to find the VAR.

This specification is valid for any distribution, discrete or continuous, fat or thin tailed. Figure 5–1, for instance, reports J.P. Morgan's distribution of daily revenues in 1994.

To compute the VAR of revenues, assume that daily revenues are identically and independently distributed. We can then derive the VAR at the 95 percent level from the 5 percent left-side "losing tail" from the histogram.

From this graph, the average revenue is about $5.1 million. There is a total of 254 observations; therefore, we would like to find W^* such that the number of observations to its left is $254 \times 5\% = 12.7$. We have 11 observations to the left of $-\$10m$, and 15 to the left of $-\$9m$. Interpolating, we find $W^* = -\$9.6m$. The VAR of daily revenues, measured relative to the mean, is VAR $= E(W) - W^* = \$5.1m - (-\$9.6m) = \$14.7m$. If one wishes to measure the VAR in terms of absolute dollar loss, the VAR is then $9.6m.

1.3 VAR for Parametric Distributions

The VAR computation can be simplified considerably if the distribution can be assumed to be normal. When this is the case, the VAR figure can be derived directly from the portfolio standard deviation, using a multiplicative factor that depends on the confidence level. This approach is sometimes called *parametric* as it involves estimation of a parameter, the standard deviation, instead of just reading the quantile off the empirical distribution.

FIGURE 5–1

Distribution of Daily Revenues

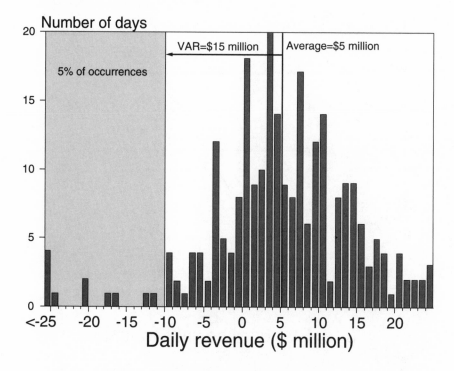

First, we need to translate the general distribution $f(w)$ into a standard normal distribution $\Phi(\epsilon)$, where ϵ has mean of zero and standard deviation of unity. We associate W^* with the cutoff return R^* such that $W^* = W_0(1 + R^*)$. Generally, R^* is negative and can also be written as $-|R^*|$. Further, we can also associate R^* with a standard normal deviate $\alpha > 0$ by setting

$$-\alpha = \frac{-|R^*| - \mu}{\sigma}. \tag{5.5}$$

It is equivalent to set

$$1 - c = \int_{-\infty}^{W^*} f(w)\,dw = \int_{-\infty}^{-|R^*|} f(r)\,dr = \int_{-\infty}^{-\alpha} \Phi(\epsilon)\,d\epsilon \tag{5.6}$$

Thus the problem of finding a value at risk is equivalent to finding the deviate α such that the area to the left of it is equal to $1 - c$. This is made possible by turning to tables of the *cumulative standard normal distribution function,* which is the area to the left of a standard normal variable with value equal to d:

FIGURE 5–2

Cumulative Normal Probability Distribution

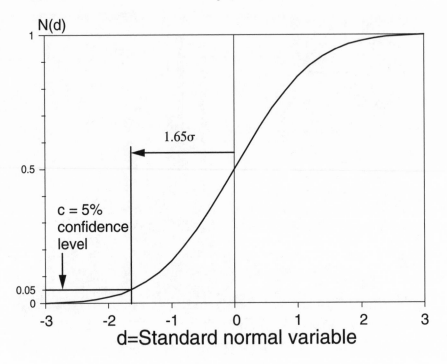

$$N(d) = \int_{-\infty}^{d} \Phi(\epsilon)d\epsilon. \tag{5.7}$$

This function also plays a key role in the Black–Scholes option pricing model. Figure 5–2 graphs the cumulative density function (cdf) $N(d)$, which increases monotonically from 0 (for $d = -\infty$) to 1(for d $= +\infty$), going through 0.5 as d passes through 0.

To find the VAR of a standard normal variable, select the desired confidence level on the vertical axis, say 5 percent. This corresponds to a value of $\alpha = 1.65$ below 0. We then retrace our steps, back from the α we just found to the cutoff return R^* and VAR. From equation (5.5), the cutoff return is

$$R^* = -\alpha\sigma + \mu. \tag{5.8}$$

For more generality, assume now that the parameters μ and σ are expressed on an annual basis. The time interval considered is Δt, in years.

Replacing in (5.1), we find the VAR below the mean as

$$\text{Value at risk (mean)} = -W_0 (R^* - \mu) = W_0 \alpha \sigma \sqrt{\Delta t}. \qquad (5.9)$$

In other words, the VAR figure is simply a multiple of the standard deviation of the distribution, times an adjustment factor that is directly related to the confidence level.

When VAR is defined as an *absolute* dollar loss, we have

$$\text{Value at risk (zero)} = -W_0 R^* = W_0 (\alpha \sigma \sqrt{\Delta t} - \mu \Delta t). \qquad (5.10)$$

This method generalizes to other cumulative probability functions as well as the normal, as long as all of the uncertainty is contained in σ. Other distributions will entail different values of α. The normal distribution is just particularly easy to deal with, since it adequately represents many empirical distributions. This is especially true for large, well-diversified portfolios but certainly not for portfolios with heavy option components and exposures to a small number of financial risks.

1.4 Comparison of Approaches

How well does this approximation work? For some distributions, the fit can be quite good. Consider for instance the daily revenues in Figure 5–1. The standard deviation of the distribution is $9.2m$. According to equation (5.9), the normal-distribution VAR is $\alpha \times (\sigma W_0) = 1.65 \times \$9.2m = \$15.2m$. Note that this number is very close to the VAR obtained from the general distribution, which was $14.7m$.

Indeed, Figure 5–3 presents the cumulative distribution functions (cdf) obtained from the histogram in Figure 5–1 and from its normal approximation. The actual cdf is obtained by summing, starting from the left, all numbers of occurrences in Figure 5–1, then scaling by the total number of observations. The normal cdf is the same as that in Figure 5–2, with the horizontal axis scaled back into dollar revenues, using equation (5.8). The two lines are generally very close, suggesting that the normal approximation provides a good fit to the actual data.

1.5 Conversion of VAR Parameters

Using the normal distribution, measures of VAR depend on two parameters: the selected horizon (which defines $\sigma \Delta t$) and the confidence level (which defines α). Both can be adjusted as desired. As an example, we can

FIGURE 5–3

Comparison of Cumulative Distributions

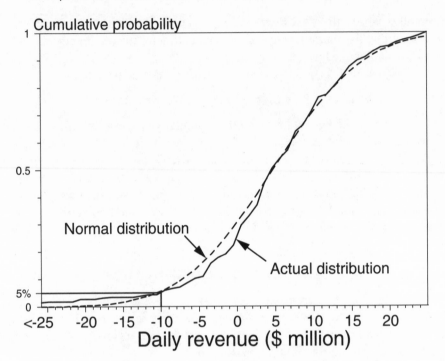

convert the RiskMetrics risk measures into the Basle Committee internal model measures. RiskMetrics provides a 95 percent confidence interval (1.65σ) over one day. The Basle proposal defines a 99 percent confidence interval (2.33σ) over 10 days. The adjustment takes the following form:

$$VAR_{BC} = VAR_{RM} \frac{2.33}{1.65} \sqrt{10} = 4.45 \ VAR_{RM}.$$

Therefore the VAR under the Basle proposal is more than four times the VAR from the RiskMetrics system. This adjustment, as will be demonstrated later, is valid only when positions are assumed constant and the portfolio does not contain options.

More generally, Table 5–1 shows how the Basle parameters translate into combinations of confidence levels and horizons, taking an annual volatility of 12.16 percent which is that of the DM/$ exchange rate. These combinations are such that they all produce the same value for $\alpha\sigma\sqrt{\Delta t}$. For instance, a 99 percent confidence level over two weeks produces the

TABLE 5-1

Equivalence between Horizon and Confidence Level Normal Distribution, Annual Risk=12.16% (Basle Parameters: 99% Confidence over Two Weeks)

Confidence Level c (%)	Number of SD α	Horizon Δt	Actual SD $\sigma\sqrt{\Delta t}$	Cutoff Value $\alpha\sigma\sqrt{\Delta t}$
Baseline:				
99	−2.326	2 weeks	2.381	−5.54
57.56	−0.456	1 year	12.160	−5.54
81.89	−0.911	3 months	6.079	−5.54
86.78	−1.116	2 months	4.964	−5.54
95	−1.645	4 weeks	3.367	−5.54
99	−2.326	2 weeks	2.381	−5.54
99.95	−3.290	1 week	1.684	−5.54
99.99997	−7.153	1 day	0.766	−5.54

same VAR as a 95 percent level over four weeks. Or, conversion into a weekly horizon requires a confidence level of 99.95 percent.

The measure of value at risk is defined only in a probabilistic sense. It gives the worst loss at the 99 percent confidence level. Interpreted differently, a loss worse than the VAR will occur about 1 percent of the time on average, or two to three days in a calendar year. To provide near-absolute insurance against bankruptcy, regulators have adopted a multiplicative factor $k = 3$ that must be applied to the resulting VAR_{BC}, which yields more than 13 times the daily RiskMetrics VAR. This factor accounts for the possibility of large losses even under normal market conditions and, possibly, for a host of additional risks not modeled by the usual application of VAR. This further underscores the point that the choice of the confidence level is a matter of convention, since resulting VARs are multiplied by an arbitrary factor anyway.

2 VERIFYING VAR

We now have seen how to estimate essential parameters for the measurement of VAR, means, standard deviations, and quantiles from actual data. These estimates, however, should not entirely be taken for granted. They are affected by "estimation error," which is the natural sampling variability due to the limited sample size. This is the case, for example, when the relevant parameters are estimated from a historical series of T observations, as in the "historical-simulation" method, which is described in Chapter 10.

For model validation, bank regulators and model users must beware the effect of estimation error. Suppose, for instance, that a bank regulator observes daily estimates of VAR reported by a bank as well as subsequent returns. The issue is, How can the regulator detect systematic biases in the reporting of VAR? The problem is that, since VAR is reported only at a specified confidence level, we expect the figure to be exceeded in some instances, for example in 5 percent of the observations at the 95 percent confidence level. But surely, we will not observe exactly 5 percent excess deviations. A greater percentage could occur due to bad luck, perhaps 6–8 percent. At some point, however, if the frequency of deviations becomes too large, say 10–20 percent, the regulator must conclude that the problem lies with the model, not bad luck, and impose penalties on a bank that willfully understates its VAR.

The same dilemma faces VAR users. Their model is useful only insofar as it predicts risk well. If there are many more large losses than expected, at some point the user must go back to the drawing board and examine what went wrong. The issue is how to make this decision.

2.1 Model Verification Based on Failure Rates

The simplest method to verify the accuracy of the model is to record the *failure rate*, which gives the proportion of times VAR is exceeded in a given sample. Suppose a bank provides a VAR figure at the 5 percent left-tail level ($p = 1 - c$) for a total of T days. The regulator then counts how many times the actual loss exceeds the previous day's VAR. Assume that N is the number of times the loss is exceeded. We want to know, at a given confidence level, whether N is too small or too large under the null hypothesis that $p = 0.05$. Let us set, for instance, the confidence level at 95 percent.[1]

---

1. Note that this number is not related to the quantitative level p selected for the VAR figure, which could be, for instance, $p = 0.01$. This confidence level refers to the decision rule to reject the model. It is generally set at a 95 percent level because this corresponds to two standard errors under a normal distribution.

TABLE 5-2

Model Verification: Nonrejection Regions
Number of Failures at 0.05 Level

Probability Level p	Nonrejection Regions for Number of Failures, N		
	T = 255 days	T = 510 days	T = 1000 days
0.01	$N < 7$	$1 < N < 11$	$4 < N < 17$
0.025	$2 < N < 12$	$6 < N < 21$	$15 < N < 36$
0.05	$6 < N < 21$	$16 < N < 36$	$37 < N < 65$
0.075	$11 < N < 28$	$27 < N < 51$	$59 < N < 92$
0.10	$16 < N < 36$	$38 < N < 65$	$81 < N < 120$

Notes: N is the number of failures that could be observed in a sample size T without rejecting the null hypothesis that p is the correct probability, at the 5 percent level of confidence. Adapted from Kupiec (1995).

Kupiec (1995) develops confidence regions for such a test, which are reported in Table 5–2. These regions are defined by the tail points of the log-likelihood ratio

$$1 = -2\ln[(1 - p)^{T-N}p^N] + 2\ln[(1 - (N/T))^{T-N}(N/T)^N], \quad (5.11)$$

which is distributed chi-square with one degree of freedom under the null hypothesis that p is the true probability.

For instance, with one year of data ($T = 255$), we would expect to observe $N = pT = 5\% \times 255 = 13$ deviations. But the regulator will not be able to reject the null hypothesis as long as N is in the [6 < N < 21] confidence interval. Values of N greater than or equal to 21 indicate that the VAR model underrepresents the probability of large losses; values of N less than or equal to 6 indicate that the VAR model is overly conservative.

The table also shows that this interval, expressed as a proportion N/T, shrinks as the sample size increases; for example, going from [6/255 = 0.024, 21/255 = 0.082] for $T = 255$ to [37/1000 = 0.037, 65/1000 = 0.065] for $T = 1000$. With more data, we should be able to reject the model more easily if it is false.

The table, however, points to a disturbing fact. For small values of the VAR parameter p, it becomes increasingly difficult to confirm deviations. For instance, the 95 percent rejection region under $p = 0.01$ and $T = 255$ is [$N < 7$]. Therefore, there is no way to tell if N is abnormally small or whether the model systematically overestimates risk.

Intuitively, detection of systematic biases becomes increasingly difficult for low values of p, because these correspond to very rare events. This explains why some banks prefer to choose a higher value for p, say 5 percent (which translates into a confidence level $c = 95\%$), in order to be able to observe a sufficient number of deviations to validate the model. A multiplicative factor is then applied to translate the VAR figure into a safe capital cushion number. So far, however, there has been no research on the choice of a confidence level that permits optimal verification.

2.2 The Problem of Measurement Errors

From the viewpoint of VAR users, it is also useful to assess the degree of precision in the reported VAR. In a previous example, the daily VAR was $15 million. The question is, How confident is management in this estimate? Could we say, for example, that management is highly confident in this figure or that it is 95 percent sure that the true estimate is in a $14–16 million range? Or is it the case that the range is $5–25 million. The two confidence bands give quite a different picture of VAR. The first is very precise, the second is rather uninformative (although it tells us that it is not in the hundreds of millions of dollars.) This is why it is useful to examine measurement errors in VAR figures.

Consider a situation where VAR is obtained from the "historical-simulation" method, which uses a historical window of T days to measure risk. The problem is that the reported VAR measure is only an *estimate* of the true value and is affected by sampling variability. In other words, different choices of the window T will lead to different VAR figures.

One possible interpretation of the estimates (the view of "frequentist" statisticians) is that the estimates $\hat{\mu}$, $\hat{\sigma}$ are samples from an underlying distribution with unknown parameters μ, σ. With an infinite number of observations $T \to \infty$ and a perfectly stable system, the estimates should converge to the true values. In practice, sample sizes are limited, either because some series like emerging markets are relatively recent or because structural changes make it meaningless to go back too far in time. As some estimation error may remain, the natural dispersion of values can be measured by the *sampling distribution* for the parameters $\hat{\mu}$, $\hat{\sigma}$. We now turn to a description of the distribution of statistics upon which VAR measures are based.

2.3 Estimation Error in Means and Variances

When the underlying distribution is normal, the exact distribution of the sample mean and variance is known. The estimated mean $\hat{\mu}$ is distributed normally around the true mean

$$\hat{\mu} \sim N(\mu, \sigma^2/T), \tag{5.12}$$

where T is the number of independent observations in the sample. Note that the standard error in the estimated mean converges toward 0 at a rate of $\sigma\sqrt{1/T}$ as T increases.

As for the estimated variance $\hat{\sigma}^2$, the following ratio is distributed as a chi-square with $(T-1)$ degrees of freedom

$$\frac{(T-1)\hat{\sigma}^2}{\sigma^2} \sim \chi^2[(T-1)]. \tag{5.13}$$

In practice, if the sample size T is large enough (e.g., above 20), the chi-square distribution converges rapidly to a normal distribution, which is easier to handle:

$$\hat{\sigma}^2 \sim N\left[\sigma^2, \sigma^4 \frac{2}{(T-1)}\right]. \tag{5.14}$$

As for the sample standard deviation, its standard error in large samples is

$$se(\hat{\sigma}) = \sigma\sqrt{\frac{1}{2T}}. \tag{5.15}$$

For instance, consider monthly returns on the DM/$ rate from 1973 to 1994. Sample parameters are $\hat{\mu} = -0.21\%$, $\hat{\sigma} = 3.51\%$, with T = 264 observations. The standard error of the estimate indicates how confident we are about the sample value; the smaller the error, the more confident we are. One standard error in $\hat{\mu}$ is $se(\hat{\mu}) = \hat{\sigma}\sqrt{1/T} = 3.51\%\sqrt{1/264} = 0.22\%$. Therefore, the point estimate of $\mu = -0.21\%$ is less than one standard error away from 0. Even with 22 years of data, μ is measured very imprecisely.

In contrast, one standard error in $\hat{\sigma}$ is $se(\hat{\sigma}) = \hat{\sigma}\sqrt{1/2T} = 3.51\%\sqrt{1/528} = 0.15\%$. Since this number is much smaller than the estimate of 3.51 percent, we can conclude that the volatility is estimated with much greater accuracy than the expected return—giving some confidence in the use of VAR systems.

As the sample size increases, so does the precision of the estimate. To illustrate this point, Figure 5–4 depicts 95 percent confidence bands

FIGURE 5–4

Confidence Bands for Volatility

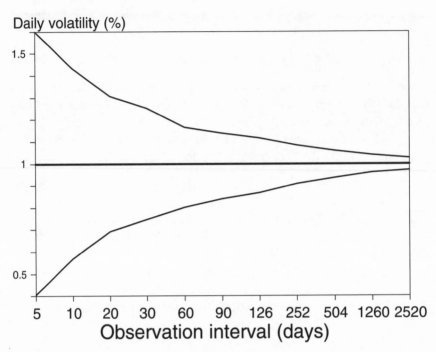

around the estimate of volatility for various sample sizes, assuming a true daily volatility of 1 percent.

With five trading days, the band is rather imprecise, with upper and lower values set at [0.41%, 1.60%]. After one year, the band is [0.91%, 1.08%]. As the number of days increases, the confidence bands shrink to the point where, after 10 years, the interval narrows to [0.97%, 1.03%]. Thus, as the observation interval lengthens, the estimate should become arbitrarily close to the true value.

Finally, $\hat{\sigma}$ can be used to estimate any quantile (an example was shown in Section 1.4). As the normal distribution is fully characterized by two parameters only, the standard deviation contains all the information necessary to build measures of dispersion. Any σ-based quantile can be derived as

$$\hat{q}(\sigma) = \alpha\hat{\sigma}. \tag{5.16}$$

At the 95 percent confidence level, for instance, we simply multiply the estimated value of $\hat{\sigma}$ by 1.65 to find the 5 percent left-tail quantile. Of course, this method will be strictly valid only if the underlying distribution is closely approximated by the normal. When the distribution is suspected to be strongly nonnormal, other methods such as kernel estimation also provide estimates of the quantile based on the full distribution.[2]

2.4 Estimation Error in Sample Quantiles

For arbitrary distributions, the cth quantile can be empirically determined from the historical distribution as $\hat{q}(c)$, as shown in Section 1.2. There is, as before, some sampling error associated with the statistic. Kendall (1994) reports that the asymptotic standard error of $\hat{q}$ is

$$\text{se}(\hat{q}) = \sqrt{\frac{c(1 - c)}{Tf(q)^2}}, \qquad (5.17)$$

where T is the sample size and $f(\cdot)$ is the probability distribution function evaluated at the quantile q. The effect of estimation error is illustrated in Figure 5–5, where the expected quantile and 95 percent confidence bands are plotted for quantiles from the normal distribution.

For the normal distribution, the 5 percent left-tailed interval is centered at 1.65. With $T = 100$, the confidence band is [1.24, 2.04], which is quite large. With 250 observations, which correspond to about one year of trading days, the band is still [1.38, 1.91]. With $T = 1250$, or five years of data, the interval shrinks to [1.52, 1.76].

These intervals widen substantially as one moves to more extreme quantiles. The expected value of the 1 percent quantile is 2.33. With one year of data, the band is [1.85, 2.80]. The interval of uncertainty is about twice that at the 5 percent interval. Kupiec (1995) points out that sample quantiles are increasingly unreliable as one goes further in the left tail; that is, from the 10 percent quantile to the 1 percent quantile.

As expected, there is more imprecision as one moves to lower left-tail probabilities, because fewer observations are involved. This is why VAR measures with very high confidence-levels should be interpreted with extreme caution.

---

2. For a further description of kernel estimation methods, see Scott (1992).

FIGURE 5–5

Confidence Bands for Sample Quantiles

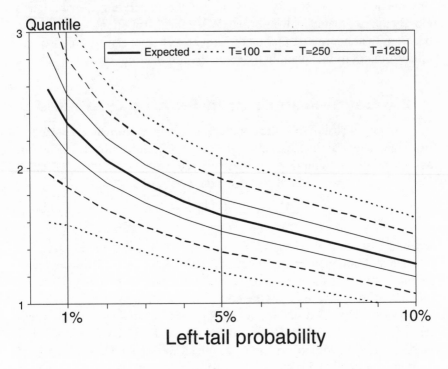

Left-tail probability

2.5 Comparison of Methods

So far, we have developed two approaches for measuring a distribution's VAR: first, by directly reading the quantile from the distribution $\hat{q}$; second, by calculating the standard deviation then scaling by the appropriate factor $\alpha\hat{\sigma}$. The issue is, Is either method superior to the other?

Intuitively, we might expect the σ-based approach to be more precise. Indeed, $\hat{\sigma}$ uses information about the whole distribution (in terms of all squared deviations around the mean), while a quantile uses only the ranking of observations and the two observations around the estimated value. And, in the case of the normal distribution, we know exactly how to transform $\hat{\sigma}$ into an estimated quantile, using α. For other distributions, the value of α may be different, but we should still expect a performance improvement since the standard deviation uses all of the sample information.

TABLE 5–3

Confidence Bands for VAR Estimates
Normal Distribution, T = 250

	VAR Confidence Level c	
	99%	95%
Exact quantile	2.33	1.65
Confidence band:		
sample $\hat{q}$	[1.85, 2.80]	[1.38, 1.91]
σ-based $\alpha\hat{\sigma}$	[2.24, 2.42]	[1.50, 1.78]

Table 5–3 compares 95 percent confidence bands for the two methods.[3] The σ-based method leads to substantial efficiency gains relative to the sample quantile. For instance, at the 95 percent VAR confidence level, the interval around 1.65 is [1.38, 1.91] for the sample quantile; this is reduced to [1.50, 1.78] for $\alpha\hat{\sigma}$, which is quite narrower than the previous interval.

A number of important conclusions can be derived from these numbers. First, there is substantial estimation error in the estimated quantiles, especially for high confidence levels, which are associated with rare events and hence difficult to verify. Second, parametric methods provide a substantial increase in precision, as the sample standard deviation contains far more information than sample quantiles.

3 CONCLUDING THOUGHTS

In this chapter, we have seen how to measure VAR using two alternative methodologies. The general approach is based on the empirical distribution and its sample quantile. The parametric approach, in contrast, attempts to fit a parametric distribution such as the normal to the data; VAR is then directly measured from the standard deviation. Systems such as RiskMetrics are based on a parametric approach.

In both cases, we have seen that long periods may be required to verify the accuracy of VAR models. Hence, the verification process will be time-consuming, even more so if models are frequently altered. With a new model, the data collection process will start again from scratch and

---

3. For extensions to other distributions such as the student, see Jorion (1996).

long periods may be required before the new model can be accepted. The parametric approach, however, provides notably more precise estimates.

Returning to the $15.2 million VAR figure at the beginning of the chapter, we can now assess the precision of this number. Using the parametric approach based on a normal distribution [see Equation (5.15)], the standard error of this number is $\alpha \times se(\hat{\sigma}) = 1.65 \times \$9.2m \,(1/\sqrt{2 \times 254})$ = $0.67. Therefore, a two-standard error confidence band around the VAR estimate is [$13.8m, $16.6m]. This narrow interval should provide reassurance that the $15 million VAR estimate indeed is meaningful.

CHAPTER 6

Fixed-Income Toolkit

Risk management—the "Theory of Particle Finance."

Charles Sanford, chairman of Bankers Trust

Risk management has been called the *theory of particle finance*. Indeed the first step in understanding risk is to decompose each product into its fundamental building blocks. A convertible bond, for instance, will be decomposed into an equity component and a bond component. At the building block level, exposures can be classified into a finite number of categories of risk, whose behavior is easy to characterize. The second step consists of aggregating the exposures of all securities in the portfolio into these categories. In the third step, total portfolio risk is constructed from the combination of exposures to risk factors and the joint characteristics of these risk factors.

As the number of risk factors increases, so should the precision of risk measures. In the fixed income market, for instance, a one-factor model provides a first approximation to movements in bond prices. Finer granularity can be obtained by considering additional risk factors, such as slope and curvature.

Thus the humble fixed-coupon bond can be subjected to different levels of disaggregation into risks. But the first step is to decompose bond payments into cash flows, which can be evaluated by appropriate discounting. This decomposition will also carry into derivatives, most of which contain fixed-income components. This chapter, therefore, develops a toolkit essential for the analysis of the fixed-income market in the context of risk management.

Section 1 reviews the implications of the term structure of interest rates for risk management. We show that zero-coupon rates (spot rates) are natural "primitive" factors for valuing bonds and therefore for measuring risk in the bond market. We explain how these can be obtained.

Risk management involves making predictions about movements in risk factors. Section 2 explains how forward rates can be used to forecast future spot rates. The term structure of forward rates provides a reference path for future spot rates in Monte Carlo simulations, which will be discussed further in Chapter 11.

Section 3 develops the concept of duration, which corresponds to a one-factor linear risk model of interest rates. We show the link between duration and value at risk. Finally, Section 4 defines *convexity*, the second-order factor in exposure of bonds to changes in interest rates.

1 THE TERM STRUCTURE OF INTEREST RATES

1.1 Bond Valuation

A fixed-income security is a government, corporate, or municipal bond that generates a predefined stream of payments. Because the payments are fixed, the value of bonds fluctuates with changes in interest rates, creating the potential for loss.

To introduce notations, let us write the market value of a bond P as the present value of future cash flows:

$$P = \sum_{t=1}^{T} \frac{C_t}{(1 + y)^t},$$
(6.1)

where

C_t = the coupon or principal payment or both in period t,
t = the number of periods (annual, semiannual, or other) to each payment,
T = the number of periods to final maturity,
y = the yield to maturity for this particular bond.

This pricing method uses discretely compounded yields, such as every half-year for most government bonds. Alternatively, yields can be *continuously* compounded, in which case the valuation is

$$P = \sum_{t=1}^{T} C_t e^{-y^c t}.$$
(6.2)

The two approaches are exactly equivalent, as long as the appropriate yields ($y^c \neq y$) are used in each formulation.

These definitions are tautologies. They implicitly define the discount rate y as the *internal rate of return* that equates the present value of the cash flows to the market value of the bond. For any bond, one can report its market price or, given the bond cash flows, its unique yield. The real question is whether this yield can be related to prevailing market conditions.

1.2 The Yield Curve

The term structure of interest rates represents the relationship, at a given point in time, between time to maturity and yield to maturity on fixed-income securities within a given risk class.

The traditional representation of the term structure is based on *par yield* bonds; that is, using the yield to maturity of bonds with a coupon close to their yield. For instance, one could take the most recently issued 2-year, 5-year, 7-year, and 10-year notes and 30-year bonds to infer yields going from 2 to 30 years. The advantage of this method is that the selected bonds, called *on the run*, are quite liquid and their prices accurately reflect market conditions. This method, however, ignores the information contained in other outstanding bonds. Some approaches attempt to fit a *yield curve* through the yields of all outstanding issues.

1.3 The Zero-Coupon Curve

Fitting a yield curve using bonds with different coupons, however, is unsatisfactory. The problem is that observed yields do not represent future returns unless all coupons can be reinvested at the same rate, which is highly unlikely.

Consider a pure discount bond, which has only one cash flow equal to the face value of the bond. Its price is

$$P = \frac{P_F}{(1 + y_T)^T}.$$ (6.3)

In this case, the yield to maturity is well-defined since it corresponds to the T period compounded return on the bond $y_T = R_T$.

In contrast, a coupon bond has many cash flows prior to maturity and can be decomposed into a series of pure discount bonds:

$$P = \frac{C_1}{(1 + R_1)} + \frac{C_2}{(1 + R_2)^2} + \ldots + \frac{C_N}{(1 + R_T)^T} + \frac{P_F}{(1 + R_T)^T}.$$ (6.4)

where R_i, $i = 1, \ldots, T$ are the *spot* rates making up the term structure at time t. The *zero-coupon curve*, or *spot curve*, represents the snapshot of spot rates plotted against time.

A zero-coupon curve is theoretically more appealing than the usual yield curve. It represents a set of primitive prices from which the value of fixed-income securities can be derived. Unfortunately, active markets for zero-coupon bonds (called *strips*) only exist in the United States and France and are relatively recent. Therefore, the spot rate curve is generally estimated from outstanding coupon-paying bonds, using the same decomposition as in equation (6.4).

1.4 Modeling the Term Structure

VAR models usually are based on estimates of spot rates at various maturities. The question is, How were these derived? Two methods can be used, one based on bootstrapping, and the other on interpolating a smooth function.

For the *bootstrapping* method, we need to observe a sample of coupon-paying bonds with equally spaced maturities. For instance, assume that we observe a one-year bond yielding 4.000 percent and a two-year par bond yielding 4.604 percent; coupons are paid once a year. The first bond is a zero, hence the one-year spot rate $R_1 = 4.00\%$. To find the second-year zero rate, we use (or bootstrap) the information from the first bond. The price on the two-year bond is

$$100 = \frac{4.604}{(1 + 0.0400)} + \frac{104.604}{(1 + R_2)^2}.$$

Solving for R_2, we find $R_2 = 4.618\%$. Next, we could use the information in R_1, R_2 to solve for R_3, and so on. In practice, this method works only if the observer has access to a full range of bonds expiring at regular intervals. Also, it ignores information contained in other bonds.

The second approach in empirical estimation of the term structure is to construct a spot-rate curve that is sufficiently smooth yet uses all the available data. To do this, the first step is to define a "discount function" as the present value of a dollar paid in the future

$$D(t) = (1 + R_t)^{-t},$$

for which a functional form must be chosen.

For instance, it is convenient to choose a cubic function:

$$D(t) = a_0 + a_1 t + a_2 t^2 + a_3 t^3, \tag{6.5}$$

which may be allowed to have different parameters a_{ij} across fixed ("knot") points $i = 1, \ldots, K, t_i < t < t_{i+1}$. This functional form consists of cubic functions "splined" at a number of knot points and is sufficiently flexible to fit most curves. To ensure continuity and smoothness of the spline curve, the function value and its first and second derivatives are restricted to be the same at the knot points. In addition, the discount function is set equal to 1 at time 0.

Second, the theoretical prices of the sample of selected bonds are computed from this discount function. For instance, if a bond pays the cash flows c_n, $n = 1, \ldots, N$ at respective times t_n, the model price is set at the present value of the future cash flows:

$$\hat{P} = \sum_n c_n D(t_n).$$

In this equation, the values of a are unknown. By collecting terms, the price can be written as a linear function of the spline parameters:

$$\hat{P} = a_0 f_0(c) + a_1 f_1(c) + a_2 f_2(c) + \ldots \tag{6.6}$$

For example, the previous two-bond portfolio yields the following equations:

Bond 1: $100 = 104.00\,(a_0 + a_1 + a_2 + a_3)$,
Bond 2: $100 = 4.60\,(a_0 + a_1 + a_2 + a_3)$
$\qquad\qquad + 104.60\,(a_0 + a_1 2 + a_2 2^2 + a_3 2^3).$

Collecting terms for the second bond, we have

$$100 = (4.60 + 104.60)\,a_0 + (4.60 + 104.60 \times 2)\,a_1$$
$$+ (4.60 + 104.60 \times 2^2)\,a_2 + (4.60 + 104.60 \times 2^3)\,a_3.$$

These equations are linear in the parameters a and can be solved in the usual fashion.

Additional parameters can be introduced, if so desired, to account for systematic deviations from this relationship. For instance, "on the run," or most recently issued, bonds usually sell at slightly higher prices than neighboring issues, which reflects a liquidity premium. In some markets, differential taxation of income and capital gains leads investors to prefer low-coupon bonds, which translates into higher prices than for high-coupon bonds. All of these effects can be accounted for by additional variables in the model (6.6).

The parameters a can be estimated by comparing the theoretical prices $\hat{P}$ with the market prices P for the selected bonds. For instance, one could choose to minimize the square of discrepancies between observed market prices and model prices. Because the cubic spline is linear in the values of a, the parameters can be computed by simply running a linear regression of the market prices on the model prices expressed as a linear function of the parameters of interest.

Figure 6–1, for example, shows the fit between market and theoretical prices for a sample of Treasury issues. Model prices are based on a cubic spline with three knot points. The fit is generally quite good, with average pricing errors around 5 to 10 cents, which is on the order of bid-ask spreads.

Cubic splines can be estimated easily using conventional regression packages and have been used by McCulloch (1975) with satisfactory results. Vasicek and Fong (1982), however, argue that cubic splines are inherently less well suited to fitting exponential curves like term structures and propose replacing equation (6.5) by exponential splines. Although theoretically more appropriate, the latter are more difficult to estimate because they involve a nonlinear optimization.[1]

The final step consists of recovering R_t from the estimated discount function $D(t)$. Figure 6–2 graphs the Treasury curve prevailing on October 4, 1995. The usual yield curve, consisting of par yield bonds, is upward sloping. The "strip" curve, based on the market prices of stripped issues, lies generally above the yield curve. These curves, however, are based on the prices of only a limited number of issues, which could be affected by liquidity considerations. A full-blown term structure model considers the prices of all outstanding issues and is less likely to be affected by supply and demand considerations for a particular issue. The third line describes the J.P. Morgan's zero-coupon curve on that day. The curve is similar to the strip curve but somewhat smoother. Most important, the term structure

---

1. These "empirical" term structures sometimes lead to an irregular term structure of forward rates. A smoother forward curve can be obtained by combining the sample information with a "reasonable" interest rate process, such as the mean-reversion model that underlies theories of the term structure.

FIGURE 6–1

Fitting Market Prices

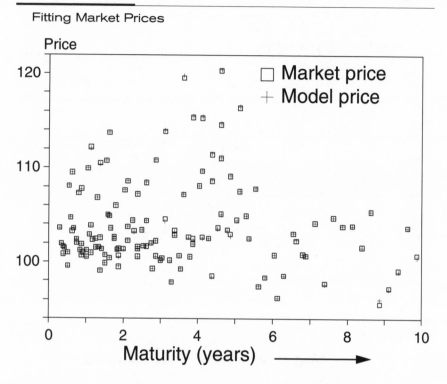

approach can be applied to any market, even those that contain no tradeable zero-coupon bonds.

1.5 Bond Risk Decomposition

The pure term structure permits us to decompose any bond into its component cash flows and then to reconstruct cash flows by maturity. This is the approach of particle finance applied to value at risk.

Table 6–1 shows how to decompose a two-bond portfolio, consisting of a $100m 6 percent five-year par bond and a $100m 4 percent one-year par bond. The left columns lay out the cash flows across time and the middle column contains the one- to five-year spot rates. From this information, we can construct the present value of the total portfolio cash flows sorted by five maturity buckets. Thus, the portfolio has an exposure of

FIGURE 6-2

Spot and Yield Curves

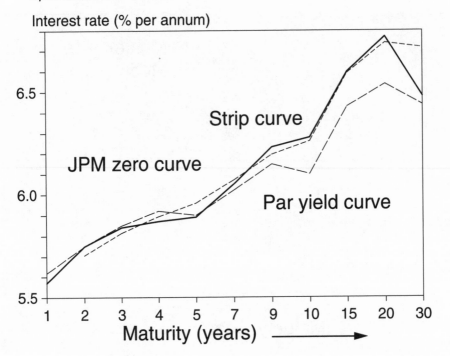

TABLE 6-1

Attributing Cash Flows to Maturity Buckets

	Cash Flows				Present Value of Cash Flows		
	Bond 1	Bond 2					
Maturity	$100m	$100m		Spot			Total
Bucket	6%	4%	Total	Rate			
(year)	5-year	1-year	Portfolio	(%)	Bond 1	Bond 2	Portfolio
1	6	104	110	4.000	5.77	100.00	105.77
2	6	0	6	4.618	5.48	0.00	5.48
3	6	0	6	5.192	5.15	0.00	5.15
4	6	0	6	5.716	4.80	0.00	4.80
5	106	0	106	6.112	78.79	0.00	78.79
Sum					100.00	100.00	200.00

$105.77m to movements in the one-year spot rate, about $5m to the two-to four-year rates, and $78.79m to the five-year rate. Chapter 11 will explain how the VAR of this portfolio can be constructed from this information, which is to be combined with the risk characteristics of the one- to five-year spot rates.

2 THE INFORMATION IN FORWARD RATES

2.1 The Forward Curve

The zero-coupon curve allows market observers to measure easily *forward rates*, which give a dynamic picture of future movements in interest rates.

Consider, for instance, one-year and two-year spot rates. An investor has the choice to lock in a two-year investment at the two-year rate observable now or to invest for a term of one year and roll over at the future one-year rate prevailing in a year. Assuming risk neutrality, one would expect the two investment alternatives to give the same payoff:

$$(1 + R_2)^2 = (1 + R_1)(1 + E[R_{1,1}]), \tag{6.7}$$

where $E[R_{1,1}]$ is the one-year rate expected in a year. But we can always define the one- to two-year forward rate $F_{1,2}$ from

$$(1 + R_2)^2 = (1 + R_1)(1 + F_{1,2}). \tag{6.8}$$

According to the *expectation* hypothesis of interest rates, forward rates are the best forecasts of future spot rates:

$$E[R_{1,1}] = F_{1,2}. \tag{6.9}$$

More generally, the T-period spot rate can be written as a geometric average of the spot and forward rates:

$$(1 + R_T)^T = (1 + R_1)(1 + F_{1,2}) \ldots (1 + F_{T-1,T}). \tag{6.10}$$

where $F_{i,i+1}$ is the forward rate of interest prevailing now (at time t) over a horizon of i to $i + 1$.

The forward rate also measures the slope of the term structure. In the simple two-period model, we can expand both sides of equation (6.8). After simplification and neglecting cross-product terms, we have

$$F_{1,2} \approx R_2 + (R_2 - R_1). \tag{6.11}$$

Therefore, with an upward sloping term structure, R_2 is above R_1, and $F_{1,2}$ will be also above R_2, providing a guiding path for the future movements of interest rates.

With continuous compounding, the definition of forward rates is more straightforward. Equation (6.8) can be generalized to any combination of periods τ_1 and τ_2:

$$e^{[R_2 \tau_2]} = e^{[R_1 \tau_1]} \, e^{[F_{1,2}(\tau_2 - \tau_1)]} \tag{6.12}$$

which defines the forward rate as

$$F_{1,2}(\tau_2 - \tau_1) = R_2 \tau_2 - R_1 \tau_1. \tag{6.13}$$

In other words, equation (6.11) becomes an exact equality.

When the "pure" term structure (the spot rate curve) is flat, the spot curve is identical to the par yield curve and the forward curve. In general, the curves differ. Figure 6–3 displays the case of an upward sloping term

FIGURE 6–3

Upward-Sloping Term Structure

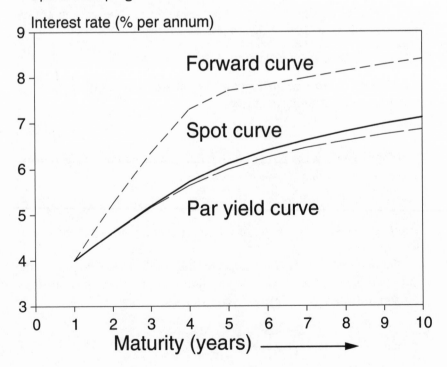

FIGURE 6–4

Downward-Sloping Term Structure

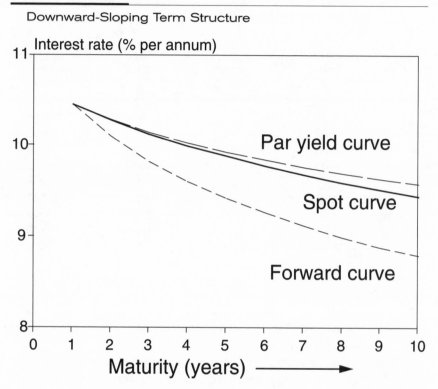

structure. It shows the yield curve is below the spot curve while the forward curve is above the spot curve. With a downward-sloping term structure, as shown in Figure 6–4, the yield curve is above the spot curve, which is above the forward curve.

Table 6–2 details the spot rates, forward rates and yields in Figure 6–3. It can be verified, for instance, that the one- to two-year forward rate satisfies $(1 + 4\%)^2 = (1 + 4.618\%)(1 + F_{1,2})$. The par yield is obtained as the coupon payment that ensures that the market value of the bond is also its face value.

2.2 Forecasting with the Forward Curve

The issue of whether the expectations hypothesis is indeed appropriate has been subject to much debate among financial economists. In the context of risk management, forward rates can simply be used to lock in future

TABLE 6–2

Spot and Forward Rates and Par Yields

Maturity (year) i	Spot Rate R_i	Forward Rate $F_{i,i+1}$	Par Yield y_i	Discount Function $D(t_i)$
1	4.000	4.000	4.000	0.9615
2	4.618	5.240	4.604	0.9136
3	5.192	6.350	5.153	0.8591
4	5.716	7.303	5.640	0.8006
5	6.112	7.712	6.000	0.7433
6	6.396	7.830	6.254	0.6893
7	6.621	7.980	6.451	0.6383
8	6.808	8.130	6.611	0.5903
9	6.970	8.270	6.745	0.5452
10	7.112	8.400	6.860	0.5030

interest rates without having to take a stand on the controversy. The class of models that rely on observed forward rates to price assets has become known as *no-arbitrage* models.

The information contained in forward rates is described in Figure 6–5, where only three periods are considered. Forward rates provide information about the sequence of future one-year spot rates, $F_{1,2}$, $F_{2,3}$, as well as about future term structures, such as next year's spot rates $F_{1,2}$, $F_{1,3}$.

This information is essential for the pricing of fixed-income instruments. And pricing is essential for understanding risk, as risk derives from changes in the valuation of securities.

Consider for instance a three-year floating-rate note, paying interest annually on a principal of $P_F = 1$. Suppose the first coupon payment is about to be set, and we observe the term structure R_1, R_2, R_3. The value of this note depends on three future one-year rates:

$$P = \frac{E[R_{0,1}]}{(1 + R_1)} + \frac{E[R_{1,2}]}{(1 + R_2)^2} + \frac{E[R_{2,3}] + 1}{(1 + R_3)^3}. \qquad (6.14)$$

We replace each future rate by the appropriate forward rate:

$$P = \frac{R_1}{(1 + R_1)} + \frac{F_{1,2}}{(1 + R_2)^2} + \frac{F_{2,3} + 1}{(1 + R_3)^3}. \qquad (6.15)$$

FIGURE 6-5

Forward Rates as Term Structure Forecasts

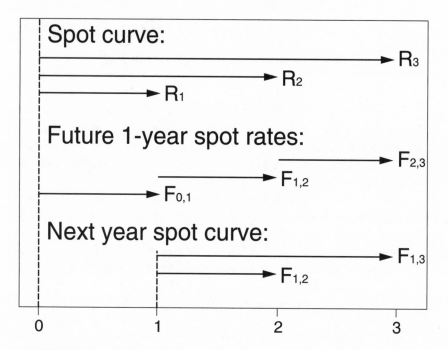

Expanding to a common denominator,

$$P = \frac{R_1\,(1 + F_{1,2})(1 + F_{2,3}) + F_{1,2}\,(1 + F_{2,3}) + F_{2,3} + 1}{(1 + R_3)^3}, \quad (6.16)$$

which simplifies to

$$P = \frac{(1 + F_{2,3})\,(1 + F_{1,2})\,(1 + R_1)}{(1 + R_3)^3} = 1. \quad (6.17)$$

Therefore, the current value of the floater is equal to the par value, as expected. But the same exercise could be repeated in a year, with two remaining coupon payments. The floater would still be valued at par. Therefore, the floater has no risk. As will be seen later, interest rate swaps typically contain a position in a floater. Just before a reset, this leg of the swap has zero VAR.

More generally, a coupon-paying bond or more complicated structures can be priced on any target date using information in forward rates.

Consider a three-year bond initially valued at par, $P_0 = 1$. After one year, it will be priced as

$$P_1 = \frac{C}{(1 + E[R_{1,2}])} + \frac{C + 1}{(1 + E[R_{1,3}])^2}. \tag{6.18}$$

Again replacing by forward rate information, we can write

$$P_1 = \frac{C}{(1 + F_{1,2})} + \frac{C + 1}{(1 + F_{1,3})^2}. \tag{6.19}$$

After manipulation, we can show that the future price is such that the total return on the bond, $R_B = C + (P_1 - P_0) / P_0$, is equal to the current one-year rate, R_1. This was to be expected, since in this risk-neutral world, all bonds must provide the same total return.

More generally, the distribution of future prices P_1 can be obtained from simulating future interest rates $R_{1,2}$ and $R_{1,3}$. The path of these variables is driven by two components, trend and volatility. The importance of forward rates is that they define a path along which these variables are expected to evolve.

As an illustration, consider the problem of assessing the risk of the return on a \$100m three-year bond over a one-year horizon. From Table 6–2, the one-year spot rate is 4.00 percent, and forward rates are $F_{1,2} = 5.24$ percent and $F_{1,3} = 5.79$ percent. The bond is initially selling at par with a coupon of 5.153 percent.

Assume now that changes in spot rates R_1 and R_2 are normally distributed; the two rates are perfectly correlated but their volatility differs, at 1.2 percent annually for the one-year rate and 1.0 percent for the two-year rate. Because there is only one effective source of randomness, this is a "one-factor model" of interest rates. The expected values for R_1 and R_2 are set at the forward rates 5.24 percent and 5.79 percent.

Figure 6–6 presents the distributions of 500 simulated future rates. For each joint realization of R_1 and R_2, we can compute the future value of the bond, P_1, whose distribution is graphed in the lower panel. We verify that the average values of the simulated rates, 5.24 percent (R_1) and 5.82 percent (R_2), are very close to their expected values. The distribution for R_2 is also tighter than that of R_1, which reflects its lower volatility. The bottom panel reveals the distribution of the bond price in a year. Its average value is 98.87, for a total return of $5.153\% + (98.87 - 100)/100 = 4.02\%$, which is very close to the risk-free rate of 4.00 percent, as expected.

FIGURE 6–6

Simulations of Bond Prices: Distributions

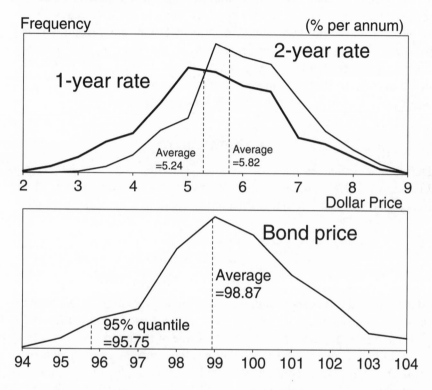

Finally, the frequency distribution also reveals the bond's VAR. The 95 percent sample quantile is 95.75. Alternatively, we can compute the VAR from the standard deviation of the distribution, which is 1.87. Assuming a normal distribution, the cutoff value is 95.76, which is very close to the previous number. Therefore, over a one-year horizon at the 95 percent level, the VAR of the bond, due to capital movements, is $(98.87 − 95.75) = $3.12 million.

More detail on this approach will be given in the chapter on Monte Carlo simulations, but suffice it to say, this method is powerful enough to accommodate multiple sources of risks, general distributions, and complex structures. If one prefers analytical tractability at the expense of lower accuracy, duration provides a particularly simple risk model and is studied next.

3 DURATION

We observe that bonds with longer maturities display greater price movements. Maturity, however, is an imperfect measure of risk because it accounts for only the repayment of principal and ignores all coupon payments. In contrast, *duration* provides a better measure of price risk, because it accounts for all payments and not only the principal. Duration also measures the sensitivity of an asset's price to movements in yields. This is why duration is such a valuable tool for risk management.

3.1 Definition

Duration is a characteristic of an asset. Duration was first defined by Macaulay in 1938 as the weighted maturity of each bond payment, where the weights are proportional to the present value of the cash flows:

$$D = \sum_{t=1}^{T} t \times w_t = \sum_{t=1}^{T} t \times \frac{C_t/(1 + y)^t}{\sum C_t/(1 + y)^t}. \qquad (6.20)$$

Table 6–1, for example, considered a five-year bond with a 6 percent coupon. Its duration can be found by multiplying the time to cash flow by the corresponding present value of the payment (discounted at the bond's yield) and then dividing the total by the value of the bond.

Table 6–3 details the computations. The present value of the payments are in the fourth column. Note that the discount factor is assumed to be the internal yield on the bond. The fifth column reports the product of

TABLE 6–3

Computing Duration

Time (year)	Payment	Yield (%)	PV of Payment	Time × PV
1	6	6.00	5.66	5.66
2	6	6.00	5.34	10.68
3	6	6.00	5.04	15.11
4	6	6.00	4.75	19.01
5	106	6.00	79.21	396.05
Sum			100.00	446.51
Duration				4.4651

time and the present value factor. Summing and dividing by 100, the price of the bond, we find a duration of 4.465 years. For the second bond in Table 6–1, which pays a coupon and the principal back in one year, the duration is exactly one year, as there are no intermediate cash payments.

3.2 Duration as Interest Rate Exposure

Redington (1952) originally suggested that duration could be used for an optimal strategy for bond investments given a definite time horizon. He pointed out that a life insurance's investment portfolio will be immune to fluctuations in interest rates if the portfolio duration is set equal to that of liabilities. Fisher and Weil (1971) actually proved that *immunization* is achieved by duration hedging.

To see the link between duration and bond price changes, recall that the market price P of a bond can be written in terms of the present value of future cash flows as

$$P = \sum_{t=1}^{T} \frac{C_t}{(1 + y)^t}. \tag{6.21}$$

The sensitivity of the bond price to instantaneous changes in yield can be found from taking the derivative of P with respect to y:

$$\frac{dP}{dy} = \sum_{t=1}^{T} \frac{(-t)C_t}{(1 + y)^{t+1}} = -\frac{1}{(1 + y)} \sum_{t=1}^{T} \frac{(t)C_t}{(1 + y)^t}. \tag{6.22}$$

Macaulay's duration is formally defined in (6.20) as the weighted-average maturity of an investment:

$$D = (1/P) \sum_{t=1}^{T} tC_t/(1 + y)^t. \tag{6.23}$$

Consequently, the sensitivity of the bond price to changes in yields is

$$(1/P)\frac{dP}{dy} = -\frac{D}{(1 + y)}. \tag{6.24}$$

This was originally proven by Fisher as far back as 1966.

If yields are small, the denominator $(1 + y)$ can be approximated by unity, and duration measures the linear relationship between a bond return and changes in yields. Otherwise, for a better approximation, the *modified duration* is

$$D^* = -(1/P)\frac{dP}{dy} = \frac{D}{(1+y)}.$$ (6.25)

Duration is always measured in units of time. If t is expressed in other units, such as semiannual terms, the resulting duration is then expressed in a number of half-years and is usually converted to years for comparison purposes.

Duration also expresses the time dimension of an investment, taking into account intervening payments, and can be interpreted as a measure of the "effective" maturity of a bond. Focusing on maturity gives an inaccurate picture of the layout of cash flows because it ignores coupon payments. Indeed only in the case of zero-coupon instruments is the maturity equal to the duration measure. If F is the face value of the "zero," setting $C_t = 0$ and $C_T = F$ in (6.1) and (6.23) yields $P = F/(1 + y)^T$ and $D = (1/P)TF/(1 + y)^T$. Replacing P in the duration measure, we see that duration simplifies to maturity $D = T$ for a zero-coupon bond.

Therefore, duration approximates changes in the prices of coupon-paying bonds by changes in the price of zero-coupon bonds. As such, it can be used to compare bonds with differing maturities, payment schedules, and interest rates. This is shown in Box 6–1.

Since duration is a measure of linear exposure, the duration of a portfolio of securities is a simple weighted average of the individual durations. If the values of x_i represent the proportions invested in N different bonds, the portfolio duration is

$$D_p = \sum_{i=1}^{N} x_i D_i,$$ (6.26)

where D_i is the duration of bond i.

For example, take a portfolio with \$100 million equally invested in a five-year bond and a one-year bond, as described in Table 6–1. The respective durations are 4.465 years and 1 year. The net portfolio duration is then $0.5 \times 4.465 + 0.5 \times 1 = 2.733$ years.

As will be discussed later, this formula is strictly valid only if the term structure is flat; that is, if y is the same across all maturities. If this is not the case, the portfolio duration is only an approximation. For more precision, one can separate the cash flows for each bond in the portfolio and solve for the unique discount rate for the portfolio. Duration can then be computed as before from the individual cash flows.

A major feature of duration is that it is a dynamic measure. Unlike maturity, which moves in lockstep with time, duration does not evolve uniformly over time. For instance, just after a coupon payment, duration

---

BOX 6-1

USING DURATION TO COMPUTE RISK

Duration is a good first-order measure of a portfolio's exposure to interest rate risk. It is much more appropriate than maturity, especially when the portfolio is leveraged or involves more complex instruments such as structured notes.

In October 1992, Merrill Lynch sent a letter to Bob Citron, the treasurer of the Orange County Investment Pool (OCIP), warning that the effective duration of the portfolio was *seven* years. The high duration was due to the high leverage of the portfolio, which was achieved through reverse repurchase agreements. These allowed Citron to buy some $20 billion of securities with only $7.5 billion in investor's money. The portfolio was invested in a variety of notes with maturities going up to five years, with an average duration of 2.6 years. The 2.7-to-1 leverage ratio increased the effective duration to 7.

From 1989 to 1993, interest rates fell dramatically, which led to large gains for the OCIP investors. But in 1994, rates went up by about 3 percent. This created a loss of

$$\text{Dollar loss} = \text{dollar value} \times \text{duration} \times \text{yield change}$$
$$= \$7.5 \text{ billion} \times 7 \text{ years} \times 3\%$$
$$= \$1.575 \text{ million}$$

which is quite close to the actual loss of $1.6 billion suffered by the pool.

---

suddenly increases; duration also changes faster for bonds with high coupon payments or when current yields are low. As a result, portfolio managers who attempt immunization must always keep track of the current duration and periodically rebalance their portfolio.

3.3 Duration and Risk

Duration can be used to translate yield volatility into price volatility. Yield volatility is generally thought to be more stable than price volatility, but ultimately, this is an empirical issue. From equation (6.25), we derive the relative change in prices as a function of the change in yield:

$$\frac{dP}{P} = -D^* \, dy, \qquad (6.27)$$

and therefore

$$\sigma\left(\frac{dP}{P}\right) = D^* \, \sigma(dy). \tag{6.28}$$

For instance, assume the 10-year zero spot rate is 8.00 percent, with an annual volatility of changes in rates of 0.94. The annual return volatility is then

$$\sigma\left(\frac{dP}{P}\right) = \frac{10}{1 + 0.08} \times 0.94 = 8.70\%.$$

Price and yield volatility therefore can be directly computed from each other. Sometimes the yield volatility is expressed as $\sigma(dy/y)$. The adjustment into return volatility is then $\sigma(dP/P) = D^* \, y\sigma(dy/y)$.

3.4 Duration and Value at Risk

Duration is directly linked to value at risk. Indeed, VAR accounts for the exposure of a portfolio to a risk factor (duration) as well as the probability of an adverse move. In Chapter 1, we computed the VAR of a $100 million portfolio invested in a five-year note. Over the last 40 years, the 95 percent cutoff level for one-month returns was -1.7 percent. There was only a 5 percent chance that the portfolio would fall by more than $100 million times -1.7 percent, or $1.7 million. Therefore, the value at risk was $1.7 million.

The dollar loss can also be obtained by multiplying duration by the increase in yield. Assume that five-year notes carry a duration of 4.5 years. If the worst increase in yields over a month at the 5 percent level is 0.38 percent, then the worst loss is given by

Worst dollar loss		duration	×	dollar portfolio value	×	worst yield increase
	=	duration	×	portfolio value	×	yield increase
	=	4.5 years	×	$100m	×	0.38%

which is also $1.7 million. Therefore, value at risk is directly related to the concept of duration through yield volatility.

3.5 Limitations of Duration

Duration has emerged as an essential tool to measure interest rate exposure and manage interest rate risk.

However, Macaulay duration is strictly valid as a measure of exposure only for "parallel" and small movements in yields. First, yield movements need to be parallel, since the same yield change is applied to all intervening coupon payments whatever their maturity. Other measures of duration have been developed for other types of movements in the yield curves; unfortunately, they are valid only under the assumed term structure shift. Second, yield movements need to be small for the linear approximation to be valid. Each of these assumptions is now examined.

Parallel Moves in Yields

Duration is limited to a specific stochastic process for the term structure, a one-factor model. Since each cash flow is discounted at the same rate, Macaulay's duration assumes a flat term structure and "parallel" movements in the entire term structure. Since the term structure is rarely flat, changes in discount rates are usually not equal to changes in the yield to maturity.

In practice, duration is used in conjunction with a yield change for a maturity similar to that of the bond under scrutiny. One would not want, for instance, to multiply the duration of a 30-year bond by the change in the three-month rate to estimate the price movement. Instead, the change in the 30-year rate is more appropriate.

Even so, while it is true that long-duration bonds are more price sensitive to a given change in yield to maturity than short-duration bonds, it is also true that short-duration yields are more volatile than are long-duration yields. As a result, both duration and yield volatility must be considered in evaluating the riskiness of a bond.

Table 6–4 compares measures of duration and yield volatility for U.S. bonds with maturities varying from 1 to 30 years. Duration is based on 8 percent par coupon bonds. Yield volatility generally decreases with maturity. For instance, two-year volatility is 1.24 percent per annum versus only 0.94 percent for 30-year yields. Risk is not strictly proportional to duration. The ratio of 30-year to 2-year duration is $11.26/1.78 = 6.33$, while the ratio of 30-year to 2-year risk is $10.58/2.22 = 4.77$. More generally, this example shows that the volatility of yields is not uniform across maturities, which is why the duration model is only approximate. In contrast, VAR methods or factor models, as described in Chapter 8, can fully account for both duration and yield volatility.

Small Yield Changes

A second limitation of duration is that it is a *linear* approximation of interest rate exposure. It is valid only with infinitesimal changes in yields, even when the term structure is flat and undergoes parallel shifts. When

TABLE 6–4

Duration and Yield Volatility (8% yield, 8% coupon bonds)

Maturity (years)	Duration (years)	Yield Volatility (% per annum)	Risk (% per annum)
1	0.93	1.17	1.08
2	1.78	1.24	2.22
3	2.59	1.24	3.21
5	3.99	1.18	4.70
7	5.21	1.12	5.82
10	6.71	1.05	7.04
30	11.26	0.94	10.58

there are large shocks to the term structure, higher-order terms in the price derivative must be incorporated into the valuation. This is why convexity is sometimes also considered a second-order measure of exposure.

4 CONVEXITY

While duration is useful for predicting the effect of interest rate changes on the value of fixed-income accounts, it should only be regarded as a first-order approximation valid for small changes in yield. Further precision can be obtained by considering convexity.

4.1 Definition

Convexity is a second-order effect that describes the way in which duration changes as yield changes. The convexity measure can be obtained by differentiating equation (6.21) twice with respect to yield and dividing by price:

$$C = -\frac{dD^*}{dy} = \frac{1}{P}\frac{d^2P}{dy^2} = \frac{1}{P}\frac{1}{(1+y)^2}\sum_{t=1}^{T}\frac{t(t+1)C_t}{(1+y)^t}. \quad (6.29)$$

Convexity is measured in units of periods squared.

To see why convexity may be important, we can approximate a bond rate of return, or relative change in bond price, by a Taylor expansion with two terms:

$$(1/P)dP \approx (1/P) \frac{dP}{dy} dy + (1/2P) \frac{d^2P}{dy^2} (dy)^2$$

$$= -D^*dy + (1/2)C(dy)^2. \qquad (6.30)$$

When changes in yield are small, the convexity term can be ignored. Otherwise, we can rewrite the previous formula as $-[D^* - (1/2)Cdy]dy$.

This shows that convexity causes duration to increase in response to a decrease in rates and to decrease in response to an increase in rates. As convexity is *positive* for option-free bonds, the true price–yield curve lies above the duration line. This effect is advantageous because it implies that bond prices rise more than by the linear approximation and decrease less than by the linear approximation.

The greater the convexity, the more beneficial this effect. However, bonds with higher convexity will also be more sought after and therefore may be more expensive. Like in option positions, the price of convexity depends on the volatility in yields. If yields are expected to stay stable, then convexity will not be valued highly.

For a given yield and duration, the lower the coupon, the lower is the convexity. Hence, zero-coupon bonds have the lowest convexity for a given duration. On the other hand, *barbell* portfolios, composed of short-term and long-term bonds mixed so as to maintain the same duration as the zero, display much greater convexity. But as in the case of duration, the quality of these approximations hinges on parallel moves in the term structure.

4.2 Improving the Price Approximation

Figure 6–7 presents the actual bond price changes resulting from changes in yields for an 8 percent par bond. Also displayed are the estimates of price changes using duration alone and using a combination of duration and convexity.

Duration alone provides a reasonable estimate of bond price changes when the interest rate changes are small. For instance, as rates increase by 2 percent, the price error due to the duration approximation is (87.54 − 85.89), or a 165 basis points understatement. As rates drop by 2 percent, the price error becomes (114.87 − 114.13), or a 74 basis points understatement. The approximation is not bad, considering that the bond price itself changed by about 1,400 basis points.

When both duration and convexity are used together, the predicted price is far more accurate over a broader spectrum of rate changes. As rates

FIGURE 6-7

Price Approximations

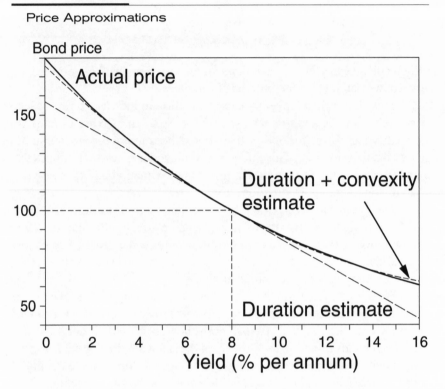

increase by 2 percent, the price error due to the duration/convexity approximation is (87.54 − 87.07), or only 47 basis points. As rates drop by 2 percent, the price error is (114.87 − 115.33), or only 46 basis points. As Figure 6–7 shows, convexity can substantially improve on duration approximation for large rate changes.

As was the case for duration, the convexity of a portfolio of fixed-income instruments can be derived from a simple weighted average of the components of the portfolio convexity. If x_i is the proportion invested in bond i with convexity C_i, portfolio convexity can be approximated by

$$C_p = \sum_{i=1}^{N} x_i C_i. \qquad (6.31)$$

The next chapter will show how VAR can be measured for nonlinear instruments.

CHAPTER 7

Derivatives

The concept of derivatives stems back at least to the Bible. In Genesis, God began creation by separating light from darkness.

Andrew Davidson, head of a derivatives research firm.

Derivative instruments allow users to disaggregate risks, to bear those they can manage and transfer those they are unwilling to bear. By providing controlled exposure to financial risks, they have created the impetus for modern risk-management methods. This chapter focuses on the characteristics of derivatives relevant for computing value at risk.

A *derivatives contract* can generally be defined as "a private contract deriving most of its value from some underlying asset, reference rate, or index—such as a stock, bond, currency, or a commodity." Derivatives range from simple building blocks such as linear contracts (forwards, futures, and swaps) to complex products such as some structured notes or exotic options. Any asset with a derivative feature can be priced as the sum of various components. For instance, a callable government bond is equivalent to a position in a straight government bond plus a short position in a call option. The bond's VAR can be reconstructed from the VAR of its components.

Section 1 shows how forwards and futures can be decomposed into "primitive" building blocks to compute VAR. The pricing and risk of swaps is explained in Section 2. Next, Section 3 describes options. Linear VAR models adequately describe the risks of linear derivatives such as forwards and swaps; however, they can badly represent the risks of options because of their nonlinear nature. The risk of assets with option components must be modeled with higher-order terms or alternatively with simulation methods. Section 4 provides a worked-out example of VAR computations for an option position used by Leeson.

1 FORWARDS AND FUTURES

The simplest class of derivatives consists of forward and futures contracts. These are private agreements to exchange a given asset at a fixed point in the future. The terms of the contract are the quantity, date, and price at which the exchange will be done.

Generally, the *forward price* is set so that the value of the contract itself is zero at initiation. To review the pricing of forwards, we define the following variables:

S_t = spot price of a security,
F_t = forward price of a security,
r = risk-free rate,
y = asset yield,
τ = time to maturity.

1.1 Pricing Forwards

In what follows, we shall use continuous compounding, in which case the present value of a dollar paid at expiration is defined as $e^{-r\tau}$. To price a forward contract, we consider that investors have two alternatives, which are economically equivalent: (1) Buy $e^{-y\tau}$ units of the asset at the price S_t and hold for one period, or (2) enter a forward contract to buy one unit of the asset in one period. Under alternative (1), the investment will grow, with reinvestment of dividend, to exactly one unit of the asset after one period. Under alternative (2), the contract costs nothing but we need to set aside enough cash to pay F_t in the future. After one year, the two alternatives lead to a position in one unit of the asset.

Therefore, their initial cost must be identical. This leads to the fundamental relationship between forward and spot prices, known as the *cost of carry:*

$$F_t e^{-r\tau} = S_t e^{-y\tau}. \tag{7.1}$$

This formula is quite general. It includes

- Futures on assets such as stock indices that make a continuous dividend payment,

- Futures on foreign currencies, where the dividend becomes the foreign-currency interest rate $y = r^*$,
- Futures on commodities, where the convenience yield, or benefit from holding the cash commodity, can be interpreted as an implicit dividend payment,
- Futures on commodities with storage costs, such as gold and silver, in which case the storage cost s can be viewed as a negative dividend.

Assume now that we want to price an outstanding forward contract, where the purchase price K was set previously. By following the same steps as before, the investment in the asset itself can be replicated by buying the existing forward contract (which has value f_t) and setting aside the present value of the purchase price K :

$$f_t = S_t e^{-y\tau} - K e^{-r\tau}, \tag{7.2}$$

where

K = purchase price set in contract,
f_t = current value of contract.

This formula is central to the measurement of risks for forward contracts. It shows that, even if the initial investment is zero, the holder of the contract may be subject to substantial fluctuations in value (as in Box 7–1). Hence the need to control risk.

1.2 Risks of Forward Contracts

The risk of positions in forward contracts can be established by differentiating equation (7.2) with respect to the various sources of risks to which the contract is exposed. These sources of risk include the underlying spot price, the domestic interest rate, and the asset yield:

$$df = \frac{\partial f}{\partial S}\, dS + \frac{\partial f}{\partial r}\, dr + \frac{\partial f}{\partial y}\, dy = e^{-y\tau}\, dS + K e^{-r\tau}\, \tau dr - S e^{-y\tau}\, \tau dy. \tag{7.3}$$

This shows how a forward contract can be decomposed into constituent components to compute VAR. Risk arises from the exposure to each source of risk (such as $e^{-y\tau}$) and from joint movements in sources of risk (such as dS).

This can be transformed further. Consider, for instance, a contract on a foreign currency. The yield is then the foreign currency interest rate $y = r^*$.

BOX 7-1

SHOWA SHELL: LOSSES ON CURRENCY FORWARDS

In February 1993, Showa Shell, an affiliate of the Royal Dutch/Shell Oil Group, announced it had lost about 125 billion yen in forward contracts ($1.05 billion). This was more than three times the company's profit of 40 billion yen the year before.

Showa Shell purchases oil in dollars, which it resells to domestic customers. Apparently, starting in 1990, some employees entered forward contracts in excess of the company's limit. The problem was compounded by Japanese accounting rules, which allowed traders to "roll over" their forward contracts into new ones, without having to realize losses (no marking to market). The company locked in forward rates around 145 yen to the dollar. By December 1992, the dollar had gone down to 125 yen. With a position of $6.4 billion, the loss can be computed from equation (7.2). Abstracting from the time value of money, the loss per contract is $f_t = S_t - K$, for a total of $6.4 (125 - 145), or 128 billion yen.

In April 1992, the Ministry of Finance banned rollovers of forward contracts. It is not clear, however, whether the new rule was enforced. One year later, another company, Kashima Oil, lost 153 billion yen ($1.45 billion) in similar foreign exchange trading.

Suppose now that the basic risk factors are defined in terms of relative changes in the spot price (dS/S) and of relative changes in the prices of zero-coupon bonds (dP/P) and (dP^*/P^*). The bond price changes can be expressed in terms of changes in yields as $dP = -\tau e^{-r\tau} dr$, or $(dP/P) = -\tau dr$, and equation (7.3) can be written as

$$df = (Se^{-r^*\tau}) \frac{dS}{S} - (Ke^{-r\tau})\frac{dP}{P} + (Se^{-r^*\tau})\frac{dP^*}{P^*}. \qquad (7.4)$$

1.3 VAR of Linear Contracts

This decomposition into exposures on different risk factors is the first step in the "theory of particle finance." The second step is the reconstruction of total risk from individual components.

Consider, for instance, a situation where the risk of the bills is negligible in relation to that of the spot price. In other words, there is only one source of risk, S. The "delta" of this position is such that $df = \Delta dS$, where $\Delta = e^{-r^*\tau}$.

The VAR of the forward contract is directly related to the VAR of the underlying asset, $\text{VAR}(dS) = \alpha\sigma\,(dS)$, where α is a function of the selected confidence level. The contract VAR is simply a linear function

$$\text{VAR}(df) = |\Delta| \times \text{VAR}(dS). \tag{7.5}$$

More general, the forward contract can be viewed as a "portfolio" of exposures on risk factors. Its VAR is related to the volatilities and correlations of the various risk factors, as explained in the next chapter.

2 SWAPS

Swaps are agreements by two parties to exchange cash flows in the future according to a prearranged formula. The first swap contract was arranged in 1981. At that time, the World Bank raised $290 million in fixed-rate loans and swapped it for liabilities in Swiss francs and Deutsche marks. Since then, the market for swaps has grown very rapidly, reaching trillions of dollars.

Currency swaps involve the exchange of currencies. To illustrate a currency swap, consider two institutions that wish to borrow in different currencies. IBM, for instance, wishes to raise ¥10,000 million over 10 years in Japanese yen, and the World Bank (WB) wishes to raise $100 million over the same period in U.S. dollars. The spot rate is 100 yen to the dollar. Assume that respective capital costs are

	Yen	Dollar
World Bank	5.0%	9.5%
IBM	6.5%	10.0%

Note that the World Bank has access to cheaper capital in the two markets: it has an "absolute" advantage, using the parlance of international trade. However, perhaps because it has easier access to the yen market, the World Bank has a "comparative" advantage in issuing yen-denominated debt. Relative to IBM, its funding costs are 1.5 percent cheaper in yen and only 0.5 percent cheaper in dollars.

This provides the basis for a swap which will be to the mutual advantage of both parties. If both institutions issue funds in their final desired currency, the total cost will be 9.5% (dollar cost for WB) + 6.5% (yen cost for IBM) = 16.0%. In contrast, the total cost of raising capital where each has a comparative advantage is 5.0% (yen cost for WB) + 10.0% (dollar cost for IBM) = 15.0% The gain to both parties from entering a swap is 16.0 − 15.0 = 1.0%. For instance, the following swap splits the benefit equally between the two parties:

World Bank	Yen	Dollar
Issue debt	Pay 5.0%	
Enter swap	Receive 5.0%	Pay 9.0%
Net		Pay 9.0%

The bank issues yen debt at 5.0 percent, then enters a 10-year swap whereby it promises to pay 9.0 percent in dollars in exchange for receiving 5.0 percent interest payments in yen. Its effective funding cost in dollars therefore is 9.0 percent, which is less than the 9.5 percent if it had raised funds directly in dollars. IBM benefits similarly. This example illustrates how institutions use swaps to lower funding costs. Since 1981, the World Bank estimates that swaps have saved $845 million in borrowing costs.

An *interest rate swap* is a mechanism for transforming a cash-flow stream from fixed to floating or vice versa, or from floating against a certain index to floating against another index. Interest swaps involve swapping only the interest payments on the respective loans. No principal needs to change hands. The exchange of cash flows is commonly done on a *net* basis, where only the net amount is transferred between parties on each payment date.

Interest rate swaps can be combined with currency swaps to transform a fixed liability in one currency into a floating liability in another currency. Swaps now include commodity swaps, equity index swaps, differential swaps, credit swaps, and so on.

2.1 Pricing Swaps

Swaps can generally be priced in two ways: either as the difference in the present value of the two streams of cash flows or as a portfolio of forward contracts corresponding to each exchange of funds.

Consider for instance the currency swap just described. The value of the swap to the World Bank is a long yen bond minus a dollar bond. Defining S as the dollar price of the yen and P and P^* as the dollar and yen bonds, we have

$$V = S(\$/¥)\, P^*(¥) - P(\$). \tag{7.6}$$

Note the similarity with (7.2). If there is only one cash flow, the yen bond is a zero. Its value is then $P^* = P_F^* e^{-r^*\tau}$, where P_F^* is the face value in yen. Similarly, the dollar bond with face value P_F is worth $P = P_F e^{-r\tau}$. The value of the swap is now $V = SP_F^* e^{-r^*\tau} - P_F e^{-r\tau}$. The valuation of the forward contract in (7.2) relates to one unit of the foreign currency. Adjusting for principal payment, we have

$$(V/P_F^*) = Se^{-r^*\tau} - (P_F/P_F^*)\, e^{-r\tau},$$

which is identical to the valuation of the forward contract if one sets $K = (P_F/P_F^*)$.

Going back to the general case, define the bond value as $P(C, y, P_F)$ where the coupon is C, the yield is y, and the face value is P_F. Using these data, the swap to the bank is initially worth

$$V = (1/100)\, P(5\%, 5\%, ¥10000) - P(9\%, 9\%, \$100)$$
$$= (1/100)10000 - 100 = 0.$$

As with forward contracts, the initial value of the swap is zero.

The market value of the swap is affected by changes in exchange rates and interest rates. Suppose, for instance, that the Bank of Japan lowers rates by 1 percent, which moves the spot rate to 110 yen to the dollar. The new value of the swap is now

$$V = (1/110)\, P(5\%, 4\%, ¥10000) - P(9\%, 9\%, \$100)$$
$$= (1/110)10811 - 100 = -\$1.72m.$$

The swap lost value because of the long position in the yen that depreciated. Some of this was offset by a higher value for the yen bond, but the net effect was a loss.

Interest rate swaps can be priced in a similar fashion. Assume company A makes floating-rate payments in exchange for receiving fixed-rate payments. If B_F is the value of the fixed-rate bond and B_f is the value of the floating-rate bond, the value of the swap is $V = B_F - B_f$.

At the beginning of its life, the value of the swap is zero, and $B_F = B_f$. If interest rates fall, A's swap will be more valuable, since it receives higher coupons than prevailing market yields. B_F will increase to the present value of fixed cash flows, using the appropriate discount rates, while

B_f will barely change, because interest payments are reset at regular intervals. In fact, just before a reset, B_f will behave exactly like a cash investment, with fair value equal to the principal.

2.2 Risks of Swaps

The risks of swaps parallel those of forward contracts. In the case of a currency swap, movements in value can be due to movements in the spot exchange rate and in the local and domestic yields $V = V(S, r, r^*)$, where r is the yield to maturity on the domestic bond, and r^* is the yield to maturity on the foreign currency bond. Using the duration approximation and continuous compounding,

$$dV = \frac{\partial V}{\partial S} \, dS + \frac{\partial V}{\partial r} \, dr + \frac{\partial V}{\partial r} \, dr*$$

$$= P*dS + S(-D*P*)dr* + DPdr. \qquad (7.7)$$

The risk of an interest rate swap depends on the timing of the reset on the floating-rate leg. With continuous resetting, this leg has no risk. In practice, the coupon may be reset every six months, for instance. Just before a reset period, the movement in value of an interest rate swap is solely due to the fixed-leg component:

$$dV = \frac{\partial P}{\partial r} \, dr = -DPdr. \qquad (7.8)$$

Just after the reset, the floating-rate note becomes a short-term fixed-rate note.

As before, the duration approximation can be improved upon by considering nonparallel movements in the term structure. Later, we will explain how to attribute the cash flows to separate sectors of the term structure.

3 OPTIONS

Options are valuable hedging and speculative instruments because of the flexibility they offer. An option confers the right to buy (a call option) or to sell (a put option) a designated quantity of an asset at a specified price, called the *strike price*, at or before a designated expiration date.

At expiration, a call option will be exercised only if it ends up in the money, that is if the spot price S_T is higher than the strike price K. Its value therefore is $c_T = \text{Max}(S_T - K, 0)$. In contrast, a put option will be exercised at expiration only if the spot price is below the strike price. Its value therefore is $p_T = \text{Max}(K - S_T, 0)$. The nonlinear pattern of options, however, causes serious difficulties for computing value at risk.

In what follows, we shall focus on conventional European calls and puts. Unlike American options, European options can be exercised only when they expire. Since the introduction of these basic options in 1973, the financial engineering industry has created a myriad of other instruments with different payoffs. These "exotic options" sometimes have no closed-form solution, in which case their exposure to risk factors must be found by numerical methods. But, as these risk factors are generally the same as those for conventional options, the principles developed here can be directly extended to other options.

3.1 Pricing Options

Evaluating options is as much an art as a science. The issue with options is whether the *premium* is fairly priced. This search for pricing led to the well-known Black-Scholes (BS) option pricing model, possibly the most successful model in applied economics. The derivation of the model is based on the following assumptions.

Black-Scholes Model Assumptions:

1. The price of the underlying asset is continuous and follows a random walk process called *geometric Brownian motion.*
2. The interest rate and variance are known and constant.
3. Capital markets are perfect (short sales are allowed, there are no transaction costs or taxes, and markets operate continuously.)

The most important assumption behind the model is that prices are continuous. This rules out discontinuities in the sample path, such as jumps, which invalidate the continuous hedging argument behind the BS model. The random walk assumption also rules out mean reversion in the asset price, or convergence to a fixed value. Therefore, the BS model is not strictly applicable to the fixed-income market, where bond prices converge to face values. In practice, the model may provide a good approximation for options on medium- to long-term bonds, which mature much later than the option term.

Based on these assumptions, Black and Scholes (1973) derived a closed-form formula for European options on a nondividend-paying stock. The key point in their derivation is that a position in the option is strictly equivalent to a "delta" position in the underlying asset. Therefore, a portfolio combining the asset and the option in appropriate proportions is "locally" risk free. *Locally* means that the portfolio is risk free only for small movements in the spot price. By arbitrage, this portfolio must return the risk-free rate.

Merton (1973) expanded the model to the case of a stock paying a continuous dividend yield. The value of a European call is

$$c = Se^{-y\tau} N(d_1) - Ke^{-r\tau} N(d_2), \tag{7.9}$$

where $N(d)$ is the cumulative distribution function for the standard normal distribution:

$$N(d) = \int_{-\infty}^{d} \Phi(x)\, dx = \frac{1}{\sqrt{2\pi}} \int_{-\infty}^{d} e^{-\frac{1}{2}x^2}\, dx,$$

where Φ is the standard normal distribution function; $N(d)$ is also the area to the left of a standard normal variable with value equal to d. The actual values of d_1 and d_2 are

$$d_1 = \frac{\ln(Se^{-y\tau}/Ke^{-r\tau})}{\sigma\sqrt{\tau}} + \frac{\sigma\sqrt{\tau}}{2}, d_2 = d_1 - \sigma\sqrt{\tau}.$$

The expression $\sigma\sqrt{\tau}$ measures the volatility over the life of the option; if the volatility is measured on a per annum basis, then T must be expressed in number of years.

By put-call parity, the European put option value is

$$p = Se^{-y\tau}[N(d_1) - 1] - Ke^{-r\tau}[N(d_2) - 1]. \tag{7.10}$$

It is essential to note that the expected rate of return on the underlying asset does not appear in the pricing model. This reflects the fundamental observation by Black and Scholes that the option can be priced using an arbitrage argument, by constructing a portfolio of the stock and call that is locally risk free. As a result, the risk premium on the asset, if any, must disappear from the final valuation formula.

As in the case of futures contracts, the valuation model applies to any asset making a continuous payment. Since foreign currencies pay a continuous rate of interest, which can be interpreted as a "dividend" yield, the BS model can be directly extended to currency options, as shown by Garman and Kohlhagen (1983). The model also applies to options on futures. As demonstrated by Black (1976), futures allow investors to take a position in an asset without up-front payment. Their savings therefore are the risk-free rate of interest. The Black model is simply the BS model where the futures is imputed on a yield equal to the risk-free rate.

The model also can be easily extended to valuing the option to exchange an asset B for another asset A. Margrabe (1978) has shown that the valuation formula is similar to the BS model, except that K is replaced by the price of asset B (S_B), and the risk-free rate by the yield on asset B (y_B). The volatility σ is now that of the difference between the two assets, which therefore also involves the correlation coefficient.

3.2 Risks of Options

The BS option pricing model relates the value of an option to several risk factors: $c = f(S, \sigma, r, y)$. Option values also depend on the time to expiration, but in a deterministic fashion. Generally, movements in the option value can be written as

$$dc = \frac{\partial f}{\partial S}\, dS + (1/2)\, \frac{\partial^2 f}{\partial S^2}\, dS^2 + \frac{\partial f}{\partial \sigma}\, d\sigma + \frac{\partial f}{\partial r}\, dr + \frac{\partial f}{\partial y}\, dy + \frac{\partial f}{\partial t}\, dt. \quad (7.11)$$

The major risk factor is the underlying asset price. The BS derivation showed that holding a call option is equivalent to holding a fraction of the underlying asset, where the fraction dynamically changes over time. This observation justifies the linear approximation for computing the VAR of a portfolio that includes derivatives such as options. For a better fit, the second partial difference also can be considered, much like convexity for bonds.

This equivalence is illustrated in Figure 7–1, which displays the current value of a call as a function of the current spot price. The long position in one call is replicated by a partial position in the underlying asset. The size of the position increases when the stock price increases, as in a graduated stop-loss order. The fraction to hold is also called the *hedge ratio*, or *delta* (Δ) of the option. This dynamic equivalence, however, is valid only if the model and assumptions used to create the hedge ratio are correct.

Since the BS formula is of closed form, the partial derivative of a call option with respect to the spot price can be written explicitly as

$$\Delta = \frac{\partial c}{\partial S} = e^{-y\tau} N(d_1), \quad (7.12)$$

which is always positive and below unity.

FIGURE 7–1

Dynamic Replication of a Call Option

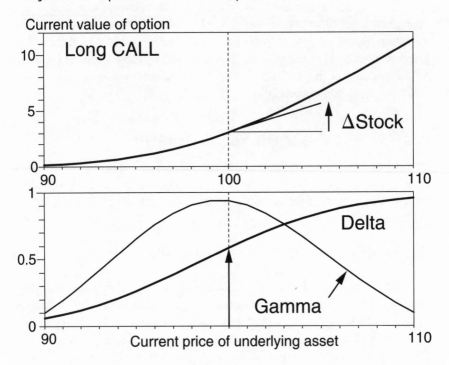

The bottom panel in Figure 7–1 shows how the delta varies with the spot price. The essential feature of this figure is that delta varies substantially with the spot price (and also with time). As the spot price increases, the option becomes *in the money* and behaves similarly to an outright position in the stock, moving nearly one for one with the stock ($\Delta \to 1$). As the spot price decreases, the option becomes *out of the money,* with a delta close to zero.

The delta of a put option is

$$\Delta = \frac{\partial p}{\partial S} = e^{-y\tau} [N(d_1) - 1], \tag{7.13}$$

which is always negative. As shown in Figure 7–2, holding a put option is equivalent to a *short* position in the stock in the amount Δ.

FIGURE 7–2

Dynamic Replication of a Put Option

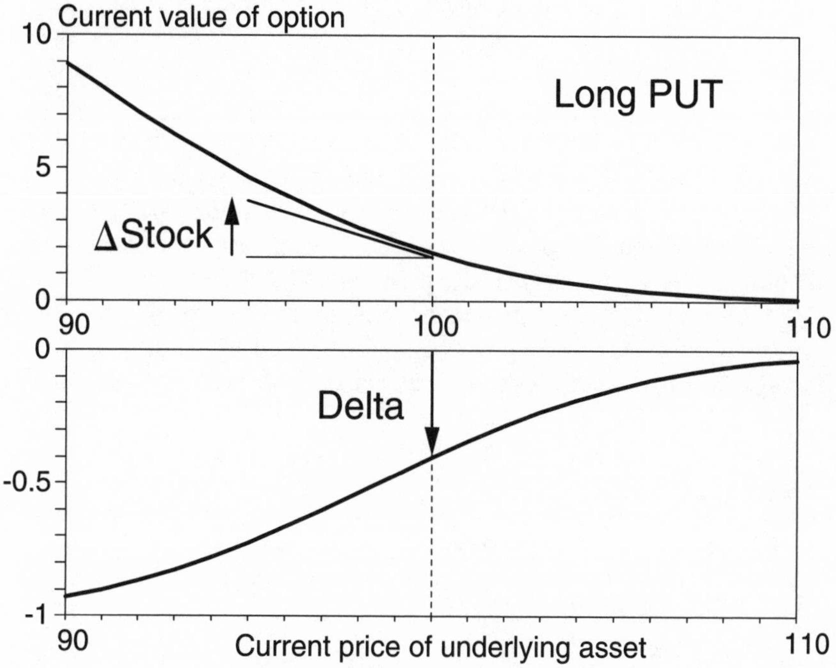

The great advantage of deltas is that they are additive. Traders hold many different options in their inventory. It would be impractical to try to hedge every one of them individually. Instead, option "books" are summarized by their total portfolio delta, obtained as

$$\Delta \hat{p} = \sum_{i=1}^{N} x_i \Delta_{\mathrm{i}}, \qquad (7.14)$$

where x_i is the number of options of type i in the portfolio. Traders then can hedge their net portfolio delta.

Options are nonlinear functions of underlying spot prices. Therefore, linear or delta hedging may fail for large moves, which is why it is useful to examine the quadratic component of options. As for bond valuation, the change in the value of the option can be written as a Taylor series

$$dc = \Delta dS + \frac{1}{2}\,\Gamma dS^2 + \ldots \qquad (7.15)$$

For a European call or put, gamma (Γ) can be derived analytically as

$$\Gamma = \frac{\partial^2 c}{\partial S^2} = \frac{e^{-y\tau}\,\Phi\,(d_1)}{S\sigma\,\sqrt{\tau}.} \qquad (7.16)$$

Figure 7–1 displays the call option gamma. At-the-money options have the highest gamma, which means that the delta changes very fast as S changes. In-the-money options have low gammas, since the option is essentially equivalent to a position in the stock. Similarly, out-of-the-money options have low gammas because their delta is close to 0.

How well does delta-gamma hedging work? Figure 7–3 provides an answer. It compares the approximations provided by delta hedging and delta-gamma hedging to the actual call price. Delta hedging is useful only

FIGURE 7–3

Delta-Gamma Approximation for a Long Call

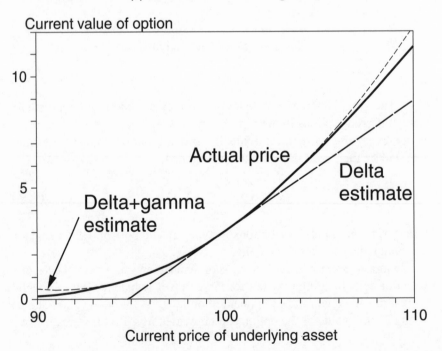

for small movements from the initial value of $100. With a price of $94, which is about one standard deviation down, the linear approximation gives a negative value (which is impossible for an option), understating the true option by 94 cents. At a spot price of $106, the delta approximation is $6.54, which is 104 cents below the true value.

Delta-gamma hedging, as expected, provides a much better approximation over a wide range of spot prices. The only drawback of this method is that it tends to overestimate the true option value for extreme movements. At $S = \$94$, it overestimates the true option premium by 5 cents only. At $S = \$106$, the error is 15 cents.

Thus, gamma extends to options the concept of convexity developed for bonds. Whereas conventional bonds offer positive convexity, options can create positive or negative convexity. Positive convexity is beneficial because it implies that the value of the asset decreases slower and increases faster relative to a linear approximation. In contrast, negative convexity can be dangerous because it implies faster price falls and slower price increases than otherwise.

Figure 7–4 associates convexity with option positions. Buying options, both calls and puts, leads to positive convexity. Selling options implies taking on negative convexity. Because negative convexity is harmful, it can be assumed only on payment of a premium. Thus the option premium can be viewed as the price of convexity. However, it should be clear by now that high gammas invalidate linear VAR models.

Options are strange instruments. The BS analysis has shown that their fair value does not depend on the expected change in the spot price. However, they are extremely sensitive to volatility. Options therefore can be viewed as volatility bets, in contrast with positions in the cash or forward markets, which are directional bets.

The sensitivity of an option to volatility is called the option *vega* (sometimes also called *lambda*). Vega is the partial derivative of the option price with respect to the volatility. For European calls and puts, we have

$$\Lambda = \frac{\partial c}{\partial \sigma} = Se^{-y\tau} \sqrt{\tau}\, \Phi\,(d_1). \qquad (7.17)$$

Since Λ must be positive, long positions in options respond positively to volatility increases and decrease in price as volatility decreases. In addition, given that Λ follows the usual bell shape of $\Phi\,(x)$, at-the-money options are the most sensitive to volatility.

FIGURE 7-4

Convexity

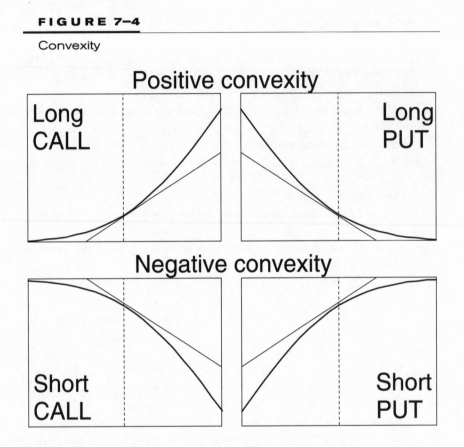

Options are also sensitive to movements in interest rates and yields, although the typical exposure to these risk factors is less than for the spot price or the volatility. A European call's exposure to interest rate, also called *rho*, is

$$\rho = \frac{\partial c}{\partial r} = Ke^{-r\tau}\,\tau\,N(d_2). \qquad (7.18)$$

For a put,

$$\rho = \frac{\partial p}{\partial r} = -Ke^{-r\tau}\,\tau\,N(-d_2). \qquad (7.19)$$

The exposure to the yield on the asset, for calls and puts, respectively, is

$$\rho^* = \frac{\partial c}{\partial y} = -Se^{-y\tau}\, \tau N(d_1), \tag{7.20}$$

$$\rho^* = \frac{\partial p}{\partial y} = Se^{-y\tau}\, \tau N(-d_1). \tag{7.21}$$

Finally, for completeness, we should mention the effect of *time decay*. For a European call, the variation in option value due to the passage of time, *theta*, is

$$\Theta = \frac{\partial c}{\partial t} = -\frac{\partial c}{\partial \tau}$$

$$= -\frac{Se^{-y\tau}\, \sigma \Phi\,(d_1)}{2\sqrt{\tau}} + ySe^{-y\tau} N(d_1) - rKe^{-r\tau} N(d_2). \tag{7.22}$$

For most options, Θ is generally negative, which means that the option loses value as time goes by. The derivative is always negative for American options, which give their holder the choice to exercise early.

To summarize the risk of option positions, Table 7–1 presents partial derivatives for a typical European call. The Γ, Λ, Θ measures are all highest when the option is at the money ($K = 100$). Such options have the most nonlinear patterns. The table also shows that changes in the spot price, among all variables, have the greatest effect on option values.

TABLE 7–1

Derivatives for a European Call (Parameters: $S = \$100$, $\sigma = 20\%$, $r = 5\%$, $y = 3\%$, $\tau = 3$ month)

	Variable	Unit	Strike		
			$K = 90$	$K = 100$	$K = 110$
c		Dollars	11.02	4.22	1.05
		Change per			
Δ	Spot price	dollar	0.868	0.536	0.197
Γ	Spot price	dollar	0.020	0.039	0.028
Λ	Volatility	(% per annum)	0.103	0.198	0.139
ρ	Interest rate	(% per annum)	0.191	0.124	0.047
$\rho^{\cdot}$	Asset yield	(% per annum)	−0.220	−0.135	−0.049
Θ	Time	day	−0.014	−0.024	−0.016

3.3 VAR of Nonlinear Contracts

Because option contracts are nonlinear functions of underlying risk factors, their VAR cannot reliably be based on their delta only. We now develop an improved approximation to an option's VAR based on the delta-gamma approximation.

Taking the variance of both sides of the quadratic approximation (7.15), we obtain

$$V(dc) = \Delta^2 V(dS) + (\frac{1}{2}\Gamma)^2 V(dS^2) + 2(\Delta\frac{1}{2}\Gamma) Cov(dS, dS^2).$$
(7.23)

If the variable dS is normally distributed, all of its odd moments are 0, and the last term in the equation vanishes. Under the same assumption, one can show that $V(dS^2) = 2V(dS)^2$, and the variance simplifies to

$$V(dc) = \Delta^2 V(dS) + \frac{1}{2} [\Gamma V(dS)]^2.$$
(7.24)

Defined as before, σ is the volatility of returns in the price, $\sigma(dS/S)$. Then the VAR of the option is

$$\text{VAR}(dc) = \alpha \sqrt{\Delta^2 S^2 \sigma^2 + \frac{1}{2} [\Gamma S^2 \sigma^2]^2},$$
(7.25)

which demonstrates the nonlinear relationship between the VAR of the underlying asset and the option's VAR. When $\Gamma = 0$, this simplifies to the VAR of linear contracts in equation (7.5). Equation (7.25), it should be noted, provides only an approximation to the true VAR. The exact VAR can be measured only from the actual distribution of option payoffs.

4 LEESON'S STRADDLE

The Barings story provides a good illustration of the shortcoming of delta hedging. Barings's downfall came from a big bet on the Nikkei 225, an index of Japanese stocks, that amounted to the staggering long position of $7 billion. These were implemented by holding, by the end of February 1995, unusually large futures positions on the Osaka, Tokyo, and Singapore exchanges. The VAR of this portfolio, including positions in bond futures, will be examined in more detail in Chapter 8.

Since futures are highly leveraged instruments, Barings did not need to put down the full $7 billion. Instead, Leeson posted margins with the exchange and was subject to variation margins as the contracts accumulated gains or losses. Leeson also sold options, about 35,000 calls and puts each on Nikkei futures. This position, known as a *short straddle,* is about delta neutral since the positive delta from the call is offset by a negative delta from the put, assuming most of the options were at the money.

In effect, the option position creates a potential for large losses. The position in calls is equivalent to 35,000 times the multiplier for the contract, which is 500 yen, divided by the yen/dollar exchange rate, which is about 100 yen. Therefore, variations in the position are equivalent to the option delta times variations in the Nikkei index times $0.175 million. Based on this information, Figure 7–5 displays the potential payoff from this position, abstracting from the initial receipt of

FIGURE 7–5

Leeson's Straddle

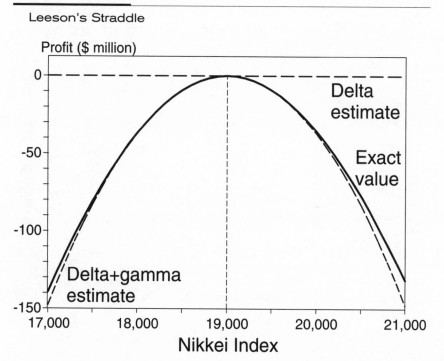

the option premium. At the current index value of 19,000, the delta VAR for this position is close to 0.

Of course, reporting a zero VAR is highly misleading. Any move up or down has the potential to create a large loss. A drop in the index to 17,000, for instance, would lead to a loss of about $150 million. Figure 7–5 compares the actual value of the straddle with the delta-gamma approximation. As in the case of duration plus convexity, this second-order approximation provides increased accuracy.

The risks involved are described in Figure 7–6, which plots the frequency distribution of profits on the straddle. This distribution is obtained from combining possible moves in the stock index over a day with the payoff function in Figure 7–5. The underlying risk factor is assumed to be normally distributed with a daily volatility of 1.26 percent.

FIGURE 7–6

Distribution of One-Day Profit for Straddle

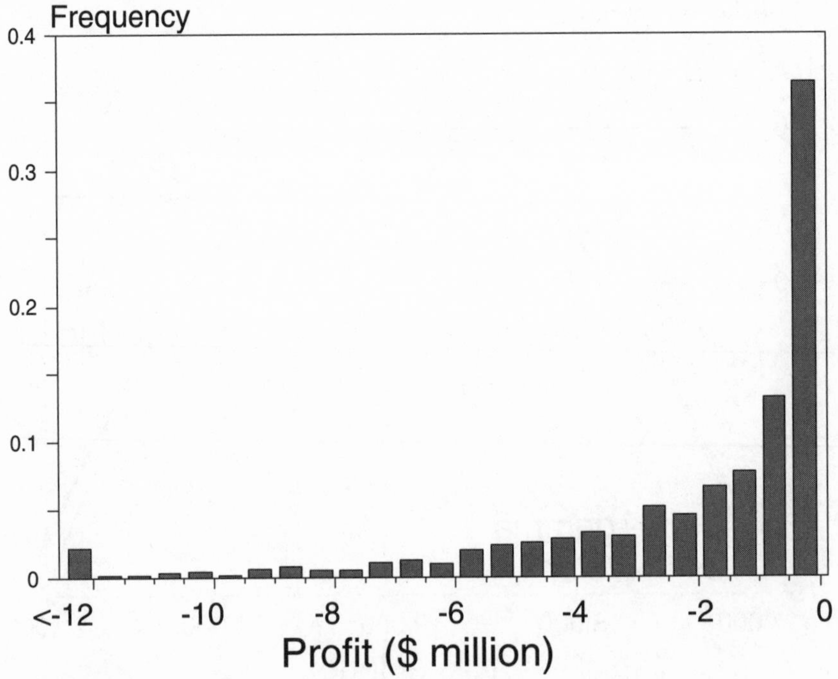

The distribution of profits looks quite different from the usual symmetric Gaussian distribution. The distribution of profits attains its most likely value at zero but is quite skewed to the left, which indicates large potential losses. Yet the delta model reports a VAR of zero. In this case, the delta approximation fails miserably.

The VAR of this position can be directly evaluated from the distribution. The mean and standard deviation are $-\$2.3m$ and $\$3.0m$, respectively; the 5 percent left quantile is $-\$8.6m$. Therefore, relative to the expected value, VAR $= 8.6 - 2.3 = \$6.3m$. Using a normal approximation to the true distribution, VAR $= 1.65 \times 3.0 = \$5.0m$. This number understates the true VAR, as expected given the asymmetry of this distribution.

The distribution can be approximated by the delta-gamma approach. Here, the net gamma of a position in one call and put is $\Gamma = 0.000422$. The total gamma is $\$0.175m \times 0.000422 = \$0.0000739m$. With a delta of zero, the expected return at the one-day horizon is

$$E(dc) = \frac{1}{2} \Gamma[\sigma(dS)]^2 = \frac{1}{2} \$0.0000739m\,(19{,}000 \times 0.0126)^2 = -\$2.1m,$$

which is very close to the actual mean of $-\$2.3m$.

As for the position VAR, it can be obtained from equation (7.25). With $\alpha = 1.65$ at the 95 percent confidence level, the VAR is

$$\text{VAR} = \alpha \sqrt{\frac{1}{2}[\Gamma S^2 \sigma^2]^2}$$

$$= 1.65 \sqrt{\frac{1}{2}\,[\$0.0000739m \times 19{,}000^2 \times 0.0126^2]^2} = \$4.9m$$

which is also very close to the approximation of $\$5.0m$. Relative to the linear approximation, which completely masked the market risk of the straddle, this is a substantial improvement.

And, indeed, the option position contributed to Barings's fall. As January 1995 began, the historical volatility on the Japanese market was very low, around 10 percent, and Leeson generated cash income by selling options. At the time, the Nikkei was hovering around 19,000. The option position would have been profitable if the market had been stable. Unfortunately, this was not so. The Kobe earthquake struck Japan on January 17 and led to a drop in the Nikkei to 18,000, shown in Figure 7–7. To make things worse, options became more expensive as market volatility increased. Both the long futures and the straddle lost money. As losses accumulated, Leeson increased his positions to recoup the losses, but to no avail. On February 27, the Nikkei dropped further to 17,000. Unable to meet the mounting margin calls, Barings went bust.

FIGURE 7–7

The Nikkei's Fall

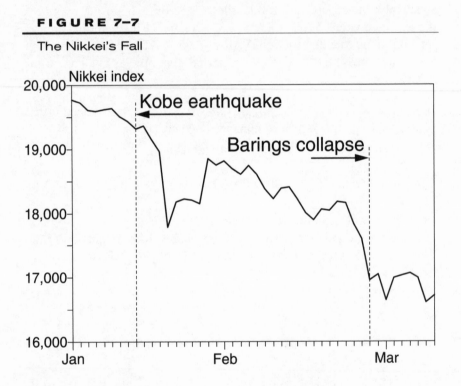

Portfolio Risk

Trust not all your goods to one ship.

Erasmus

The previous chapters have focused on single financial instruments. Absent any insight into the future, prudent investors should diversify across sources of financial risks. This was the message of portfolio analysis laid out by Harry Markowitz in 1959. Thus, the concept of value at risk, or portfolio risk, is not new. What is new is the systematic application of VAR to many sources of financial risks, including derivatives, culminating with one number that applies to the whole corporation.

As will be seen in Chapter 10, there are many approaches to measuring VAR. The shortest road assumes that asset returns are linearly related to each other. Indeed the "delta-normal" method is a direct application of traditional portfolio analysis based on variances and covariances.

This chapter provides a brief review of portfolio analysis. Section 1 relates VAR measures to total portfolio risk and shows how VAR can be decomposed into "incremental" components. Incremental VAR allows users to identify the asset that contributes most to their total risk. Section 2 presents a fully worked-out example of VAR computations, using Barings's fatal positions. One drawback of linear VAR models is that the size of the covariance matrix increases geometrically with the number of assets. Section 3 develops simplifications to the covariance matrix based on the diagonal and factor models.

1 PORTFOLIO VAR

1.1 Definitions

A portfolio can be characterized by positions on a certain number of risk factors. Once the decomposition is established, the portfolio return is a *linear* combination of the returns on underlying assets, where the weights are given by the relative dollar amounts invested at the beginning of the period. Therefore, the VAR of a portfolio can be reconstructed from a combination of the risks of underlying securities.

Define the portfolio return from t to $t + 1$ as

$$R_{p,t+1} = \sum_{i=1}^{N} w_{i,t} R_{i,t+1}, \tag{8.1}$$

where the weights $w_{i,t}$ were established at the beginning of the period and sum to unity. To shorten notation, the portfolio return can be written using *matrix notation*, replacing strings of numbers by a single vector:

$$R_p = [w_1\, w_2 \ldots w_N] \begin{bmatrix} R_1 \\ R_2 \\ . \\ . \\ . \\ R_N \end{bmatrix} = w'R, \tag{8.2}$$

where w' represents the transposed vector (i.e., horizontal) of weights and R is the vertical vector containing individual asset returns.

By extension of the formulas in Chapter 4, the portfolio expected return is

$$E(R_p) = \mu_p = \sum_{i=1}^{N} w_i \mu_i \tag{8.3}$$

and the variance is

$$V(R_p) = \sigma_p^2 = \sum_{i=1}^{N} w_i^2 \sigma_i^2 + \sum_{i=1}^{N} \sum_{j=1, j \neq 1}^{N} w_i w_j \sigma_{ij}$$

$$= \sum_{i=1}^{N} w_i^2 \sigma_i^2 + 2 \sum_{i=1}^{N} \sum_{j<i}^{N} w_i w_j \sigma_{ij}. \tag{8.4}$$

This sum accounts not only for the risk of the individual securities σ_i^2, but also for all different cross-products, which add up to a total of $N(N-1)/2$ different covariances.

As the number of assets increases, it becomes difficult to keep track of all covariance terms, which is why it is easier to use matrix notation. The variance is

$$\sigma_p^2 = [w_1 \ldots w_N] \begin{bmatrix} \sigma_1^2 & \sigma_{12} & \sigma_{13} & \cdots & \sigma_{1N} \\ \vdots & & & & \\ \sigma_{N1} & \sigma_{N2} & \sigma_{N3} & \cdots & \sigma_N^2 \end{bmatrix} \begin{bmatrix} w_1 \\ \vdots \\ w_N \end{bmatrix}.$$

Defining Σ as the covariance matrix, the portfolio variance can be written more compactly as

$$\sigma_p^2 = w' \Sigma w. \tag{8.5}$$

Using a normal distribution, the VAR measure is then $\alpha \sigma_p$ times the initial investment.

Lower portfolio risk can be achieved through low correlations or a large number of assets. To see the effect of N, assume that all assets have the same risk and that all correlations are the same, that equal weight is put on each asset. Figure 8–1 shows how portfolio risk decreases with the number of assets.

Start with the risk of one security, which is assumed to be 12 percent. When ρ is equal to 0, the risk of a 10-asset portfolio drops to 3.8 percent; increasing N to 100 drops the risk even farther to 1.2 percent. Risk tends asymptotically to zero. More generally, portfolio risk is

$$\sigma_p = \sqrt{\sigma \frac{1}{N} + \left(1 - \frac{1}{N}\right)\rho}, \tag{8.6}$$

which tends to $\sigma\sqrt{\rho}$ as N increases. So, when $\rho = 0.5$, risk decreases rapidly from 12 percent to 8.9 percent as N goes to 10, but then converges much more slowly toward its minimum value of 8.5 percent. Correlations are essential in lowering portfolio risk.

Covariances can be estimated from sample data as

$$\hat{\sigma}_{ij} = \frac{1}{(T-1)} \sum_{t=1}^{T} (x_{t,i} - \hat{\mu}_i)(x_{t,j} - \hat{\mu}_j). \tag{8.7}$$

Covariance is a measure of the extent to which two variables move linearly together. If two variables are independent, their covariance is equal to 0. A positive covariance means that the two variables tend to move in the same direction; a negative covariance means that they tend to move in opposite directions.

FIGURE 8–1

Risk and Number of Securities

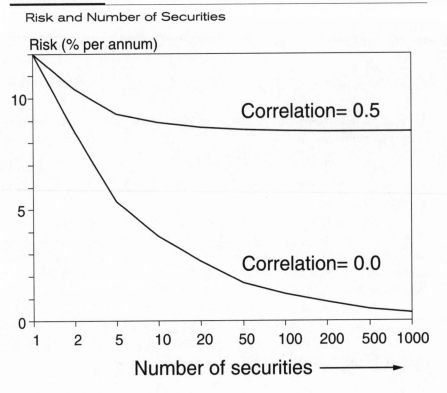

The magnitude of covariance, however, depends on the variances of the individual components and is not easily interpreted. The *correlation coefficient* is a more convenient, scale-free, measure of linear dependence:

$$\rho_{12} = \sigma_{12}/(\sigma_1\sigma_2).\qquad(8.8)$$

The correlation coefficient ρ always lies between -1 and $+1$. When equal to unity, the two variables are said to be perfectly correlated. When 0, the variables are uncorrelated.

Correlations help to diversify portfolio risk. With two assets, the "diversified" portfolio variance is

$$\sigma_p^2 = w_1^2\,\sigma_1^2 + w_2^2\,\sigma_2^2 + 2w_1w_2\rho_{12}\sigma_1\sigma_2.\qquad(8.9)$$

For simplicity, assume now that both assets have the same volatility. When the correlation is 0, equation (8.9) reduces to

$$\sigma_p^2 = V(R_1 + R_2) = w_1^2\,\sigma_1^2 + w_2^2\,\sigma^2 = (w_1^2 + w_2^2)\,V(R).\qquad(8.10)$$

The portfolio risk must be lower than individual risk.

When the correlation is exactly unity, equation (8.9) reduces to

$$V[w_1R_1 + w_2R_2] = w_1^2V[R] + w_2^2V[R] + 2w_1w_2V[R] \qquad (8.11)$$
$$= (w_1 + w_2)^2V[R]$$
$$= V[R],$$

since the portfolio weights sum to unity. Generally, the "undiversified" VAR is the sum of individual VAR measures—diversification into perfectly correlated assets does not pay.

So far, nothing was said about the distribution of the portfolio return. Ultimately, we would like to translate the portfolio variance into a VAR measure. To do so, we need to know the distribution of the portfolio return. In the "delta-normal" model, all individual security returns are assumed normally distributed. This is particularly convenient since the portfolio, a linear combination of normal random variables, is then also normally distributed. At a given confidence level, the portfolio VAR is value at risk = $\alpha\sigma_p$.

1.2 Incremental VAR

An important aspect of calculating VAR is to understand which asset, or combination thereof, contributes most to risk. Armed with this information, users can alter positions to modify their VAR most efficiently.

For this purpose, individual VARs are not sufficient. Volatility measures the uncertainty in the return of an asset, taken in isolation. When this asset belongs to a portfolio, however, what matters is the contribution to portfolio risk.

Suppose now that an existing portfolio is made up of $N - 1$ securities, numbered as $j = 1, \ldots, N - 1$. A new portfolio is obtained by adding one security, called i. The marginal contribution to risk is measured by differentiating equation (8.4) with respect to w_i :

$$\frac{\partial\sigma_p^2}{\partial w_i} = 2w_i\sigma_i^2 + 2\sum_{j=1, j\neq i}^{N} w_j\sigma_{ij}$$

$$= 2\,\text{Cov}\left(R_i, w_iR_i + \sum_{j\neq i}^{N} w_jR_j\right) = 2\,\text{Cov}(R_i, R_p). \qquad (8.12)$$

We note that $\partial\sigma_p^2 / \partial w_i = 2\sigma_p\partial\sigma_p / \partial w_i$. The sensitivity of the relative change in portfolio volatility to a change in the weight is then

$$\frac{\partial \sigma_p}{\sigma_p \partial w_i} = \frac{\text{Cov}(R_i, R_p)}{\sigma_p^2} = \beta_i. \tag{8.13}$$

Therefore, β measures the contribution of one security to total portfolio risk. This is also called the *systematic risk* of security i vis-à-vis portfolio p. Using matrix notation, β is

$$\beta = \frac{\Sigma w}{(w'\Sigma w)}.$$

Beta risk is the basis for the capital asset pricing model (CAPM), developed by Sharpe (1964). According to the CAPM, well-diversified investors want to be compensated for the systematic risk of securities only. In other words, the risk premium on all assets should depend on beta only. Whether this is an appropriate description of capital markets or not has been the subject of much of finance research in the last 20 years. Even though this proposition is much debated, the fact remains that systematic risk is a useful statistical measure of portfolio risk.

The measure of β is particularly useful for decomposing a portfolio's VAR into sources of risk. We can expand the portfolio variance into

$$\sigma_p^2 = w_1\left(w_1\sigma_1^2 + \sum_{j=1, j\neq 1}^{N} w_j\sigma_{1j}\right) \tag{8.14}$$

$$+ w_2\left(w_2\sigma_2^2 + \sum_{j=1, j\neq 2}^{N} w_j\sigma_{2j}\right) + \cdots$$

This is also

$$\sigma_p^2 = w_1 \text{Cov}(R_1, R_p) + w_2 \text{Cov}(R_2, R_p) + \cdots \tag{8.15}$$
$$= w_1(\beta_1\sigma_p^2) + w_2(\beta_2\sigma_p^2) + \cdots$$
$$= \sigma_p^2\left(\sum_{i=1}^{N} w_i\beta_i\right),$$

which shows that the portfolio variance can be decomposed into a sum of components each due to asset i. Using a similar decomposition, we write

$$\text{VAR} = \text{VAR}\left(\sum_{i=1}^{N} w_i\beta_i\right) = \text{VAR}_1 + \text{VAR}_2 + \cdots \tag{8.16}$$

Here we decomposed the total VAR into incremental measures. This provides vital information, as risk should be viewed in relation to the total portfolio and not in isolation. An example of such a decomposition is presented next.

2 BARINGS: AN EXAMPLE IN RISKS

VAR can be used to measure total portfolio risk and incremental contributions to this risk. Barings's collapse is such an example. Leeson was reported to be long about $7.7 billion worth of Japanese stock index (Nikkei) futures and short $16 billion worth of Japanese government bond (JGB) futures. Unfortunately, official reports to Barings showed "nil" risk.

The top panel of Table 8–1 displays monthly volatility measures and correlations for positions in the 10-year zero JGB and the Nikkei index.[1] The correlation between Japanese stocks and bonds is negative, indicating that increases in stock prices are associated with decreases in bond prices, or interest rates increases. The last column displays positions, which are reported in millions of dollar equivalents.

To compute the VAR, we first construct the covariance matrix Σ from the correlations. Next, we compute the vector Σx, which is in the first column of the bottom panel. For instance, the -2.82 entry is found from $x_1\sigma_1^2 + x_2\sigma_{12} = -\$16,000 \times 0.000139 + \$7,700 \times (-0.000078) = -2.82$. The next column reports $x_1(\Sigma x)_1$ and $x_2(\Sigma x)_2$, which sum to the total portfolio variance of 256,193.8, for a portfolio volatility of $\sqrt{256,194} = \$506m$. At the 95 percent confidence level, Barings's VAR was $1.65 \times \$506$, or $835 million.

This represents the worst monthly loss at the 95 percent confidence level under normal market conditions. Leeson's total loss was reported at $1.3 billion, which is comparable to the VAR reported here. The difference is because the position was changed over the course of the two months, there were other positions (such as short options), and also due to bad luck. In particular, on January 23, 1995, one week after the Kobe earthquake, the Nikkei index lost 6.4 percent. Based on a monthly volatility of 5.83 percent, the daily VAR of Japanese stocks at the 95 percent level should be 2.5 percent. Therefore, this was a very unusual move—even though we expect to exceed VAR in 5 percent of situations.

---

1. We assume that the risk of JGB futures is approximated by that of a 10-year zero-coupon bond. In reality, risk is somewhat less because the duration of this bond is less than 10 years.

TABLE 8–1

Barings's Risks

	Risk (%) σ	Correlation Matrix		Covariance Matrix Σ		Positions (m) x
10-yr JGB	1.18	1	−0.114	0.000139	−0.000078	($16,000)
Nikkei	5.83	−0.114	1	−0.000078	0.003397	$7,700
Total						$8,300

Asset	Total VAR		Incremental VAR		
			β_i	for $1m	for x_i
i	$(\Sigma x)_i$	$x_i'(\Sigma x)_i$	$(\Sigma x)_i/(x'\Sigma x)$	β_i VAR	$\beta_i x_i$ VAR
10-yr JGB	−2.82	45138.8	−0.0000110	($0.00920)	$147.15
Nikkei	27.41	211055.1	0.0001070	$0.08935	$688.01
Total		256193.8			$835.16
Risk = σ_p		506.16			
VAR = $\alpha\sigma_p$(m)		$835.16			

The incremental risk of each leg is also revealing. With a negative correlation between bonds and stocks, a hedged position would typically be long the two assets. Instead, Leeson was short the bond market, which market observers were at a loss to explain. A trader said, "This does not work as a hedge. It would have to be the other way round."[2] Thus, Leeson was increasing his risk from the two legs of the position.

This is formalized in the rightmost panel of the table, which displays the incremental VAR computation. The β column is obtained by dividing each element of Σx by $x'\Sigma x$, for instance −2.82 by 256194 to obtain −0.000011. Multiplying by the VAR, we obtain the marginal change in VAR due to increasing the bond position by $1 million, which is −$0.00920 million. Similarly, increasing the stock position by $1 million increased the VAR by $0.08935.

---

2. *Financial Times* (March 1, 1995).

Overall, the incremental VAR due to the total bond position is $147.15 million, and the incremental VAR due to the stock position is $688.01 million. By construction, these two numbers add up to the total VAR of $835.16 million. This shows that most of the loss was due to the Nikkei exposure and that the bond position made things even worse.

3 SIMPLIFYING THE COVARIANCE MATRIX

So far, we have shown that correlations are essential driving forces behind portfolio risk. When the number of assets is large, however, the measurement of the covariance matrix becomes increasingly difficult. With 10 assets, for instance, we need to estimate $10 \times 11/2 = 55$ different variance and covariance terms. With 100 assets, this number climbs to 5,500. The number of correlations increases geometrically with the number of assets. For large portfolios, this causes real problems: (1) The portfolio VAR may not be positive, and (2) correlations may be imprecisely estimated.

This section examines the extent to which such problems can affect VAR measures and proposes some solutions. For many users, however, such problems may not be relevant because they have no control over the measurement of inputs. Until such users encounter zero VAR measures, this section can be safely skipped.

3.1 Zero VAR Measures

The VAR measure derives from the portfolio variance, which is computed as

$$\sigma_p^2 = w' \Sigma w. \tag{8.17}$$

The question is, Is this product guaranteed to be always positive?

Unfortunately, not always. For this to be the case, we need the matrix Σ to be *positive definite*.[3] This will be verified under two conditions: the number of historical observations T must be greater than the number of assets N, and the series cannot be linearly correlated. The first condition states that, if a portfolio consists of 100 assets, there must be at least 100 historical observations to ensure that, whatever portfolio is selected, the

---

3. Abstracting from the obvious case where all elements of w are 0.

portfolio variance will be positive. The second condition rules out situations where an asset is exactly equivalent to a linear combination of other assets.

An example of a non-positive-definite matrix is obtained when two assets are identical ($\rho = 1$). In this situation, a portfolio consisting of \$1 on the first asset and $-\$1$ on the second will have exactly zero risk.

In practice, this problem is more likely to occur with a large number of assets that are highly correlated (such as zero-coupon bonds or currencies fixed to each other). In addition, positions must have been precisely matched with assets to yield zero risk. This is most likely to occur if the weights have been *optimized* on the basis of the covariance matrix itself. Such optimization is particularly dangerous since it can create positions that are very large, yet apparently offset each other with little total risk.

If users notice that VAR measures appear abnormally low in relation to positions, they should check whether small changes in correlations lead to large changes in their VARs.

3.2 Diagonal Model

A related problem is that, as the number of assets increases, it is more likely that some correlations will be measured with error. Some models can help simplifying this process by providing a simpler structure for the covariance matrix. One such model is the *diagonal model,* originally proposed by Sharpe in the context of stock portfolios.[4]

The assumption is that the common movement in all assets is due to one common factor only, the market. Formally, the model is

$$R_i = \alpha_i + \beta_i R_m + \epsilon_i, \qquad E[\epsilon_i] = 0,$$

$$E[\epsilon_i R_m] = 0, \quad E[\epsilon_i \epsilon_j] = 0, \quad E[\epsilon_1^2] = \sigma_{\epsilon,i}^2. \tag{8.18}$$

The return on asset i is driven by the market return R_m and an idiosyncratic term ϵ_i, which is not correlated with the market nor across assets. As a result, the variance can be decomposed as

$$\sigma_i^2 = \beta_i^2 \sigma_m^2 + \sigma_{\epsilon,i}^2. \tag{8.19}$$

---

4. Note that this model is often referred to as the CAPM, which is not correct. The diagonal model is simply a simplification of the covariance matrix and says nothing about expected returns, whose description is the essence of the CAPM.

The covariance between two assets is

$$\sigma_{i,j}^2 = \beta_i \beta_j \sigma_m^2, \tag{8.20}$$

which is solely due to the common factor. The full covariance matrix is

$$\Sigma = \begin{bmatrix} \beta_1 \\ \vdots \\ \beta_N \end{bmatrix} [\beta_1 \ldots \beta_N] \sigma_m^2 + \begin{bmatrix} \sigma_{\epsilon,1}^2 & \cdots & 0 \\ \vdots & & \vdots \\ 0 & \cdots & \sigma_{\epsilon,N}^2 \end{bmatrix}.$$

Written in matrix notation, the covariance matrix is

$$\Sigma = \beta\beta'\sigma_m^2 + D_\epsilon. \tag{8.21}$$

As the matrix D_ϵ is diagonal, the number of parameters is reduced from $N \times (N + 1)/2$ to $2N + 1$ (N for the betas, N in D and one for σ_m). With 100 assets, for instance, the number is reduced from 5,500 to 201, a considerable improvement.

Furthermore, the variance of large well-diversified portfolios simplifies even further, reflecting only exposure to the common factor. The variance of the portfolio is

$$\text{Var}(R_p) = \text{Var}(w'R) = w'\Sigma w = (w'\beta\beta'w)\sigma_m^2 + w'D_\epsilon w. \tag{8.22}$$

The second term consists of $\sum_{i=1}^{N} w_i^2 \sigma_{\epsilon,i}^2$. But this term becomes very small as the number of securities in the portfolio increases. For instance, if all the residual variances are identical and have equal weights, this second term is $[\sum_{i=1}^{N}(1/N)^2]\sigma_\epsilon^2$, which converges to 0 as N increases. Therefore, the variance of the portfolio converges to

$$\text{Var}(R_p) \rightarrow (w'\beta\beta'w)\sigma_m^2, \tag{8.23}$$

which depends on one factor only. This approximation is particularly useful when assessing the VAR of a portfolio consisting of many stocks. It has been adopted by the Basle Committee to reflect the market risk of well-diversified portfolios.

As an example, consider three stocks, General Motors (GM), Ford, and Hewlett Packard (HWP). The top panel in Table 8–2 displays the full covariance matrix for monthly data. This matrix can be simplified by estimating a regression of each stock on the U.S. stock market. These regressions are displayed in the second panel of the table, which shows betas of 0.806, 1.183, 1.864, respectively. GM has the lowest beta; HWP has the highest systematic risk. The market variance is $V(R_m) = 11.90$. The bottom panel in the table reconstructs the covariance matrix using the diagonal

TABLE 8-2

The Diagonal Model

	Covariances			Correlations		
	GM	**FORD**	**HWP**	**GM**	**FORD**	**HWP**
Full matrix						
GM	72.17			1		
FORD	43.92	66.12		0.636	1	
HWP	26.32	44.31	90.41	0.326	0.573	1
Regression						
β_i	0.806	1.183	1.864			
$V(R_i)$	72.17	66.12	90.41			
$V(\epsilon_i)$	64.44	49.46	49.10			
$\beta_i^2 V(R_m)$	7.73	16.65	41.32			
Diagonal model						
GM	72.17			1		
FORD	11.35	66.12		0.164	1	
HWP	17.87	26.23	90.41	0.221	0.339	1

approximation. For instance, the variance for GM is taken as $\beta_1^2 \times V(R_m)$ + $V(\epsilon_1)$, which is $0.806^2 \times 11.90 + 64.44 = 7.73 + 64.44 = 72.17$. The covariance between GM and Ford is $\beta_1 \beta_2 V(R_m)$, which is $0.806 \times 1.183 \times 11.90 = 11.35$.

The last three columns in the table report the correlations between pairwise stocks. Actual correlations are all positive, as are those under the diagonal model. Although the diagonal model matrix resembles the original covariance matrix, the approximation is not perfect. For instance, the actual correlation between GM and Ford is 0.636. Using the diagonal model, the correlation is driven by exposure to the market and is 0.164, which is lower than the true correlation. This is because the market is the only source of common variation. Whether this model produces acceptable approximations depends on the purpose at hand; we will compute actual VAR numbers in Chapter 11. But there is no question that the diagonal model provides a considerable simplification.

3.3 Factor Models

If a one-factor model is not sufficient, better precision can be obtained with multiple-factor models. Equation (8.18) can be generalized to K factors:

$$R_i = \alpha_i + \beta_{i1}R_1 + \ldots + \beta_{iK}R_K + \epsilon_i, \qquad (8.24)$$

where $R_1, \ldots, R_K$ are factors independent of each other. In the previous three-stock example, the covariance matrix model can be improved with a second factor, such as transportation industry, that would pick up the higher correlation between GM and Ford. With multiple factors, the covariance matrix acquires a richer structure

$$\Sigma = \beta_1\beta'_1\sigma_1^2 + \ldots + \beta_K\beta'_K\sigma_K^2 + D_\epsilon. \qquad (8.25)$$

The total number of parameters is $(K + N \times K + N)$, which may still be considerably less than for the full model. With 100 assets and five factors, for instance, the number is reduced from 5,500 to 605, which is no minor decrease.

Factor models are also important because they can help us decide on the number of VAR building blocks for each market. Consider, for instance, a government bond market that displays a continuum of maturities ranging from one day to 30 years. The question is, How many VAR building blocks do we need to represent this market adequately?

To illustrate, consider the U.S. Treasury market. Table 8–3 presents monthly VARs of zero-coupon bonds as well as correlations, for maturities going from 1 to 30 years. Under the RiskMetrics convention, VAR corresponds to 1.65 standard deviations. With strictly parallel moves in the term structure, VAR should increase linearly with maturity. In fact, this is not the case. Longer maturities display slightly less VAR than under a linear relationship. The 30-year zero, for instance, has a VAR of 11.12 instead of the value of 14.09 extrapolated from the 1-year maturity ($0.470 \times 30/1$).

Particularly interesting are the very high correlations, confirming the presence of one major factor behind bond returns. Correlations are high for close maturities but tend to decrease with the spread between maturities. The lowest value, 0.644, is obtained between the 1-year and 30-year zeroes. Could this pattern of correlation be simplified to just a few common factors?

Table 8–4 provides an answer. The first three components for the correlation matrix of U.S. bond returns are presented in Table 8–4, based on principal component analysis.[5] The most striking feature of the table is

---

5. Intuitively, principal components breaks down a matrix into a series of simplified matrices of the type $\beta\beta'$ due to one factor. It attempts to find a series of vectors β that provide the best explanation of diagonal terms and are orthogonal to each other.

TABLE 8–3

Risk and Correlations for U.S. Bonds (monthly VAR at 95 % level)

Term (year)	VAR (%)	1Y	2Y	3Y	4Y	5Y	7Y	9Y	10Y	15Y	20Y	30Y
1	0.470	1										
2	0.987	.897	1									
3	1.484	.886	.991	1								
4	1.971	.866	.976	.994	1							
5	2.426	.855	.966	.988	.998	1						
7	3.192	.825	.936	.965	.982	.990	1					
9	3.913	.796	.909	.942	.964	.975	.996	1				
10	4.250	.788	.903	.937	.959	.971	.994	.999	1			
15	6.234	.740	.853	.891	.915	.930	.961	.976	.981	1		
20	8.146	.679	.791	.832	.860	.878	.919	.942	.951	.991	1	
30	11.119	.644	.761	.801	.831	.853	.902	.931	.943	.975	.986	1

TABLE 8–4

Principal Components of Correlation Matrix: U.S. Bonds

Maturity (year)	Percentage of Variance Explained by			Total Variance Explained
	Factor 1 "Level"	Factor 2 "Slope"	Factor 3	
1	72.2	17.9	9.8	99.8
2	89.7	7.8	0.5	98.0
3	94.3	4.5	0.7	99.5
4	96.5	2.2	1.0	99.7
5	97.7	1.1	0.9	99.7
7	98.9	0.0	0.4	99.3
9	98.2	0.7	0.2	99.1
10	98.1	1.2	0.1	99.4
15	94.1	5.3	0.2	99.6
20	87.2	11.0	0.9	99.1
30	83.6	14.5	0.9	99.0
Average	91.9	6.0	1.4	99.3

that the first factor provides an excellent fit to movements of the term structure. The average explanatory power is very high, at 91.9 percent. This common factor can be defined as a yield "level" variable and it explains why duration is a good measure of interest rate risk.

The second factor explains an additional 6.0 percent in movements. Since it has the highest explanatory power and highest loadings for short and long maturities, it describes the "slope" of the term structure. Finally, the last factor is much less important. It seems to be most related to one-year rates, perhaps because of different characteristics of money market instruments. Together, the three factors explain an impressive 99.3 percent of all return variation.

This decomposition shows that the risk of a bond portfolio can be usefully summarized by its exposure to two factors only. For instance, the portfolio can be structured so that the net exposure to the two factors is very small. This will considerably improve upon duration hedging, yet requires no forecast of future twists in the yield curve. In other words, we need only two primitive risk factors to represent movements in the yield curve.

CHAPTER 9

Forecasting Risks and Correlations

Preparing the future is building the present.

Antoine de Saint-Exupéry

Chapter 4 described the risk of basic financial variables such as interest rates, exchange rates, and equity prices. A reader looking more closely at the graphs would notice that risk appears to change over time. This is quite obvious for exchange rates, which displayed much more variation after 1973. Bonds yields were also more volatile in the early 1980s. These periods corresponded to structural breaks: Exchange rates started to float in 1973, and the Federal Reserve abruptly changed monetary policies in October 1979. Even during other periods, volatility seems to *cluster* in a predictable fashion.

The observation that financial market volatility is predictable has important implications for risk management. If volatility increases, so will value at risk. Investors may want to adjust their portfolios to reduce their exposure to those assets whose volatility is predicted to increase. Also, predictable volatility means that assets directly depending on volatility, such as options, will change in value in a predictable fashion. Finally, in a rational market, equilibrium asset prices will be affected by changes in volatility. Investors who can reliably predict changes in volatility should be able to better control financial markets risks.

The purpose of this chapter is to present techniques to forecast variation in risk and correlations. Users who have no control over the inputs or do not care to know how these were generated could skip this chapter and directly advance to Chapter 10, which compares approaches to VAR.

Section 1 presents recent developments in time-series models that capture time variation in volatility. A particular application of these models is the exponential approach adopted by J.P. Morgan for the Risk-Metrics system. Section 2 extends univariate models to correlation forecasts. Finally, Section 3 argues that time-series models are inherently inferior to forecasts of risk contained in option prices.

1 MODELING TIME-VARYING RISK

1.1 Risk or Outliers?

As an illustration, we will walk through this chapter focusing on the U.S. dollar/British pound ($/BP) exchange rate measured at daily intervals. Movements in the exchange rate are displayed in Figure 9–1. The 1990–1994 period was fairly typical, covering narrow trading ranges and

FIGURE 9–1

Spot Rate:British Pound versus Dollar

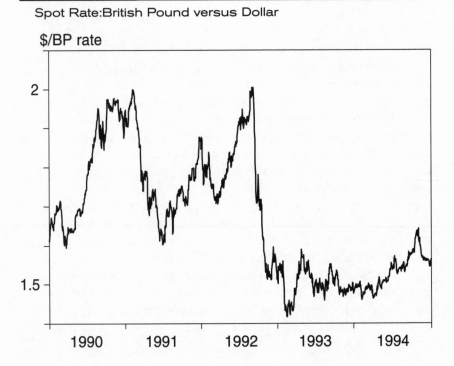

wide swings. September 1992 was particularly tumultuous. After vain attempts by the Bank of England to support the pound against the German mark, sterling exited the European Monetary System. There were several days with very large moves. On September 16 alone, the pound fell by 6 cents. Hence, we can expect interesting patterns in volatility.

Over this period, the average daily volatility was 0.694 percent, which translates into 11.02 percent per annum (using a 252-trading day adjustment). This risk measure, however, surely was not constant over time. In addition, time variation in risk could explain the fact that the empirical distribution of returns does not quite exactly fit a normal distribution.

Figure 9–2 compares the normal approximation to the actual empirical distribution of the $/BP exchange rate. Relative to the normal model, the actual distribution contains more observations in the center and in the tails.

FIGURE 9–2

Distribution of the $/BP Rate

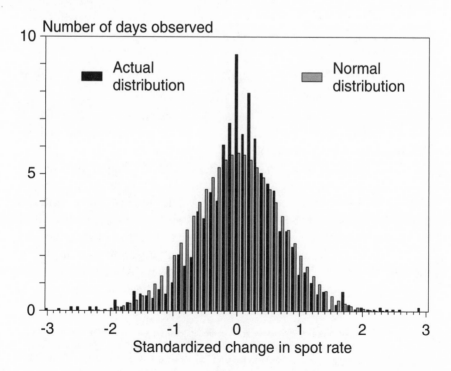

These fat tails can be explained by two alternative viewpoints. The first view is that the true distribution is stationary and indeed contains fat tails; in which case a normal approximation is clearly inappropriate. The other view is that the distribution does change through time. As a result, in times of turbulence, a stationary model could view large observations as outliers, when they are really drawn from a distribution with temporarily greater dispersion.

In practice, both explanations carry some truth. This is why forecasting variation in risk is particularly fruitful for risk management. In this chapter, we focus on traditional approaches based on "parametric" time-series modeling.[1]

1.2 Moving Averages

A very crude method, but employed widely, is to use a *moving window*, of fixed length, to estimate volatility. For instance, a typical length is 20 trading days (about a calendar month) or 60 trading days (about a calendar quarter).

Assuming that we observe returns r_t over M days, this volatility estimate is constructed from a moving average

$$\sigma_t^2 = (1/M)\sum_{i=1}^{M} r_{t-i}^2. \qquad (9.1)$$

Here, we focus on raw returns instead of returns around the mean. This is because, for most financial series, ignoring expected returns makes little difference for volatility estimates.

Each day, the forecast is updated by adding information from the preceding day and dropping information from $(M+1)$ days ago. All weights on past returns are equal and set to $(1/M)$. While simple to implement, this model has serious drawbacks.

Most important, it ignores the dynamic ordering of observations. In particular, recent information receives the same weight as older information, but recent data should be more relevant. Also, if there was a large return M days ago, dropping this return as the window moves one

---

1. Other methods exist, however. For instance, multivariate density estimation (MDE) is a nonparametric model that appears to be quite flexible, as described by Boudoukh, Richardson, Stanton, and Whitelaw (1995). Also, risk estimators do not have to necessarily rely solely on daily closing prices. Parkinson (1980) has shown that using the information in the extreme values (daily high and low) leads to an estimator that is twice as efficient as the usual volatility.

day forward will substantially affect the volatility estimate. As a result, moving-average measures of volatility tend to look like "plateaus" of width *M* when plotted against time.

Figure 9–3 displays 20-day and 60-day moving averages for our $/BP rate. Movements in the 60-day average are much more stable than for the 20-day average. This is understandable because longer periods decrease the weight of any single day. But is it better? This approach leaves wholly unanswered the choice of the moving window. Longer periods increase the precision of the estimate but could miss underlying variation in volatility.

1.3 GARCH Estimation

This is why volatility estimation has moved toward models that put more weight on recent information. The first such model was the generalized autoregressive heteroskedastic (GARCH) model proposed by Engle and Bollerslev.

FIGURE 9–3

Moving-Average (MA) Volatility Forecasts

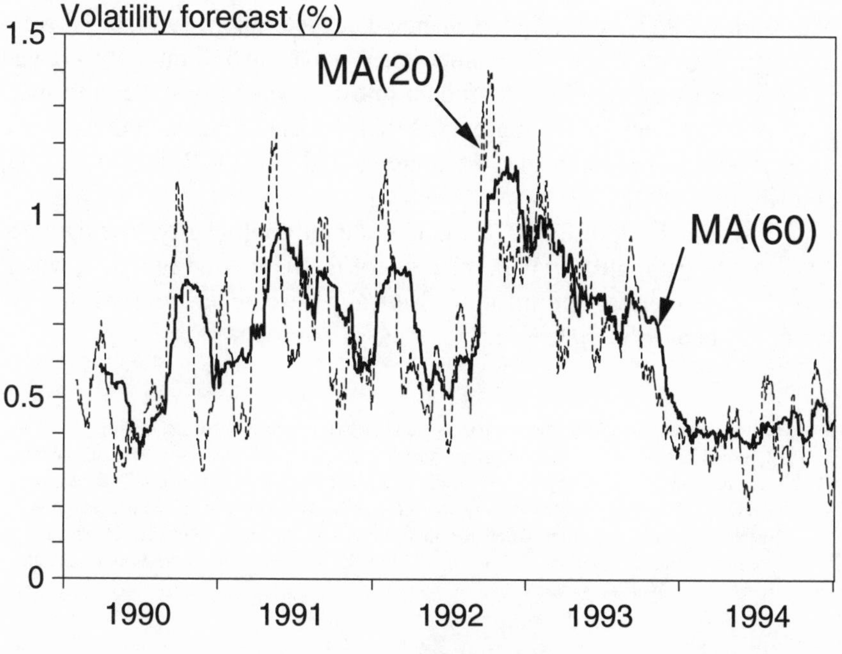

The GARCH model assumes that the variance of returns follows a predictable process. The *conditional* variance depends on the latest innovation but also on the previous conditional variance. Define h_t as the conditional variance, using information up to time $t - 1$, and r_{t-1} as the previous day's return. The simplest such model is the GARCH $(1,1)$ process:

$$h_t = \alpha_0 + \alpha_1 r_{t-1}^2 + \beta h_{t-1}. \tag{9.2}$$

The average, unconditional variance is found by setting $E[r_{t-1}^2] = h_t = h_{t-1} = h$. Solving for h, we find

$$h = \frac{\alpha_0}{1 - \alpha_1 - \beta}. \tag{9.3}$$

For this model to be stationary, the sum of parameters $\alpha_1 + \beta$ must be less than unity. This sum is also called the *persistence*, for reasons that will become clear later on.

The beauty of this specification is that it provides a parsimonious model, with few parameters, that seems to fit the data quite well.[2] GARCH models have become a mainstay of time-series analysis of financial markets, which systematically display volatility clustering. Literally hundreds of papers have applied GARCH models to stock return data (see French, Schwert, and Stambaugh, 1987), to interest rate data (see Engle, Lilien, and Robins, 1987), to foreign exchange data (see Hsieh, 1988, or Giovannini and Jorion, 1989). Econometricians have also frantically created many variants of the GARCH model, most of which provide only marginal improvement on the original GARCH model. Readers interested in a comprehensive review of the literature should consult Bollerslev, Chou, and Kroner (1992).[3]

The drawback of GARCH models is their nonlinearity. The parameters must be estimated by maximization of the likelihood function, which involves a numerical optimization. Typically, researchers assume that the scaled residual, $\epsilon_t = r_t/\sqrt{h_t}$ has a normal distribution.

---

2. For the theoretical rationale behind the success of GARCH models, see Nelson (1990).

3. GARCH models have other interesting properties. The returns r_t can be serially uncorrelated but are not independent as they are nonlinearly related through second moments. This class of models is also related to chaos theory. Recent work has revealed that many financial prices display "chaotic" properties. Often, the nonlinearities behind chaos theory can be traced to the time variation in variances. Thus, GARCH models explain some of the reported chaotic behavior of financial markets.

TABLE 9–1

Risk Models: Daily Data, 1990–1994

Parameter	Currency $/BP	Currency DM/$	Currency DM/BP	U.S. Stocks	30-year Bond	Bond Market
σ (% pa)	11.33	11.48	7.08	12.02	9.72	3.78
α_0	0.00695	0.01185	0.00316	0.00233	0.00410	0.00067
α_1	0.0678	0.0507	0.0979	0.0213	0.0256	0.0132
β	0.9186	0.9260	0.8908	0.9740	0.9634	0.9749
Persistence						
$(\alpha_1 + \beta)$	0.9864	0.9767	0.9887	0.9953	0.9890	0.9881

Table 9–1 presents the results of the estimation for a number of financial series over the 1990–1994 period. There are wide differences in the level of volatility across series, yet for all of these series, the time variation in risk is highly significant. The persistence parameter is also rather high, on the order of 0.97–0.99.

Figure 9–4 displays the GARCH forecast of volatility for the $/BP rate. It shows increased volatility in the fall of 1992. Afterward, volatility decreases progressively over time, not in the abrupt fashion observed in Figure 9–3.

The practical use of this information is illustrated in Figure 9–5, which shows daily returns along with conditional 95 percent confidence bands. This model appears to capture variation in risk adequately. Most of the returns fall within the 95 percent band. The few outside the bands correspond to the remaining 5 percent of occurrences.

1.4 Long-Horizon Forecasts

The GARCH model can also be used to compute the volatility over various horizons. Assume that the model is estimated using daily intervals. To compute a monthly volatility, we first decompose the multiperiod return into daily returns as in equation (4.19):

$$r_{t,T} = r_t + r_{t+1} + r_{t+2} + \cdots + r_T.$$

If returns are uncorrelated across days, the long-horizon variance as of $t - 1$ is

FIGURE 9–4

GARCH Volatility Forecast

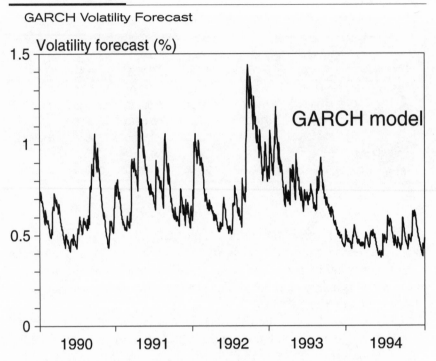

$$E_{t-1}[r_{t,T}^2] = E_{t-1}[r_t^2] + E_{t-1}[r_{t+1}^2] + E_{t-1}[r_{t+2}^2] + \cdots + E_{t-1}[r_T^2].$$

After some manipulation, the forecast of variance τ days ahead is

$$E_{t-1}[r_{t+\tau}^2] = \alpha_0 \frac{1 - (\alpha_1 + \beta)^\tau}{1 - (\alpha_1 + \beta)} + (\alpha_1 + \beta)^\tau h_t.$$

Figure 9–6 displays the effect of different persistence parameters $(\alpha_1 + \beta)$ on the variance. We start from the long-run value for the variance, 0.51. Then a shock moves the conditional variance to twice its value, about 1.02. High persistence means that the shock will decay slowly. For instance, with a persistence of 0.986, the conditional variance is still 0.90 after 20 days. With a persistence of 0.8, the variance drops very close to its long-run value after 20 days only. The marker on each line represents the average daily variance over the next 25 days. High persistence implies that the average variance will remain high.

FIGURE 9–5

Returns and GARCH Confidence Bands

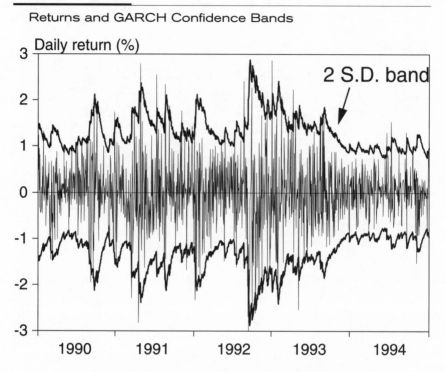

1.5 The RiskMetrics Approach

RiskMetrics takes a pragmatic approach to modeling risk.[4] Variances are modeled using an *exponential* forecast. Formally, the forecast for time t is a weighted average of the previous forecast, using weight λ, and of the latest squared innovation, using weight $(1 - \lambda)$

$$h_t = \lambda h_{t-1} + (1 - \lambda) r_{t-1}^2. \tag{9.4}$$

Here, the λ parameter is called the *decay* factor, and must be less than unity.

This model can be viewed as a special case of the GARCH process, where α_0 is set to 0, and α_1 and β sum to unity. The model therefore allows

---

4. For more detail on the methodology, see J. P. Morgan's *Technical Manual*.

FIGURE 9–6

Mean Reversion for the Variance

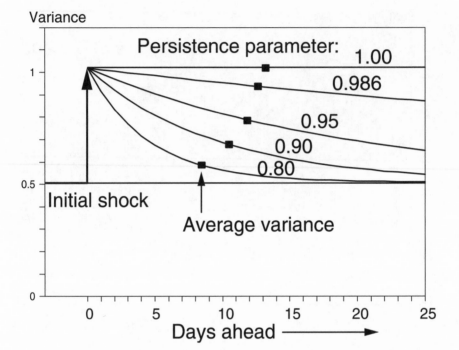

for persistence. As shown by Figure 9–7, it appears to produce results that are very close to those from the GARCH model.

The exponential model is particularly easy to implement because it relies on one parameter only. Thus, it is more robust to estimation error than other models. In addition, as was the case for the GARCH model, the estimator is *recursive*; the forecast is based on the previous forecast and the latest innovation. The whole history is summarized by one number, h_{t-1}. This is in contrast to the moving average, for instance, where the last M returns must be used to construct the forecast.

The only parameter in this model is the decay factor λ. In theory, this could be found from maximizing the likelihood function. Operationally, this would be a daunting task to perform every day for more than 450 series in the RiskMetrics database. An optimization has other shortcomings. The decay factor may vary not only across series, but also over time, thus

FIGURE 9–7

Exponential Volatility Forecast

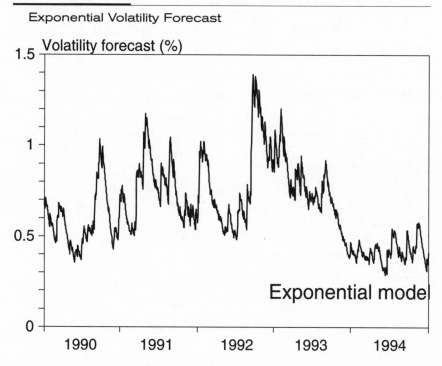

losing consistency over different periods. In addition, different values of λ create incompatibilities for the covariance terms and may lead to coefficients of correlations greater than unity, as we shall see later. In practice, RiskMetrics uses only one decay factor for all series, which is set at 0.94 for daily data.

RiskMetrics also provides risk forecasts over monthly horizons, defined as 25 trading days. In theory, the exponential model should be used to extrapolate volatility over the next day, then the next, and so on until the 25th day ahead as was done previously for the GARCH model. Herein lies the rub.

The persistence parameter for the exponential model is unity. Therefore, there is no mean reversion and the monthly volatility should be the same as the daily volatility. In practice, the estimator is identical to (9.4), except that it defines innovations as the 25-day variance. After experimenting with the data, J. P. Morgan chose $\lambda = 0.97$ as the optimal decay factor. Therefore, the daily and monthly specifications are inconsistent with each other. However, they are both easy to use, they approximate the behavior of actual data quite well and are robust to misspecifications.

2 MODELING CORRELATIONS

Correlation is of paramount importance for portfolio risk, even more so than individual variances. To illustrate the estimation of correlation, we pick two series: the dollar/British pound exchange rate, and the dollar/Deutsche mark rate.

Over the 1990–1994 period, the average daily correlation coefficient was 0.7732. We should expect, however, some variation in the correlation coefficient because this time period covers fixed and floating exchange rate regimes. On October 8, 1990, sterling became pegged to the mark within the European Monetary System (EMS). This lasted until the turmoil of September 1992, during which time sterling left the EMS and again floated against the mark.

As in the case of variance estimation, various methods can be used to capture time variation in correlation: moving average, GARCH, and exponential.

2.1 Moving Averages

The first method is based on moving averages (MAs), using a fixed window of length M. Figure 9–8 presents estimates based on a MA(20) and MA(60). Correlations start low, around 0.5, then increase to 0.9 as sterling enters the EMS. During the September 1992 crisis, correlations drop sharply, then go back to the pre-EMS pattern. The later drop in correlation would have been disastrous for positions believed to be nearly riskless on the basis of EMS correlations.

These estimates are subject to the same criticisms as before. Moving averages place the same weight on all observations within the moving window and ignore the fact that more recent observations may contain more information than older ones. In addition, dropping observations from the window sometimes has severe effects on the measured correlation.

FIGURE 9–8

Moving-Average (MA) Correlation: $/BP and $/DM

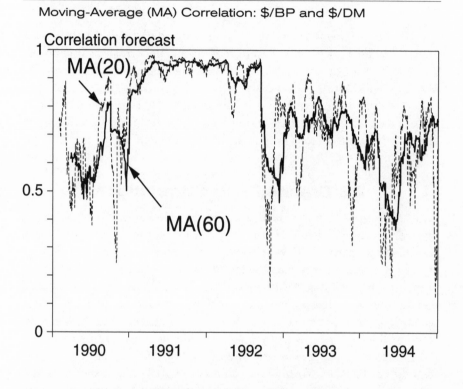

2.2 Exponential Averages

In theory, GARCH estimation could be extended to a multivariate frame-work. The problem is that the number of parameters to estimate increases exponentially with the number of series. With two series, for instance, we need to estimate nine terms, three α_0, α_1, β parameters for each of the three covariance terms. For larger samples of securities, this number quickly becomes unmanageable.

Here shines the simplicity of the RiskMetrics approach. Covariances are estimated, much like variances, using an exponential weighing scheme:

$$h_{12,t} = \lambda h_{12,t-1} + (1 - \lambda)r_{1,t-1}r_{2,t-1}. \qquad (9.5)$$

As before, the decay factor λ is arbitrarily set at 0.94 for daily data and 0.97 for monthly data. The conditional correlation is then

$$\rho_{12,t} = \frac{h_{12,t}}{\sqrt{h_{1,t} h_{2,t}}}.$$ (9.6)

Figure 9–9 displays the time variation in the correlation between the pound and the mark. The pattern of movements in correlations seems not too different from the MA model, plotting somewhere between the MA(20) and MA(60).

Note that the reason why J.P. Morgan decided to set a common factor λ across all series is to ensure that all estimates of ρ are between -1 and 1. Otherwise, there is no guarantee that this will always be the case.

2.3 Crashes and Correlations

Low correlations help to reduce portfolio risk. However, it is often argued that correlations increase in periods of global turbulence. If true, such statements are particularly worrisome, because increasing correlations occurring at a time of increasing volatility would defeat the diversification properties of portfolios. Measures of VAR based on historical data would then seriously underestimate the actual risk of failure since, not only would risk be understated, but so would correlations. This double blow could well lead to returns that are way outside the range of forecasts.

Indeed, we expect the structure of the correlation matrix to depend on the type of shocks affecting the economy. Global factors, such as the oil crises and the Gulf War, create increased turbulence and increased correlations. Longin and Solnik (1995), for instance, examine the behavior of correlations of national stock markets and find that correlations typically increase by 27 percent (from 0.43 to 0.55) in periods of high turbulence. Assuming a large portfolio (where risk is proportional to $\sqrt{\rho}$), this implies that VAR should be multiplied by a factor of $\sqrt{(0.55/0.43)} = 1.13$. Thus, just because of the correlation effect, VAR measures could underestimate true risk by 13 percent.

The extent of bias, however, depends on the sign of positions. Higher correlations are harmful to portfolios with only long positions, as is typical of equity portfolios. In contrast, decreasing correlations are dangerous for portfolios with short sales. Consider our previous example where a trader is long sterling and short mark. As Figure 9–4 shows, this position would have been nearly riskless in 1991 and in the first half of 1992. But the trader would have been caught short by the September 1992 devalua-

FIGURE 9–9

Exponential Correlation: $/BP and $/DM

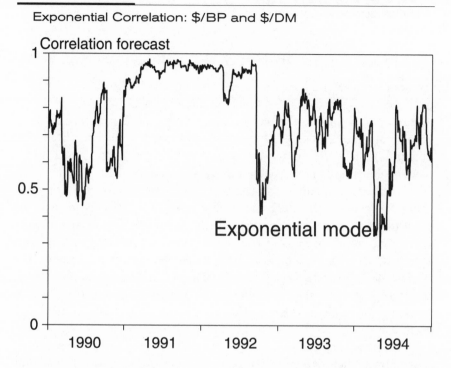

tion of the pound. Estimates of VAR based on the previous year's data would have grossly underestimated the risk of the position.

Perhaps these discomforting results explain why regulators impose large multiplicative factors to internally computed VAR measures. But these observations also point to the need for stress simulations to assess the robustness of VAR measures to changes in correlations. Robert Gumerlock, managing director of Swiss Bank Corporation, argues that, to deal with infrequent and highly disruptive events, "there is only one answer—stress simulations on extraordinary scenarios."

3 USING OPTION DATA

Measures of value at risk are only as good as the quality of forecasts of risk and correlations. Historical data, however, may not provide the best available forecasts of future risks. Situations involving changes in regimes, for instance, are simply not reflected in recent historical data. This is why it is useful to turn to *implied* forecasts contained in the latest market data.

3.1 Implied Volatilities

An important function of derivatives markets is *price discovery*. Derivatives provide information about market-clearing prices, which includes the discovery of *volatility*. Options are assets whose price is influenced by a number of factors, all of which are observable save for the volatility of the underlying price. By setting the market price of an option equal to its model value, one can recover an implied standard deviation (ISD).[5]

Implied correlations also can be recovered from triplets of options, using, for instance, the Margrabe pricing model. Correlations are also implicit in so-called quanto options, which also involve two random variables. An example of a quantity-adjusted option, for instance, would be an option struck on a foreign stock index where the foreign currency payoff is translated into dollars at a fixed rate. The valuation formula for such an option also involves the correlation between two sources of risk. So, options can potentially reveal a wealth of information about future risks and correlations.

If option markets are efficient, the ISD should provide the market's best estimate of future volatility. After all, option trading involves taking volatility bets. Expressing a view on volatility has become so pervasive in the options markets that prices are often quoted in terms of bid-ask volatility. As options reflect the market consensus about future volatility, there are sound reasons to believe that option-based forecasts should be superior to historical estimates.

The empirical evidence indeed points to the superiority of option data.[6] An intuitive way to demonstrate the usefulness of option data is to analyze the September 1992 breakdown of the European Monetary System (EMS). Figure 9–10 compares volatility forecasts during 1992, including those im-

---

5. One potential objection to the use of option volatilities is that the Black–Scholes model is, *stricto sensu*, inconsistent with stochastic volatilities. Recent research on the effect of stochastic volatilities, however, has shown that the BS model performs well for short-term at-the-money options. For further details, see Heston (1993), Duan (1995), and Bates (1995).

6. Jorion (1995a), for instance, shows that, for currency futures, option-implied volatilities subsume all information contained in time-series models.

FIGURE 9–10

Volatility Forecasts: DM/Pound

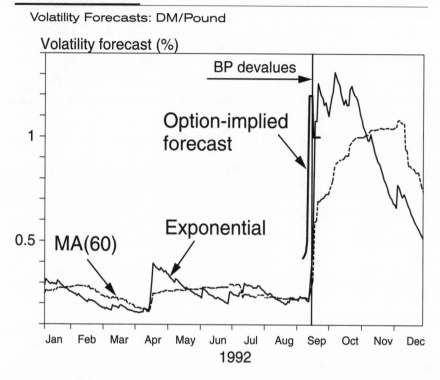

plied from DM/BP cross-options, the RiskMetrics volatility, and a moving average with a window of 60 days.

As sterling came under heavy selling pressures by speculators, the ISD moved up sharply, anticipating a large jump in the exchange rate. Indeed, sterling went off the EMS on September 16. In contrast, the Risk-Metrics volatility moved up only after the first big move, and the MA volatility changed ever so slowly. As option traders rationally anticipated greater turbulence, the implied volatility was much more useful than time-series models.

3.2 Conclusions

Overall, the evidence is that options contain a wealth of information about price risk that is generally superior to time-series models. This information is particularly useful in times of stress, when the market has access to current information simply not reflected in historical models. Therefore, my advice is as follows: *Whenever possible, value at risk should use implied parameters.*

The only drawback of option-implied parameters is that the menu of traded options is not sufficiently wide to recover the volatility of all essential financial prices. Even fewer cross-options could be used to derive implied correlations. As more and more option contracts and exchanges are springing up all over the world, however, we will be able to use forward-looking option data to measure risk. In the meantime, historical data provide a backward-looking alternative.

PART THREE

Value-at-Risk Systems

CHAPTER 10

Approaches to Measuring VAR

In practice, this works, but how about in theory?

Attributed to a French mathematician

The previous chapters have laid out the foundations for measuring value at risk. VAR summarizes the expected maximum loss over a target horizon within a given confidence interval. There are various methods to come up with VAR measures, however. The purpose of this chapter is to present and critically evaluate various approaches to VAR.

Approaches to VAR can be basically classified into two groups. The first group is based on local valuation; the best example is the *delta-normal* method, which is explained in Section 1. The second group uses full valuation. The pros and cons of local versus full valuation are discussed in Section 2. Full valuation is implemented in the *historical-simulation* method, the *stress testing* method, and the *structured Monte Carlo* method. Each of these is presented in Sections 3, 4, and 5, respectively.

This classification reflects a fundamental trade-off between correlations, which are handled more easily in the delta-normal approach, and nonlinearities. Because the delta-normal approach is so much easier to implement, a variant, called *the Greeks*, is sometimes used. This method, explained in Section 2, consists of analytical approximations to first- and second-order derivatives and is most appropriate for portfolios with limited sources of risk.

1 DELTA-NORMAL METHOD

If VAR were to be measured for a single asset, the issue would be relatively simple. The problem is that VAR must be measured for large and complex portfolios that evolve over time. Over the next period, the portfolio return can be written as

$$R_{p,t+1} = \sum_{i=1}^{N} w_{i,t} R_{i,t+1}, \qquad (10.1)$$

where the weights $w_{i,t}$ are indexed by time to recognize the dynamic nature of trading portfolios.

The delta-normal method assumes that all asset returns are normally distributed. As the portfolio return is a linear combination of normal variables, it is also normally distributed. Using matrix notations, the portfolio variance is given by

$$V(R_{p,t+1}) = w_t' \Sigma_{t+1} w_t. \qquad (10.2)$$

Thus, risk is generated by a combination of linear exposures to many factors that are assumed to be normally distributed and by the forecast of the covariance matrix Σ_{t+1}. This method involves a local approximation to price movements. It can accommodate a large number of assets and is simple to implement.

Within this class of models, two methods can be used to measure the variance-covariance matrix Σ. It can be based solely on historical data, using, for example, a model that allows for time variation in risk. Alternatively, it can include implied risk measures from options. Or it can use a combination of both. As we have seen in the previous chapter, option-implied measures of risk are superior to historical data, but are not available for every asset or pair of assets. Figure 10–1 details the steps involved in this approach.

The delta-normal method can be subject to a number of criticisms. First, it accounts poorly for *event risk*. This refers to the possibility of unusual or extreme circumstances such as stock market crashes or exchange rate collapses. The problem is that event risk does not occur frequently enough to be adequately represented by a probability distribution based on recent historical data. This is a general shortcoming of all methods using historical series.

A related, second problem is the existence of "fat tails" in the distribution of returns on most financial assets. These fat tails are particularly worrisome precisely because VAR attempts to capture the behavior of the portfolio return in the left tail. With fat tails, a model based on the normal approximation underestimates the proportion of outliers and hence the

FIGURE 10–1

Delta-Normal Method

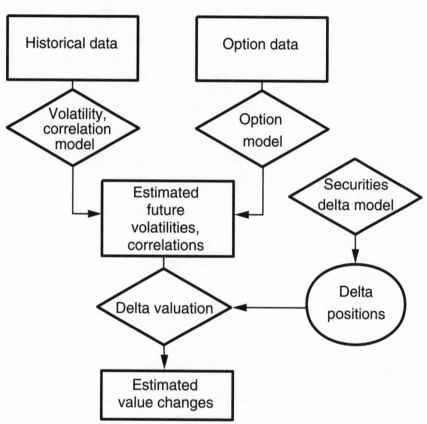

true value at risk. As discussed in Chapter 9, some of these fat tails can be explained in terms of time variation in risk. However, even after adjustment, there are still generally too many observations in the tails.

Third, the method inadequately measures the risk of nonlinear instruments, such as options or mortgages. Under the delta-normal method, option positions are represented by their "deltas" relative to the underlying asset. The price movement of an option is represented by $c_1 - c_0 = \Delta(S_1 - S_0)$. For instance, with an at-the-money call, $\Delta = 0.5$, and a long position in the option is simply replaced by a 50 percent position in the underlying asset.

Unfortunately, changes in the values of option positions depend on changes in underlying spot rates but also in the level of the spot rates.

At-the-money options, for instance, display very high convexity, which translates into unstable deltas. In other words, the linear approximation to option values is valid for only a very narrow range of underlying spot prices.

Lest we led the reader into thinking that this method is inferior, we will now show that alternative methods are no panacea because they involve a quantum leap in difficulty. The delta-normal method is computationally easy to implement. It requires only the market values and exposures of current positions, combined with risk data. Also, in many situations, the delta-normal method provides adequate measurement of market risks.

2 DELTA VERSUS FULL VALUATION

2.1 Definitions

The normal distribution assumption is particularly convenient because of the invariance property of normal variables: portfolios of normal variables are themselves normally distributed. Because portfolios are linear combinations of individual assets, the delta-normal method is fundamentally linear. Its virtue is its simplicity. The potential loss in value V is computed as

$$\Delta V = \beta_0 \times \Delta S, \tag{10.3}$$

which is the product of β_0, the portfolio sensitivity to changes in prices, evaluated at the current position V_0, and of ΔS, which is the potential change in prices. The normality assumption allows us to compute the portfolio β simply as the average of individual betas.

An essential benefit of this method is that it requires computing the portfolio value only once, at the current position V_0, which depends on current prices S_0. Hence, the delta-normal method is ideally suited to large portfolios exposed to many risk factors.

With options in the portfolio, however, the delta approach suffers from several problems.

- The portfolio delta may change very fast (high gamma).
- The portfolio delta may be different for up and down moves.
- The worst loss may not be obtained for two extreme realizations of the underlying spot rate.

An example of the latter problem is that of a purchase of a call and put. The worst payoff, which is the sum of the premiums, will be realized if the spot rate does not move. In general, it is not sufficient to evaluate the portfolio at the two extremes. All intermediate values must be checked.

The full valuation approach, therefore, requires computing the value of the portfolio for different levels of prices:

$$\Delta V = V(S_1) - V(S_0), \tag{10.4}$$

which, in theory, is more correct. Computationally, this approach may be quite demanding, since it requires marking to market the whole portfolio over a large number of realizations of underlying random variables.

Full valuation must be employed to evaluate the risk of option trading books exposed to a limited number of sources of risk. For instance, a complex portfolio of options all written on the same foreign currency can be evaluated by systematically evaluating the positions for each possible value of the exchange rate. From the full distribution of potential outcomes, VAR can be calculated using the actual percentiles of distributions.

To illustrate the result of nonlinear exposures, Figures 10–2 and 10–3 compare the process by which the profit distribution is obtained. In

FIGURE 10–2

Distribution with Linear Exposures

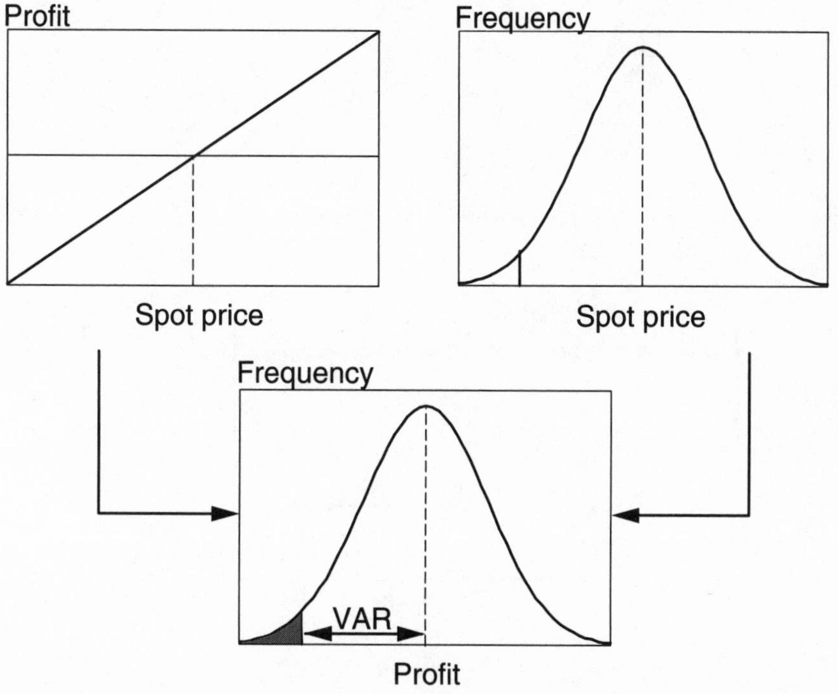

both cases, the underlying market variable is assumed to follow a normal distribution. In Figure 10–2, the payoff is a linear function of the underlying price and is displayed in the upper left side; the price itself is normally distributed, as shown in the right panel. As a result, the profit itself is normally distributed, as shown at the bottom of the figure. The VAR for the profit can be found from the exposure and the VAR for the underlying price. There is a one-to-one mapping between the two VAR measures.

In contrast, Figure 10–3 displays the profit function for a short straddle (the Leeson example), which is highly nonlinear. The resulting profit distribution is skewed to the left. Further, there is no direct way to relate the VAR of the portfolio to that of the underlying asset.

FIGURE 10–3

Distribution with Nonlinear Exposures

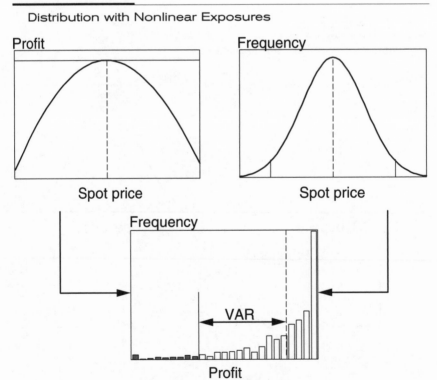

2.2 Delta-Gamma Approximations (the "Greeks")

The main drawback of the delta-normal method is that all risk types except delta risk are lost. In principle, one could add terms to capture gamma and vega risks, which are additional terms in the Taylor expansion:

$$dc = \Delta dS + \frac{1}{2}\Gamma dS^2 + \Lambda d\sigma + \ldots, \tag{10.5}$$

where Δ, Γ, and Λ are net values for the total portfolio of options, which are all written on the same underlying asset. Indeed, the 1995 Basle proposal recommends, "At a minimum, internal risk measurement systems should incorporate option price behavior through a nonlinear approximation approach involving higher-order risk factor sensitivities (such as gamma)."

Let us illustrate the $\Delta + \Gamma$ method for a simple position, such as a long or short position in a call or a put. With the delta-normal approximation, VAR is measured as in equation (7.5)

$$VAR_1 = \mid \Delta \mid (\alpha\sigma S). \tag{10.6}$$

Using higher-order terms, VAR can be measured as in equation 7.5

$$VAR_2 = \mid \Delta \mid (\alpha\sigma S) - \frac{1}{2}\Gamma(\alpha\sigma S)^2 + \mid \Lambda \mid \mid Sd\sigma \mid. \tag{10.7}$$

If Γ is negative, which corresponds to a net short position in options, the second term results in an add-on; otherwise, the second term will decrease the total VAR. The third term represents an add-on due to exposure to changes in volatility. If the net position has positive Λ, $d\sigma$ represents an adverse movement (decrease) in volatility at the c confidence level; otherwise, positions with a negative Λ, such as short option positions, will be hurt by increasing volatility.

Unfortunately, as soon as linearity is lost, the distribution of changes in the portfolio value V becomes quite complex and, in general, cannot be related to the VAR of the underlying asset. In the case of Leeson's short straddle, for instance, the worst losses are attained for both up and down moves in the underlying variable. This is why we had to resort to numerical simulations to uncover Leeson's VAR.

One possible shortcut was presented in equation (7.25), where the VAR of the option position was obtained by assuming that dS and dS^2

are normally distributed. The quality of this approximation in real-life situations, however, is still a open issue.

In theory, the $\Delta + \Gamma$ method could be generalized to many sources of risk. In a multivariate framework, the Taylor expansion is

$$dP(S) = \Delta' dS + \frac{1}{2}(dS)'\Gamma(dS)+ \ldots, \qquad (10.8)$$

where dS is now a vector of N changes in market prices, Δ is a vector of N positions, and Γ an N by N matrix of gammas with respect to the various risk factors.

One approach to finding the portfolio VAR consists of simulating movements in the market prices dS. For instance, a large number of realizations can be drawn from the distribution

$$dS \sim N(0, \Sigma), \qquad (10.9)$$

where Σ is the covariance matrix of changes in prices. Even more generally, the distribution need not be normal. For each realization, the portfolio value is computed according to equation (10.8). Note that this is still a local valuation method as the portfolio is fully valued at the initial point V_0 only. The VAR can then be found from the empirical distribution of the portfolio value.

Unfortunately, the $\Delta + \Gamma$ method is not practical with many sources of risk, as the amount of required data increases geometrically. For instance, with $N = 100$, we need 100 estimates of Δ, 5,050 estimates for the covariance matrix Σ, and an additional 5,050 for the matrix Γ, which includes the second derivatives of each position with respect to each source of risk. For such portfolios, a full Monte Carlo method provides a more direct route to VAR measurement.

2.3 Comparison of Methods

In summary, each of these methods is best adapted to a different environment:

- For large portfolios where optionality is not a dominant factor, the delta-normal method provides a fast and efficient method for measuring VAR.

- For portfolios exposed to a few sources of risk and with substantial option components, the "Greeks" method provides increased precision at a low computational cost.
- For portfolios with substantial option components (such as mortgages), a full valuation method such as Monte Carlo simulation is needed.

It should be noted that the linear/nonlinear dichotomy also has implications for the choice of the VAR horizon. With linear models, as we have seen in Chapter 4, daily VAR can be easily adjusted to other periods by simple scaling by a square root of time factor. This adjustment assumes the position is constant and that daily returns are independent and identically distributed.

This time adjustment, however, is not valid for option positions. As options can be replicated by dynamically changing positions in the underlying assets, the risk of option positions can be dramatically different from the scaled measure of daily risk. Therefore, *adjustments of daily volatility to longer horizons using the square root of the time factor are valid only when positions are constant and when optionality in the portfolio is negligible*. For portfolios with substantial option components, the full valuation method must be implemented over the desired horizon instead of scaling a daily VAR measure.

3 HISTORICAL-SIMULATION METHOD

The historical-simulation method provides a straightforward implementation of full valuation (see Figure 10–4). It consists of going back in time, such as over the last 90 days, and applying current weights to a time series of historical asset returns:

$$R_{p,\tau} = \sum_{i=1}^{N} w_{i,t} R_{i,\tau}, \qquad \tau = 1, \dots, t. \qquad (10.10)$$

Note that the weights w_t are kept at their current values. This return does not represent an actual portfolio but rather reconstructs the history of a hypothetical portfolio using the current position.

More generally, full valuation may require a set of complete prices, such as yield curves, instead of just returns. Hypothetical future prices for

FIGURE 10–4

Historical-Simulation Method

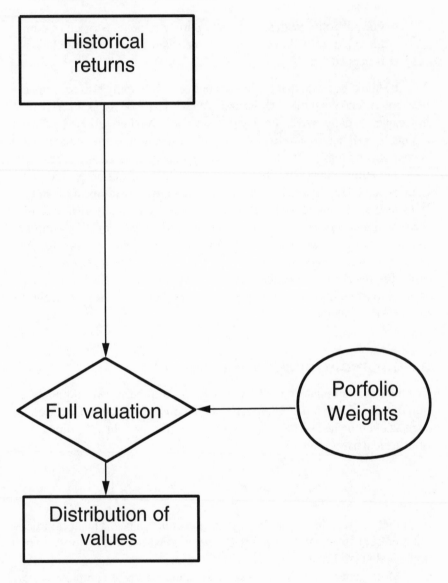

scenario τ are obtained from applying historical changes in prices to the current level of prices:

$$P^*_{i,\tau} = P_{i,0} + \Delta P_{i,\tau}, \qquad i = 1, \ldots, N. \tag{10.11}$$

A new portfolio value $P^*_{p,\tau}$ is then computed from the full set of hypothetical prices, perhaps incorporating nonlinear relationships. Note that, to capture vega risk, the set of prices can incorporate implied volatility measures. This creates the hypothetical return corresponding to observation τ:

$$R_{p,\tau} = (P^*_{p,\tau} - P_{p,0})/P_{p,0}. \tag{10.12}$$

Value at risk is then obtained from the entire distribution of hypothetical returns. Alternatively, one could assume normality and rely on the variance to compute the VAR. As was discussed in Chapter 5, smoothing the distribution using a normal approximation decreases the effect of irregularity in the distribution due to sampling variation. This provides more precise estimates of VAR as long as the actual distribution does not differ too much from the normal.

This method is relatively simple to implement if historical data have been collected in-house for daily marking to market. The same data can then be stored for later reuse in estimating VAR. As always, the choice of the sample period reflects a trade-off between using longer and shorter sample sizes. Longer intervals increase the accuracy of estimates but could use irrelevant data, thereby missing important changes in the underlying process.

The method also deals directly with the choice of horizon for measuring VAR. Returns are measured simply over intervals that correspond to the length of the horizon. For instance, to obtain a monthly VAR, the user would reconstruct historical monthly portfolio returns over, say, the last five years.

By relying on actual prices, the method allows nonlinearities and non-normal distributions. Full valuation is obtained in the simplest fashion: from historical data. The method captures gamma, vega risk, and correlations. It does not rely on specific assumptions about valuation models or the underlying stochastic structure of the market. It accounts for "fat tails" and, since it does not rely on valuation models, is not prone to model risk. The method is robust and intuitive and, as such, forms the basis for the Basle 1993 proposals on market risks.

On the other hand, the historical-simulation method is subject to a number of criticisms. Only one sample path is used. The assumption is that the past represents the immediate future fairly. And, as we demonstrated in Chapter 9, risk contains significant and predictable time variation. The historical-simulation method will miss situations with temporarily elevated volatility.

Also, the quality of the results critically hinges on the length of the historical period. As was pointed out in Chapter 5, VAR is only a statistical estimate and may be subject to much estimation error if the sample size is too short.

This approach is also subject to the same criticisms as the moving-average estimation of variances. The method puts the same weight on all observations in the window, including old data points. The measure of risk can change significantly after an old observation is dropped from the window.

A final drawback is that the method quickly becomes cumbersome for large portfolios with complicated structures. In practice, users adopt simplifications such as grouping interest rate payoffs into bands, which considerably increases the speed of computation. Regulators have also adopted such a "bucketing" approach. But, if too many simplifications are carried out, such as replacing assets by their delta equivalents, the benefits of full valuation can be lost.

4 STRESS TESTING

Stress testing takes a completely opposite approach to the historical-simulation method. This method, sometimes called *scenario analysis*, examines the effect of simulated large movements in key financial variables on the portfolio. It consists of subjectively specifying scenarios of interest to assess possible changes in the value of the portfolio.

For instance, one could specify a scenario where the yield curve shifts up by 100 basis points (bp) over a month or a doomsday scenario where a currency suddenly devalues by 30 percent. These are typical scenarios used by the traditional asset liability management (ALM) approach. Specific guidelines from the Derivatives Policy Group include

Parallel yield curve shifting by ± 100bp

Yield curve twisting by ± 25bp

Equity index values changing by ± 10 percent

Currencies moving by ± 6 percent

Volatilities changing by ± 20 percent of current values

The usefulness of these guidelines depends on whether they adequately represent typical market moves. If interest rates commonly move by more than 100bp over the period of interest, such stress tests will not be effective at identifying potential losses.

All of the assets in the portfolio are then revalued using the new environment, and the portfolio return is derived from the hypothetical component $R_{i,s}$ under the new scenario s:

$$R_{p,s} = \sum_{i=1}^{N} w_{i,t} R_{i,s}. \tag{10.13}$$

Many such exercises generate various values of $R_{p,s}$. Specifying a probability p_s for each scenario s then creates a distribution of portfolio returns, from which VAR can be measured. Figure 10–5 details the steps involved in this approach.

The advantage of this method is that it may cover situations completely absent from the historical data. In the summer of 1992, for

F I G U R E   1 0 – 5

Stress-Testing Method

instance, it would have been useful to assess the effect of a realignment in the European Monetary System. Indeed the German mark abruptly moved from 760 liras to 880 liras in September 1992. As the lira had been pegged to the mark and stable for the previous two years, historical volatilities would have completely missed the possibility of a devaluation. This is why this method is one of those recommended by the G-30 report to provide sensitivity analysis for the results (recommendation 6). Stress testing forces management to consider events that they might otherwise ignore.

Stress testing, however, is poorly adapted to measuring VAR in the same scientific sense as other methods. The method is completely subjective. Bad or implausible scenarios will lead to wrong measures of VAR. The history of some firms has shown that people may be very bad at predicting extreme situations.

Further, the choice of scenarios may be affected by the portfolio position itself. One month, the portfolio may be invested in a national fixed-income market; the scenario will then focus on interest rate shifts in this market. The following month, the portfolio may be invested mainly in currencies. If scenarios change over time, measures of risk will change just because of these changes. Also, stress testing does not specify the likelihood of worst-case situations. Expected risk should be a function not only of the losses but also of the probability of such losses to occur.

The most damning criticism of stress testing is that it handles correlations poorly, which we have shown to be an essential component of portfolio risk. Typically, stress testing examines the effect of a large move in one financial variable at a time or perhaps just a few. As the previous scenario was based on an educated guess, one could surmise that, if the Italian central bank let the lira float, short-term rates could likewise drop and the stock market rally. Beyond the effect on Italian interest rates and equity prices, it is not easy to come up with plausible scenarios for other financial variables. Thus, stress testing is not well-suited to large, complex portfolios.

This method, nevertheless, may be appropriate in situations where the portfolio depends primarily on one source of risk. The Office of Thrift Supervision (OTS), for instance, uses scenario analysis to assess the market risk of savings associations.[1] The OTS requires institutions to estimate what would happen to their economic value under parallel shifts in the

---

1. The OTS is a U.S. agency created in 1989 to supervise savings and loan associations (S&Ls).

yield curve varying from -400 to $+400$ basis points. The OTS has recently imposed a risk-based capital requirement directly linked to the interest rate exposure of savings and loan associations (S&Ls).

More sophisticated implementations of stress testing proceed in two steps. First, push up and down all risk-factor variables individually by, say, 1.65 standard deviations; compute the changes to the portfolio. Second, evaluate a worst-case scenario, where all variables are pushed in the direction that creates the worst loss. For instance, variable 1 is pushed up by $\alpha\sigma_1$, while variable 2 is pushed down by $\alpha\sigma_2$, and so on. This creates the worst possible case but completely ignores correlations. If variables 1 and 2 are highly correlated, it makes little sense to consider moves of opposite directions.

Further, looking at extreme movements may not be appropriate. Some positions such as combinations of long positions in options will lose most money if the underlying variables do not move at all.

Interestingly, stress testing is now used by regulators to evaluate the safety and soundness of the existing supervisory framework. The Commodities Futures Trading Commission (CFTC) has recently conducted stress testing exercises at futures exchanges to see how a $100 million default would be handled. The exercise revealed some flaws in the existing system, and regulations have been adjusted accordingly.

Overall, stress testing should be considered a complement rather than a replacement to other measures of VAR. Stress testing is useful to evaluate the worst-case effect of large movements in key variables. This is akin to drawing a few points in the extreme tails: useful information, but only after the rest of the distribution has been specified.

5 STRUCTURED MONTE CARLO

In contrast to scenario analysis, structured Monte Carlo (SMC) simulations cover a wide range of possible values in financial variables and fully account for correlations. SMC will be developed in more detail in a future chapter. In brief, the method proceeds in two steps. First, the risk manager specifies a stochastic process for financial variables as well as process parameters; parameters such as risk and correlations can be derived from historical or option data. Second, fictitious price paths are simulated for all variables of interest. At each horizon considered, which can go from one day to many months ahead, the portfolio is marked to market using full valuation. Each of these "pseudo" realizations is then used to compile a distribution of returns, from which a VAR figure can be measured. The method is summarized in Figure 10–6.

The Monte Carlo method is similar to the historical-simulation method, except that the hypothetical changes in prices ΔP_i for asset i in equation (10.11) are created by random draws from a stochastic process.

Monte Carlo analysis is by far the most powerful method to compute value at risk. It can account for a wide range of risks, including nonlinear price risk, volatility risk, and even model risk. It can incorporate time variation in volatility, fat tails, and extreme scenarios.

The biggest drawback of this method is its computational cost. If 1,000 sample paths are generated with a portfolio of 1,000 assets, the total number of valuations amounts to 1 million. When full valuation of assets is complex, this method quickly becomes too onerous to implement on a frequent basis.

This method is the most expensive to implement in terms of systems infrastructure and intellectual development. When the institution already has in place a system to model complex structures using simulations, how-

FIGURE 10–6

Monte Carlo Method

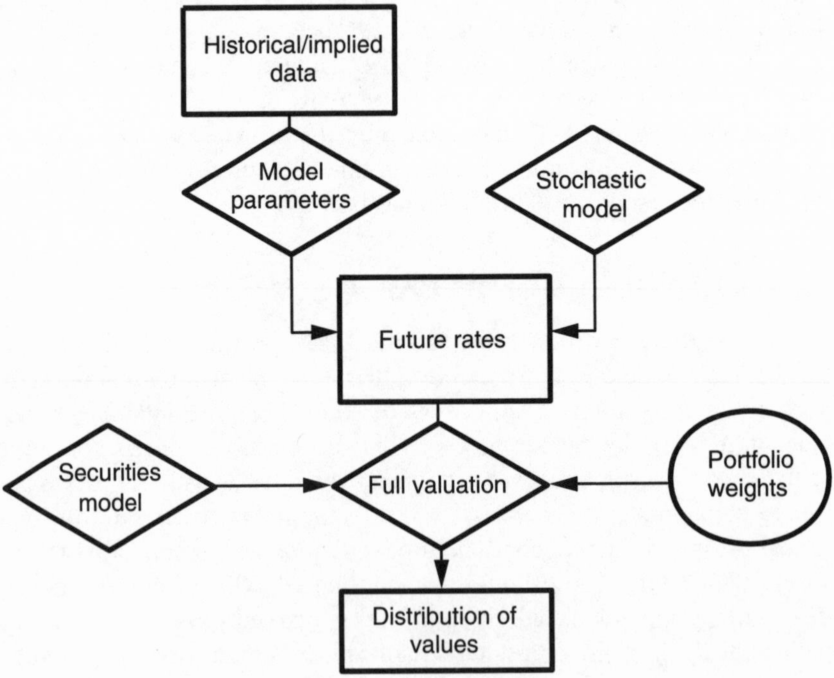

ever, implementing SMC is less costly because the required expertise is in place. Also, these are situations where proper risk management of complex positions is absolutely necessary.

Otherwise, the SMC method is relatively onerous to develop from scratch, in spite of rapidly falling prices for hardware. Perhaps, then, it should be purchased from outside vendors.

Another potential weakness of the method is that it relies on a specific stochastic model for the underlying risk factors as well as pricing models for securities such as options or mortgages. Therefore, it is subject to the risk that the models are wrong. To check if the results are robust to changes in the model, simulation results should be complemented by some sensitivity analysis.

Overall, this method is probably the most comprehensive approach to measuring market risk if modeling is done correctly. To some extent, the method can even handle credit risks. This is why a full chapter is devoted to the implementation of structured Monte Carlo methods.

6 SUMMARY

We can distinguish four separate routes to measuring VAR. At the most fundamental level, they separate into delta (or linear) valuation and full valuation. This separation reflects a trade-off between correlations, most easily handled in a linear framework, and nonlinear relationship.

Delta models can use parameters based on historical data, such as implemented by RiskMetrics, or on implied data, where volatilities are derived from options. Both methods generate a covariance matrix, to which the "delta" or linear positions are applied to find the portfolio VAR. Among full valuation models, the historical-simulation is the easiest to implement. It relies simply on historical data for securities valuation, but applies the most current weight to historical prices. The third model is the scenario, or stress testing, approach, which is based on historical data or educated guesses or both. Finally, the most complete model but also most difficult to implement, is the "structured Monte Carlo" approach, which imposes a particular stochastic process on the financial variables of interest, from which various sample paths are simulated. Full valuation for each sample path generates a distribution of portfolio values.

Table 10–1 describes the pros and cons of each method. The choice of method depends largely on the composition of the portfolio. For portfolios with no options (nor embedded options), the delta-normal method

TABLE 10-1

Comparison of Approaches to VAR

	Delta Normal	Historical Simulation	Scenarios	
			Stress Testing	Monte Carlo
Position				
Valuation	Linear	Full	Full	Full
Nonlinear assets	No	Yes	Yes	Yes
Distribution				
Historical	Normal	Actual	Subjective	Full
Time varying	Yes	No	Subjective	Yes
Implied	Possible	No	Possible	Yes
Market				
Non-normal distribution	No	Yes	Yes	Yes
Measure extreme events	Somewhat	Somewhat	Yes	Possible
Use correlations	Yes	Yes	No	Yes
Implementation				
Avoid model risk	Somewhat	Yes	No	No
Ease of computation	Yes	Somewhat	Somewhat	No
Communicability	Easy	Easy	Good	Difficult
Major pitfalls	Nonlinearities, extreme events	Time variation, extreme events	Wrong guess, correlations	Model risk

may well be the best choice. VAR is relatively easy to compute and not too prone to model risk (due to faulty assumptions or computations). The resulting VAR is easy to explain to management and the public. For portfolios with options positions, however, the method is not appropriate. Instead, users should turn to historical or Monte Carlo simulations.

The second method, historical simulation, is also relatively easy to implement and uses actual, full valuation of all securities. However, it cannot account for time variation in risk and, like the delta-normal model, can be caught short by extreme events.

The stress-testing method allows users to assess the effect of "doomsday" scenarios. It accounts for nonlinear positions and is relatively easy to implement and communicate. On the downside, stress testing usually focuses on one variable only and ignores correlations. It is also highly subjective in that the output directly depends on the input: wrong scenario, wrong value at risk.

In theory, the Monte Carlo approach can alleviate all of these technical difficulties. In can incorporate nonlinear positions, non-normal distributions, implied parameters, and even user-defined scenarios. The price to pay for this flexibility, however, is heavy. Computer and data requirements are a quantum step above the other two approaches, model risk looms large, and value at risk loses its intuitive appeal.

All of these methods present some advantages. They are also related. Monte Carlo analysis of simple positions with normal returns, for instance, should yield the same result as the delta-normal method. Perhaps the best lesson from this chapter is to check VAR measures with different methodologies and then analyze the sources of differences.

CHAPTER 11

Implementing Delta-Normal VAR

> The second [principle], to divide each of the difficulties under examination
> into as many parts as possible, and as might be necessary for its adequate
> solution.
>
> *René Descartes*

Among various approaches to measuring VAR, the delta-normal method appears to be the easiest to implement. Since the method assumes linearity, all that is required is the combination of portfolio positions and the variance–covariance matrix. The basic principle behind delta-normal VAR is presented in Section 1.

This chapter goes through several VAR examples, presented in order of increasing complexity. Section 2 shows how to determine the value at risk for a multinational corporation with cash flows in different currencies. In this example, all positions correspond to risk factors. In general, however, this is not the case, as the covariance matrix is simplified into a limited set of "primitive" risk factors. Section 3 explains how to choose such a set of factors.

We then proceed to illustrate cases where securities are broken down into their constituent components. Sections 4 and 5 explain how to decompose fixed-income instruments and derivatives into cash flows positions that we assign to various risk factors. This approach is compared to the duration method. Last, Section 6 presents various methods to measure equity risks.

1 OVERVIEW

Figure 11–1 describes a typical implementation of the delta-normal method. The first component is provided by a datafeed system, such as the

FIGURE 11-1

Implementation of Delta-Normal Method

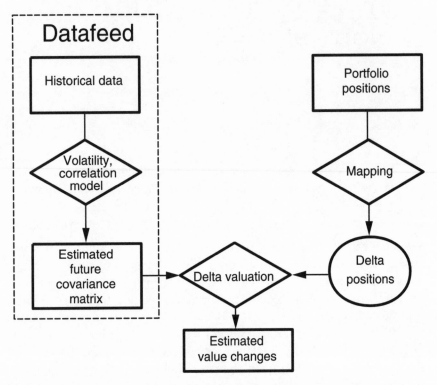

RiskMetrics system currently available on the Internet. The second component must reside locally and consists of a "mapping system" that trans-
forms the portfolio positions into weights on each of securities for which
risk is measured. The estimated change in value, or VAR, results from the
combination of these two components.

So far, we have assumed that every security in the portfolio was one
of those for which risk and correlation data are made available. Save for
the simplest portfolios, this is impractical. With tens of thousands of outstanding stocks and bonds, and an almost infinite variety of derivatives,
there is no way to cover the existing universe of securities.

As important, even a complete history of all securities would not be
relevant. The risk characteristics of bonds, for instance, change as they
age. The risk of options depends on the current price of the underlying
asset. Thus, past history may not be a useful guide to future risks.

This is why risk is typically measured for a set of "primitive" factors, such as foreign currencies, zero-coupon bonds, national equity markets, and commodities. For portfolios invested in these primitive factors only, VAR can be computed directly from the covariance matrix of factors and the vector of positions.

In most cases, portfolios also contain more complex assets. This chapter shows how to decompose securities into building blocks with delta-positions x aligned on each of the primitive risk factors. Once these are obtained, the VAR of the portfolio can be computed from the covariance matrix over the target horizon Σ and the number of standard deviations corresponding to the specified confidence level:

$$\text{Value at risk} = \sqrt{\alpha x' \Sigma x}. \tag{11.1}$$

For instance, α is set at 1.65 for a one-tail 95 percent level. Alternatively, the covariance matrix is sometimes presented in terms of the correlation matrix R, and individual volatilities σ, $\Sigma = S'RS$, where S is a matrix with the volatilities on its diagonal, but zeroes everywhere else. If the "risk" factor is then measured directly as the vector $V = (\alpha\sigma)$, the

$$\text{Value at risk} = \sqrt{x'\alpha S'RS\alpha x} = \sqrt{(x \times V)'R(x \times V)}. \tag{11.2}$$

As the RiskMetrics system provides estimates of V and R, the VAR of a portfolio can be found by, first, multiplying each position x by the associated risk and, second, pre- and post-multiplying the correlation matrix R.

2 APPLICATION TO CURRENCIES

VAR can be used to determine the exposure to financial risks such as currency risks. As an illustration, let us consider the case of a U.S. automobile manufacturer with a total of $52 billion in annual sales. The corporation has assembly facilities in Canada, which export $9.2 billion worth of vehicles to the United States annually. Direct exports from the United States to Germany amount to $1.4 billion, and to Japan $1.3 billion.

Focusing solely on exchange rates, the question is, What is the VAR of the company's cash flows over a monthly horizon? The corporation's exposure derives from the currency denomination of its costs and revenues. Simplifying to the extreme, we can translate annual cash flows into monthly numbers: −$767 million in Canadian dollars, $117 million in German marks, and $108 million in yen.

TABLE 11–1

Computing the VAR of Multinational Cash Flows (monthly VAR at 95% level)

	Risk (%)	Correlation (R)			Cash Flow
	$V = \alpha\sigma$	CAD	DEM	JPY	x
CAD	2.747	1	–0.208	–0.216	–767
DEM	6.220	–0.208	1	0.787	117
JPY	8.046	–0.216	0.787	1	108

	Total VAR		Incremental VAR	
	$(V'RV)x$	$x(V'RV)x$	β	$\beta x VAR$
CAD	–0.6717	514.97	–0.00082	$18.0
DEM	1.1505	134.23	0.00141	$4.7
JPY	1.5269	165.41	0.00187	$5.8
Total:		814.61		$28.5

Table 11–1 shows the risk and correlation of these three currencies. The volatility of the mark and yen is more than twice that of the Canadian dollar. In addition, these two currencies are highly correlated with each other. By way of contrast, the Canadian dollar is negatively correlated with the other two currencies.

The bottom panel of the table shows the computation for the VAR of total cash flows. The first column reports the vector resulting from the product $(V'RV)x$; the second column multiplies each element in the first column by the corresponding cash flow. Summing over the second column yields the total VAR, which is $28.5 million over a monthly horizon at the 95 percent level. Therefore, under normal market conditions, the company could lose as much as $28.5 million due to unfavorable movements in exchange rates.

The computations for incremental VAR are displayed in the last two columns. First, we need to compute the β_i of each cash flow, which is obtained by dividing each element in the first column by the total VAR squared (e.g., $-0.6717/814.61 = -0.00082$). As we have seen in the portfolio risk chapter, the marginal contribution to portfolio risk is ($\beta_i \times x_i \times$ VAR). This represents the proportion of total VAR due to the position x_i in currency i. By construction it adds up to the total VAR.

The incremental VAR for the Canadian dollar position is $18.0 million, against $4.7 and $5.8 for the mark and yen. It is much higher for the first currency because the position is greater, even though the Canadian dollar is less volatile than others. Note that the negative correlations indicate that the best diversification benefits will be obtained with positions of like signs in Canadian dollars and other currencies. Unfortunately, this is not the case. Sourcing is in Canadian dollars, and revenues are in other currencies. The signs of these flows increase the overall cash flow VAR.

Overall, in relation to the company's total annual profits of $5.8 billion, the risk of losses due to exchange rates is small. Other companies are not so lucky. Toyota, for instance, sells 49 percent of its vehicles outside Japan, yet produces only 20 percent outside Japan. As a result, for every fall of Y1 in the yen/dollar rate, the company's profits decrease by $100 million. Exposure to exchange rates has had a significant effect on Toyota's bottom line.

This type of information is essential to the decision of whether or not this exposure should be hedged. Hedging can be achieved with financial instruments or, in the long run, by altering marketing strategies or shifting production and sourcing across countries. Thus VAR is an essential first step toward an informed risk management system.

The next logical step in risk management is the measurement of economic risks due to financial variables, not just cash flow risks. This is much more complex for a number of reasons. First, the previous analysis assumes that quantities do not change with prices. In practice, changing prices in the foreign currency may affect demand and thus total revenues. Second, the currency of denomination is not necessarily the same as the currency of determination. For instance, the price for parts used for construction in Canada could fluctuate in line with the U.S. dollar, even though prices are invoiced in Canadian dollars. Third, and more generally, even domestic operations could be affected by exchange rates. The resurgence of U.S. automobile manufacturers can be attributed in part to the sustained appreciation of the yen, which has made Japanese cars more expensive in America. Whether these financial risks should be hedged is a more complex matter. Still, corporations and their shareholders should be aware of their exposure to financial risks.

3 CHOOSING "PRIMITIVE" SECURITIES

The previous example was straightforward because currencies are basic risk factors. In general, portfolios must be reduced to positions on a "primitive" set of securities. To a large extent, the choice of these primitive risk factors is arbitrary. More factors lead to tighter risk measurement. The trade-off is that the marginal improvement may not be worth the additional cost and complexity.

In the bond market, for instance, a one-factor model may provide a good first approximation to risk for some portfolios. For more precision, more factors can be added. The need for additional coverage depends on the complexity of the exposure to financial risk. Simple portfolios may be adequately described by one interest-rate factor. More complex positions, such as those run by government securities dealers, should account for every twist and shape of the yield curve. The degree of leverage in these portfolios is such that tracking error can be magnified to create large losses.

Another rationale for the choice of risk factors is to define sources of risk that can be readily hedged using existing exchange-listed futures contracts. This leads into the next step following exposure measurement, hedging. Sources of risk that can be hedged easily are particularly useful to identify.

A side benefit of futures contracts is that they reveal what the market views as "primitive" factors. This choice is not obvious, for there are few successful derivative contracts.[1] The key to explaining the success of exchange-listed contracts lies in understanding their economic function. Successful contracts require the following conditions:

- **Large Underlying Cash Markets**   A large underlying cash market demonstrates interest in the underlying asset. It also provides reassurance that the contract can be priced fairly in relation to the underlying asset.

- **Large Volatility of Underlying Asset**   High volatility leads to hedging needs for business-related financial risks, and also creates the possibility of fast profits for speculators. Indeed, the empirical evidence points to a strong relationship between trading volume and volatility.

- **Lack of Close Substitutes**   Derivatives are generally successful when they provide a means to hedge price risks that cannot be met with existing contracts. If the prices on two assets move in similar fashion, for instance, one derivative contract may be sufficient to hedge the two price risks. The residual risk, known as *basis risk*, may not be large enough to warrant trading in a new contract, especially if it is less liquid.

All of these conditions are directly relevant to the choice of "primitive" factors for risk management. At the very least, risk factors should in-

---

1. Silber (1981), for instance, reports that the success rate of contracts is only one out of four.

clude exchange-listed instruments, which have revealed their economic importance.

4 APPLICATION TO BOND PORTFOLIOS

Bond positions describe the distribution of money flows over time by their amount, timing, and credit quality of issuer. The risk of interest rate positions can be described by different mapping systems: principal, maturity, and cash flows. With *principal mapping*, the bond risk is associated with the maturity of the principal payment only. With *duration mapping*, the risk is associated with that of a zero-coupon bond with maturity equal to the bond duration. With *cash flow mapping*, the risk of fixed income instruments is decomposed into the risk of each of the bond cash flows.

To illustrate differences between these approaches, Table 11–2 presents monthly VARs of zero-coupon bonds as well as correlations for maturities going from one month to 30 years. Here, VAR corresponds to a 1.65 standard deviation movement. With strictly parallel moves in the

TABLE 11–2

Risk and Correlations for U.S. Zeroes (monthly VAR at 95% level)

Ver-tex	VAR (%)	1m	3m	6m	1Y	2Y	3Y	4Y	5Y	7Y	9Y	10Y	15Y	20Y	30Y
1m	0.021	1													
3m	0.064	.56	1												
6m	0.162	.50	.69	1											
1Y	0.470	.51	.67	.87	1										
2Y	0.987	.45	.52	.80	.90	1									
3Y	1.484	.44	.50	.79	.89	.99	1								
4Y	1.971	.42	.47	.76	.87	.98	.99	1							
5Y	2.426	.41	.46	.74	.86	.97	.99	1.0	1						
7Y	3.192	.39	.44	.70	.83	.94	.97	.98	.99	1					
9Y	3.913	.37	.42	.66	.80	.91	.94	.96	.98	1.0	1				
10Y	4.250	.36	.41	.65	.79	.90	.94	.96	.97	.99	1.0	1			
15Y	6.234	.33	.38	.61	.74	.85	.89	.92	.93	.96	.98	.98	1		
20Y	8.146	.30	.35	.55	.68	.79	.83	.86	.88	.92	.94	.95	.99	1	
30Y	11.119	.26	.31	.51	.64	.76	.80	.83	.85	.90	.93	.94	.98	.99	1

term structure, VAR should increase linearly with maturity. This is not the case. As pointed out in a previous chapter, longer maturities display slightly less risk than by a simple extrapolation of short maturities. Also, correlations are below unity.

4.1 Portfolio VAR

Consider now the portfolio of two bonds described in Chapter 6, a $100 million five-year par 6 percent issue and a $100 million one-year par 4 percent issue. This portfolio has a duration of 2.733 years, or average maturity of three years.

The three methods are compared in Table 11–3. Principal mapping consists of one payment at $t = 3$, duration mapping of one payment at $t = 2.733$, and cash flow mapping is described in the last column. The table lays out the present value of all portfolio cash flows discounted at the appropriate zero-coupon rate.

Three approaches are possible to compute the portfolio VAR. Principal mapping considers the timing of redemption payments only. As the average maturity of this portfolio is three years, the VAR can be found from the risk of a three-year maturity zero, which is 1.484 percent. The VAR is then $200 $\times$ 1.484% = $2.97. The only positive aspect of this method is its simplicity. This approach overstates the true risk because it ignores intervening payments.

The next step in precision is duration mapping. If the term structure always followed parallel moves, evaluating the risk of bond portfolios would be relatively simple. Duration corresponds to the maturity of a zero-coupon

TABLE 11–3

Mapping for a Bond Portfolio

Term (year)	6% 5-Year	4% 1-Year	Spot Rate	Mapping Principal	Duration	Cash Flow
1	6	104	4.000	.00	.00	105.77
2	6	0	4.618	.00	.00	5.48
2.733	—	—		—	200.00	—
3	6	0	5.192	200.00	.00	5.15
4	6	0	5.716	.00	.00	4.80
5	106	0	6.112	.00	.00	78.79
Total				200.00	200.00	200.00

bond with a life of 2.733 years. Using a linear interpolating between the two- and three-year measures, we find a risk of $0.987 + (1.484 - 0.987) \times (2.733 - 2) = 1.351\%$ for this hypothetical zero. With a $200 million portfolio, the duration-based VAR is $2.70 million, slightly less than before.

The cash flow mapping method consists of grouping all cash flows on term structure "vertices," which correspond to maturities for which volatilities are provided. Each cash flow is represented by the present value of the cash payment, discounted at the appropriate zero-coupon rate.

$$
\begin{matrix}
\text{Coupon-} \\
\text{paying} \\
\text{bond}
\end{matrix}
=
\begin{matrix}
\text{Cash flow} \\
\text{PV on} \\
\text{vertex 1}
\end{matrix}
+
\begin{matrix}
\text{Cash flow} \\
\text{PV on} \\
\text{vertex 2}
\end{matrix}
+ \ldots +
\begin{matrix}
\text{Principal} \\
\text{PV on} \\
\text{last vertex}
\end{matrix}
$$

Table 11–4 shows how to compute the portfolio VAR using cash flow mapping. The second column reports the cash flows x from Table 11–3. The third column presents the product of these cash flows with the risk of each vertex $V = \alpha\sigma$ (at the 95 percent level). With perfect correlation across all zeroes, the VAR of the portfolio would be

$$
\text{Undiversified value at risk} = \sum_{i=1}^{N} x_i V_i,
$$

TABLE 11–4

Computing the VAR of a $200 Million Bond Portfolio (monthly VAR at 95% level)

Term (year)	Cash Flows x($m)	$x \times V$ (%)	Correlation Matrix R					Var ($m)
			1Y	2Y	3Y	4Y	5Y	
1	105.77	49.66	1					
2	5.48	5.40	.897	1				
3	5.15	7.65	.886	.991	1			
4	4.80	9.47	.866	.976	.994	1		
5	78.79	191.15	.855	.966	.988	.998	1	
Total	200.00	263.35						
VAR ($m)								
Undiversified		$2.63						
Diversified								$2.57

which is 263.35%, or $2.63 million. This number represents the *undiversified* VAR. It is close to the VAR obtained from the duration approximation, which was $2.70 million. As in Chapter 8, the fact that the undiversified VAR is simply the weighted sum of individual VAR can be demonstrated for a portfolio of two assets with $\rho = 1$, as $V[x_1R_1+x_2R_2] = x_1^2\sigma_1^2+x_2^2\sigma_2^2+2x_1x_2\rho\sigma_1\sigma_2 = (x_1\sigma_1 + x_2\sigma_2)^2$. Therefore,

$$\sigma(x_1R_1 + x_2R_2) = (x_1\sigma_1 + x_2\sigma_2). \tag{11.3}$$

The right side of the table presents the correlation matrix of zeroes for maturities ranging from one to five years. To obtain the portfolio VAR, we premultiply and postmultiply the matrix by the dollar amounts (xV) at each vertex. Taking the square root, we find a VAR measure of $2.57 million. This is the most the portfolio could lose over a one-month horizon at the 95 percent confidence level.

Note that the duration VAR was $2.70 million, and the undiversified VAR was $2.63 million. These differences are due to two factors. First, risk measures are not perfectly linear with maturity, which should be the case if term structure shifts were strictly parallel. Second, diversification reduces risk even further. Thus, of the $130,000 difference in the extreme VARs ($2.70m - $2.57m$), $70,000 is due to differences in yield volatility ($2.70m - $2.63m$) and $60,000 is due to imperfect correlations.

Table 11–5 presents another approach to VAR, which is directly derived from movements in the value of zeroes, as in stress testing. Assume all zeroes were perfectly correlated. Then we could decrease all zeroes' values by their VAR. For instance, the one-year zero is worth 0.9615. Given the VAR in Table 11–1 of 0.4696, a 95 percent probability move would be for the zero to fall to $0.9615 \times (1 - 0.4696\%) = 0.9570$. If all zeroes were perfectly correlated, they should all fall by their respective VARs. This generates a new distribution of present value factors, which can be used to price the portfolio. Table 11–5 shows that the new value is $197.37 million, which is exactly $2.63 million below the original value. This number is exactly the same as the one obtained in the previous paragraph, with correlations set to unity.

The two approaches illustrate the link between computing VAR through matrix multiplication and through movements in underlying prices. Computing VAR through matrix multiplication is much more direct, however, and more important, it also allows nonperfect correlations across different sectors of the yield curve.

TABLE 11–5

Computing the VAR from the Change in Prices of Zeroes

Cash Term (year)	Old Flows ($m)	Old Zero Value	Zero PV of Flows	Zero Risk (VAR)	New Zero Value	PV of Flows
1	109	0.9615	105.77	0.4696	0.9570	105.27
2	6	0.9136	5.48	0.9868	0.9046	5.43
3	6	0.8591	5.15	1.4841	0.8463	5.08
4	6	0.8006	4.80	1.9714	0.7848	4.71
5	106	0.7433	78.79	2.4261	0.7252	76.88
Total			200.00			197.37
Loss						$2.63m

4.2 Assigning Weights to Vertices

In the previous example, each portfolio cash flow fell on one of the prese-lected vertices. In general, however, this will not be the case. Assume for instance that the portfolio consists of one cash flow with maturity of $D_p = 2.7325$ years and present value of $200 million. The question is, How should we allocate the $200 million to the adjoining vertices in a way that best represents the risk of the original investment?

A simple method consists of allocating funds according to a duration interpolation. Define x as the weight on the first vertex and D_1, D_2 as the duration of the first and second vertices. The portfolio duration D_p will be matched if $xD_1 + (1 - x)D_2 = D_p$, or $x = (D_2 - D_p)/(D_2 - D_1)$. In our case, $x = (3 - 2.7325)/(3 - 2) = 0.26675$, which leads to an amount of $53.49 million on the first vertex. The balance of $146.51 million is allo-cated to the three-year vertex.

Unfortunately, this approach may not create a portfolio with the same risk as the original portfolio. To maintain the same VAR, a different method can be employed. Define σ_1 and σ_2 as the respective volatilities, and ρ as the correlation.

The portfolio variance is

$$V[R_p] = x^2\sigma_1^2 + (1 - x)^2\sigma_2^2 + 2x(1 - x)\rho\sigma_1\sigma_2, \qquad (11.4)$$

which we set equal to the variance of the zero-coupon bond falling be-tween the two vertices. By linear interpolation of the price volatilities for two- and three-year zeroes, the portfolio volatility is $\sigma_p = 1.351\%$, as we have done before.[2] Therefore, the weight x that maintains the portfolio risk to that of the initial investment is found from solving the quadratic equation

$$(\sigma_1^2 + \sigma_2^2 - 2\rho_1\sigma_2)x^2 + 2(-\sigma_2^2 + \rho\sigma_1\sigma_2)x + (\sigma_2^2 - \sigma_p^2) = 0. \quad (11.5)$$

The solution to the equation $ax^2 + 2bx + c = 0$ is $x = (-b \pm \sqrt{b^2 - ac})/a$, which leads to the two roots $x_1 = 0.2635$ and $x_2 = 5.2168$. We choose the first root, which is between zero and unity. As shown in Table 11–6, this translates into a position of \$52.71 million on the two-year vertex and \$147.29 million on the three-year vertex.

In this example, the difference between the two approaches is minor. The actual VAR of the cash flow is \$2.702 million, against \$2.698 million for the portfolio based on duration weights. In fact, the duration approximation is exact under two conditions: (1) the correlation coefficient is unity, and (2) the volatility of each vertex is proportional to its duration ($\sigma_1 = \sigma D_1$, $\sigma_2 = \sigma D_2$, $\rho = 1$). Under these conditions, equation (11.4) simplifies to

$$V[Rp] = x^2\sigma^2 D_1^2 + (1 - x)^2\sigma^2 D_2^2 + 2x(1 - x)\sigma^2 D_1 D_2 \quad (11.6)$$

$$= \sigma^2(xD_1 + (1 - x)D_2)^2,$$

which equals $(\sigma D_p)^2$ if $xD_1 + (1 - x)D_2 = D_p$. In other words, duration matching is perfectly appropriate under these conditions. In more general cases, especially if ρ is much lower than 1, the duration approximation will fail to provide a portfolio with the same risk as that of the original cash flow.

4.3 Benchmarking a Portfolio

Finally, we illustrate how to compute VAR in relative terms; that is, relative to a performance benchmark. Table 11–7 presents the cash flow decomposition of the J.P. Morgan U.S. bond index, which has a duration of 4.62

---

2. Another approach is to interpolate yield volatilities, from which the price volatility can be obtained. Unfortunately, this method does not ensure a solution x that is always such that $0 < x < 1$. Also, there is no theory to suggest that interpolating yield volatilities is more appropriate than interpolating price volatilities.

TABLE 11-6

Assigning Weights to Vertices

Term (year)		VAR Adjustment			Duration Adjustment	
	VAR (%)	Correlation	Weight	Amount	Weight	Amount
2	0.9868		0.2635	$52.71	0.2675	$53.49
3	1.4841	0.9908	0.7365	$147.29	0.7325	$146.51
2.7325	1.3510					
Total			1.0000	$200.00	1.0000	$200.00

years. We can use the pattern of cash flows and information about risk and correlations to find the diversified VAR. Assume we are trying to benchmark a portfolio of $100 million. Over a monthly horizon, the VAR at the 95 percent level is $1.99 million. This is about equivalent to the risk of a four-year note. The undiversified VAR is $2.07 million, slightly higher.

Next, we try to match the index with two bonds. The rightmost columns in the table display the positions of two-bond portfolios with duration matched to that of the index. Since no zero-coupon has a maturity of exactly 4.62 years, the closest portfolio consists of two positions, each in a four and a five-year zero. The respective weights for this portfolio are $38 and $62 million.

Define the now vector of positions for this portfolio as x, and for the index as x_0 . The VAR of the deviation relative to the benchmark is

$$\text{Value at risk} = \alpha\sqrt{(x - x_0)'\Sigma(x - x_0)}.$$

After performing the necessary calculations, we find that the relative VAR of this duration-hedged portfolio is $0.43 million. Thus, the maximum deviation between the index and the portfolio is at most $0.43 million under normal market conditions. This potential shortfall is much less than the $1.99 million absolute risk of the index. The remaining tracking error is due to nonparallel moves in the term structure.

Relative to the original index, the tracking error can be measured in terms of variance reduction, similar to an R^2 in a regression. The variance improvement is

TABLE 11–7

Benchmarking a $100 Million Bond Index (monthly VAR at 95% level)

Vertex	Risk (%)	Position: JPM US Index ($m)	Position: Portfolio				
			1 ($m)	2 ($m)	3 ($m)	4 ($m)	5 ($m)
≤1m	0.022	1.05	0.0	0.0	0.0	0.0	84.8
3m	0.065	1.35	0.0	0.0	0.0	0.0	0.0
6m	0.163	2.49	0.0	0.0	0.0	0.0	0.0
1Y	0.470	13.96	0.0	0.0	0.0	59.8	0.0
2Y	0.987	24.83	0.0	0.0	62.6	0.0	0.0
3Y	1.484	15.40	0.0	59.5	0.0	0.0	0.0
4Y	1.971	11.57	38.0	0.0	0.0	0.0	0.0
5Y	2.426	7.62	62.0	0.0	0.0	0.0	0.0
7Y	3.192	6.43	0.0	40.5	0.0	0.0	0.0
9Y	3.913	4.51	0.0	0.0	37.4	0.0	0.0
10Y	4.250	3.34	0.0	0.0	0.0	40.2	0.0
15Y	6.234	3.00	0.0	0.0	0.0	0.0	0.0
20Y	8.146	3.15	0.0	0.0	0.0	0.0	0.0
30Y	11.119	1.31	0.0	0.0	0.0	0.0	15.2
Total		100.00	100.0	100.0	100.0	100.0	100.0
Duration		4.62	4.62	4.62	4.62	4.62	4.62
VAR ($m)							
Absolute		1.99	2.25	2.20	2.13	2.07	1.10
Relative		0.00	0.43	0.29	0.16	0.20	0.36

$$1 - \left(\frac{0.43}{1.99}\right)^2 = 95.4\%,$$

which is in line with the explanatory power of the first factor in the variance decomposition of bond returns detailed in Chapter 8.

Next, we explore the effect of altering the composition of the tracking portfolio. Portfolio 2 widens the bracket of time vertices; it consists of positions in years 3 and 7. Its tracking error VAR is $0.29 million, which is an improvement over the previous number.

Portfolio 3 consists of positions in years 2 and 9. This comes the closest to approximating the cash flow positions in the index, which has the greatest weight on the two-year vertex. The tracking error VAR is reduced further to $0.16 million. Portfolio 4 consists of positions in years

1 and 10. Now the VAR increases to \$0.20 million. This mistracking is even more pronounced for a portfolio consisting of one-month bills and 30-year zeroes, for which the residual VAR increases to \$0.36 million.

Among the portfolios considered here, the lowest tracking error is obtained with portfolio 3. Note that the absolute risk of these portfolios is lowest for portfolio 5. As correlations decrease for more distant maturities, we should expect that a duration-matched portfolio should have the lowest absolute risk for the combination of most distant maturities, such as a barbell portfolio of cash and a 30-year zero. However, minimizing absolute market risk is not the same as minimizing relative market risk.

This example demonstrates that duration hedging only provides a first approximation to interest rate risk management. If the goal is to minimize tracking error relative to an index, it is essential to use a fine decomposition of the index by maturity. Among the combinations considered here, the lowest tracking error is attained for a portfolio with cash positions that are closest to those of the index.

5 APPLICATION TO DERIVATIVES

5.1 Forward Currency Contracts

As forward or futures contracts are linear in the underlying spot rates, their risk can be easily constructed from basic building blocks. Assume for instance we are dealing with a forward contract on a foreign currency. The basic valuation formula developed in the derivatives chapter is

$$f_t = S_t e^{-r^*\tau} - Ke^{-r\tau}, \tag{11.7}$$

where S_t is the spot price, K is the contract purchase price, r is the U.S. risk-free rate, $y = r^*$ is the foreign risk-free rate, and τ is the time to maturity. A position in a forward contract can be decomposed into

Long forward contract	=	Long foreign currency spot	+	Long foreign currency bill	+	Short U.S. dollar bill

The initial investment is zero since the position in the foreign currency bill is funded by borrowing in the home currency.

Let us examine the risk of a one-year forward contract with a notional (face amount) of DEM 100 million. Table 11–8 displays pricing

TABLE 11–8

Risk and Correlations for Forward Cash Flows (monthly VAR at 95% level)

Term (year)	Price	VAR (%)	Correlations DEM Spot	DEM 1Y	USD 1Y
DEM spot	$0.6962	6.2201	1	0.1912	0.0400
Long DEM	3.9375%	0.2876	0.1912	1	0.2937
Short USD	5.8125%	0.4696	0.0400	0.2937	1
Forward	$0.7088				

information for the contract (spot, forward, and interest rates), risk, and correlations. Among the three sources of risk, the volatility of the spot contract is the highest, by far, with a 6.22 percent VAR (corresponding to 1.65 standard deviation over a month for a 95 percent confidence level). This is much greater than the 0.29 percent VAR for the DEM one-year bill, or even the 0.47 percent VAR for the USD bill. Thus, most of the risk of the forward contract is driven by the cash DEM position.

But risk is also affected by correlations. The positive correlation of 0.19 between the DEM spot and bill positions indicates that, when the DEM goes up in value against the dollar, the value of a one-year DEM investment is likely to appreciate. Therefore, higher values of the DEM are associated with lower DEM interest rates.

This positive correlation increases the risk of the combined position. On the other hand, the position is also short a one-year USD bill, which is positively correlated with the other two legs of the transaction. This should decrease the risk of the transaction. The issue is, What will be the net effect on the risk of the forward contract?

VAR provides an exact answer to this question, which is displayed in Table 11–9. But first, we have to compute the positions x on each of the three building blocks of the contract. The chapter on derivatives has shown that the risk of a forward contract is

$$df = \frac{\partial f}{\partial S}dS + \frac{\partial f}{\partial r^*}dr^* + \frac{\partial f}{\partial r}dr = e^{-r^*\tau}dS - Se^{-r^*\tau}\tau dr^* + Ke^{-r\tau}\tau dr. \quad (11.8)$$

TABLE 11-9

Computing the VAR of a DEM 100 Million Forward Contract (monthly VAR at 95% level)

Position	Present Value Factor	Cash Flows	PV of Flows x	Total VAR		Incremental VAR
				$(V'RV)x$	$x(V'RV)x$	βxVAR
DEM spot			$66.99	2606.72	17.461	$4.155
Long DEM	0.962116	DM100.00	$66.99	25.79	1.727	$0.041
Short USD	0.945067	-$70.88	-$66.99	-4.30	0.288	$0.007
Total					17.663	$4.203
VAR (m)					$4.203	

These exposures can be expressed in terms of the risk of the spot rate and of investments in the local and foreign bills. Define these as $P = e^{-r\tau}$ and $P* = e^{-r*\tau}$. If the building blocks are returns on zero-coupon bonds, $\sigma(dP/P)$, we transform dr into dP using $dP = (-\tau)e^{-r\tau}dr$ and $dP* = (-\tau)e^{-r*\tau}dr*$. The risk of the forward contract becomes

$$df = (Se^{-r*\tau})\frac{dS}{S} + (Se^{-r*\tau})\frac{dP*}{P*} - (Ke^{-r\tau})\frac{dP}{P}. \qquad (11.9)$$

This shows that the forward position can be separated into three cash flows, (1) a long spot position in DEM, worth DEM 100 m = $70.88 million in a year, or $(Se^{-r*\tau})$ = $66.99 million now; (2) a long position in a DEM investment, also worth $66.99 million now; and (3) a short position in a USD investment, worth $70.88 million in a year, or $(Ke^{-r\tau})$ = $66.99 million now.

Considering only the spot position, the VAR is $66.99 million times the risk of 6.22 percent. To compute the diversified VAR, we use the risk matrix from the data in Table 11-8 and pre- and postmultiply by the vector of positions (PV of CF column in the table).[3] The total VAR for the forward contract is $4.2027 million. This number is about the same size as that of the spot contract, because exchange rate volatility so dominates

---

3. Note that all risk measures are expressed in percent squared, which is more convenient to use. After performing all computations, we must correct for the factor of 100.

bond volatility. The slightly higher value is due to the additional effect of the one-year positions in bonds.

The risk of a forward contract includes both currency risk and interest rate risk. Longer maturities are exposed to greater interest rate risk. For instance, changing the maturity in our example from 1 year to 10 years would increase the VAR from $4.203 million to $4.867 million.

More generally, the same methodology can be used for long-term currency swaps, which are equivalent to portfolios of forward contracts. For instance, a 10-year contract to pay dollars and receive marks is equivalent to a series of 10 forward contracts to exchange a set amount of dollars into marks. To compute the VAR, the contract must be broken down into a currency risk component and a string of USD and DEM fixed-income components. As before, the total VAR will be driven by the currency component.

5.2 Forward Rate Agreements

Forward rate agreements (FRAs) are forward contracts that allow users to lock in an interest rate at some future date. The buyer of an FRA locks in a borrowing rate; the seller locks in a lending rate. In other words, the "long" receives a payment if the spot rate is above the forward rate.

Consider for instance a contract where the short leg of the FRA is defined by τ_1 year and the long leg by τ_2 year. Assume linear compounding for simplicity. As seen in Chapter 6, the forward rate is defined as the rate that equalizes the return on a τ_2-period investment with a τ_1-period investment rolled over at the forward rate

$$(1 + R_2\tau_2) = (1 + R_1\tau_1)[1 + F_{1,2}(\tau_2 - \tau_1)]. \qquad (11.10)$$

For instance, suppose that you sold a 6×12 FRA on $100 million. This is equivalent to borrowing $1 million for six months and investing the proceeds for 12 months. When the FRA expires in six months, assume that the prevailing six-month spot rate is higher than the locked-in forward rate. The seller then pays the buyer the difference between the spot and forward rate applied to the principal. In effect, this payment offsets the higher return that the investor would otherwise receive, thus guaranteeing a return equal to the forward rate. Therefore, an FRA can be decomposed into two zero-coupon building blocks:

Long 6×12 FRA = Long 6-month bill + Short 12-month bill

Table 11–10 provides a worked-out example. If the 360-day spot rate is 5.8125 percent and the 180-day rate is 5.625 percent, the forward rate must be such that

$$[1 + F_{1,2}/2] = \frac{(1 + 5.8125\%)}{(1 + 5.625\%/2)},$$

or $F = 5.836\%$. The present value of the notional $100 million in six months is $x = \$100/(1 + 5.625\%/2) = \$97.264$ million. This amount is invested for 12 months. In the meantime, what is the risk of this FRA?

Table 11–10 displays the computation of the value at risk for the FRA. The VAR of 6- and 12-month zeroes is 0.1629 and 0.4696, respectively, with a correlation of 0.8738. Applied to the principal of $97.26 million, the VAR of single zeroes would be $0.158 million and $0.457 million, respectively. If the two zeroes were not correlated, the total VAR of the FRA would be obtained from the square root of the sum of variances, which is $0.484 million.

Fortunately, the correlation substantially lowers the FRA risk. As the table shows, the largest amount the position can lose over a month at the 95 percent level is $0.327 million, which is less than the risk of a 12-month zero.

5.3 Interest Rate Swaps

Interest rate swaps allow investors to exchange interest rate flows from fixed to floating or vice versa. As was shown in Chapter 7, swaps can be decomposed into two legs, a fixed leg and a floating leg. The fixed leg can

TABLE 11–10

Computing the VAR of a $100 Million FRA (monthly VAR at 95% level)

Term (days)	PV of Flows x	Risk (%) V	Correlation Matrix R		VAR $(VRV)x$	$x(VRV)x$	Incremental VAR βxVAR
180	-$97.264	0.1629	1	0.8738	0.00039	-0.0381	-$0.116
360	$97.264	0.4696	0.8738	1	0.00149	0.1454	$0.444
Total	$0					0.1072	$0.327
VAR (m)						$0.327	

be priced as a coupon-paying bond; the floating leg is equivalent to a floating-rate note.

To illustrate, let us compute the value at risk of a $100 million five-year interest rate swap. We enter a dollar swap that pays 6.195 percent annually for five years in exchange for floating rate payments indexed to London Interbank Offer Rate (LIBOR). Initially, we consider a situation where the floating-rate note is about to be reset. Therefore, it has no risk.

Two approaches are possible for evaluating the risks of interest rate swaps. They can be viewed as a combined position in a fixed-rate bond and in a floating-rate bond or as a portfolio of forward contracts. We first value the swap as a position in two bonds, using the risk measures in Table 11–2. Details are in Table 11–11.

The second and third columns lay out the payments on both legs. The next column lists the spot rate for maturities going from one to five years. The fifth column reports the present value of the net flows, fixed minus floating. The last column presents the incremental VAR, which adds up to a total diversified VAR of $2.152 million. The undiversified VAR is obtained from summing all individual VARs; as usual, the value of $2.160 million somewhat overestimates risk.

TABLE 11–11

Computing the VAR of a $100 Million Interest Rate Swap (monthly VAR at 95% level)

Term (year)	Flow Fixed	Flow Floating	Rate (% per annum)	PV of Flows ($) x	Var of Flows $x \times V$	Incremental VAR (m)
1	−6.195	−	5.813	−5.855	−0.027	0.024
2	−6.195	−	5.929	−5.521	−0.054	0.053
3	−6.195	−	6.034	−5.196	−0.077	0.075
4	−6.195	−	6.130	−4.883	−0.096	0.096
5	−106.195	−	6.217	−78.546	−1.905	1.905
Total	−100.00					
VAR (m)						
Undiversified					$2.160m$	
Diversified						$2.152m$

This swap can also be viewed as the sum of five forward contracts, as shown in Table 11–12. The one-year contract promises payment of $100 million plus the coupon of 6.195 percent; discounted at the spot rate of 5.813 percent, this yields a present value of −$100.36. This is in exchange for $100 million now, which has no risk.

The next contract is a 1 × 2 forward contract, which promises to pay the principal plus the fixed coupon in two years, or −$106.195, million; discounted at the two-year spot rate, this yields −$94.64 million. This is in exchange for $100 million in one year, which is also $94.50 million discounted at the one-year spot rate. And so on until the fifth contract, a 4 × 5 forward contract.

Table 11–12 shows the VAR of each contract. The "undiversified" VAR of $2.401 million is the result of a simple summation of the five VARS. It overstates the true risk of the position, since it assumes perfect correlation among all five forward contracts, which is not the case. The fully diversified VAR is $2.152m, exactly the same as in the previous table. This demonstrates the equivalence of the two approaches.

Finally, we examine the change in risk after the first payment has just been set on the floating rate leg. The floating rate note (FRN) then becomes a one-year bond initially valued at par but subject to fluctuations in rates. The

TABLE 11–12

An Interest Rate Swap Viewed as Forward Contracts

Term (year)	1	1 × 2	2 × 3	3 × 4	4 × 5	VAR
			PV of Flows Contract			
1	−100.36	94.50				
2		−94.64	89.11			
3			−89.08	83.88		
4				−83.70	78.82	
5					−78.55	
VAR ($m)	$0.471	$0.571	$0.488	$0.446	$0.425	
Undiversified						$2.401m
Diversified						$2.152m

only change in the pattern of cash flows is to add $100 million to the position on year 1 (from $-\$5.855$ to $\$94.145$). The resulting VAR then decreases from $\$2.152$ million to $\$1.939$ million. More generally, the swap's VAR will converge to zero as the swap matures, dipping each time a coupon is set.

5.4 Options

A warning flag should be raised at the outset: the delta-normal method poorly measures the market risk of options. This is because options are non-linear instruments, while the delta-normal method is fundamentally linear.

Nonetheless, the risk of option positions can be approximated by a delta-equivalent position in the underlying asset:

$$dc = \Delta dS, \tag{11.11}$$

where the derivative can be obtained analytically for simple options or numerically for options that have no closed-form solution:

$$\text{Long option} = \text{Long } \Delta \text{ asset} + \text{Short } (\Delta S - c) \text{ bill}$$

For instance, assume that the delta for an at-the-money call option on an asset worth $\$100$ is $\Delta = 0.536$. The option itself is worth $\$4.2$. This option is equivalent to a $\$53.6$ position in the underlying asset financed by a loan of $\$49.4$. For portfolios of options on the same underlying asset, the market risk of the position can be captured by setting the position x to the total portfolio delta. The main drawback of this approach, of course, is that deltas change dynamically over time and, therefore, that the approximation is valid only for small movements in the underlying asset.

If one is willing to continue with the linear approximation, the risk of an option position can be illustrated using the Black-Scholes framework. Take for instance a long European call position on a foreign currency:

$$
\begin{aligned}
dc &= \frac{\partial f}{\partial S} dS + \frac{\partial f}{\partial r}*dr* + \frac{\partial f}{\partial r} dr \\
&= \Delta dS + \rho*dr* + \rho dr \\
&= e^{-r*\tau}N(d_1)dS + [-Se^{-r*\tau}\tau N(d_1)]dr* + [Ke^{-r\tau}\tau N(d_2)]dr \\
&= [Se^{-r*\tau}N(d_1)]\frac{dS}{S} + [Se^{-r*\tau}N(d_1)]\frac{dP*}{P*} - [Ke^{-r\tau}N(d_2)]\frac{dP}{P}. \tag{11.12}
\end{aligned}
$$

This formula bears a striking resemblance to that for foreign currency forwards, as in Equation (11.9). The only difference is that the positions on the spot foreign currency and the foreign currency bill are now multiplied by $N(d_1)$ and the position on the dollar bill is multiplied by $N(d_2)$.

In the extreme case, where the option is deep in the money, both $N(d_1)$ and $N(d_2)$ are equal to unity, and the option behaves exactly like a position in a forward contract. In this case, the BS model reduces to $c = Se^{-r^*\tau} - Ke^{-r\tau}$, which is indeed the valuation formula for a forward contract, as in equation (11).

Finally, note that the position on the dollar bill, $Ke^{-r\tau}N(d_2)$, is also equivalent to $Se^{-r^*\tau}N(d_1) - c = S\Delta - c$, thereby confirming that the call option is equivalent to a position of Δ in the underlying asset plus a short position of $(\Delta S - c)$ in a dollar bill. This example shows that, when $N(d)$ is relatively stable, the risk of option positions can be constructed from component building blocks using the delta-normal approach.

6 EQUITIES

Stock portfolios can be rather large, often with positions in excess of hundreds of securities. This motivates models for simplifying the covariance matrix. Chapter 8 has examined a number of such models. The issue is whether simplifications cause material errors in the measurement of VAR.

The simplest model is the "diagonal" model, where the variance of the portfolio return R_p is [see Equation (8.22)]

$$V(R_p) = (x'\Sigma x) = (x'\beta\beta'x)\sigma_m^2 + x'D_e x. \qquad (11.13)$$

To compute portfolio risk, one needs the vector of betas, which represents the systematic risks relative to a market index m, the variance of that market index σ_m^2, and the residual variances, which are captured by the diagonal matrix D_e.

A further simplification obtains if one ignores the residual risk. Risk-Metrics, for instance, provides risk measures for a number of stock markets. As the portfolio beta is

$$\beta_p = \sum_{i=1}^{N} x_i\beta_i = x'\beta, \qquad (11.14)$$

the portfolio VAR is $VAR_p = VAR_m\beta_p$. In effect, this approximation consists of ignoring the second term in equation (11.13). We refer to this model as the *beta model*.

Finally, regulators are considering a measure of VAR that is undiversified, i.e., where all correlations are set to unity. The question is, What is the effect of these approximations on the portfolio VAR?

As an example, let us go back to the three-stock portfolio described in Chapter 8. A total of $100 million is invested equally in GM, Ford, and Hewlett Packard (HWP). The VAR is computed over a monthly horizon at the 95 percent level. The first line in Table 11–13 shows the VAR of each stock, which ranges from $13.41 to $15.68 million for a $100 million position.

Next, the table displays four covariance matrices: the full model, diagonal model, beta model, and undiversified model. Their respective

TABLE 11–13

Computing the VAR of a $100 Million Stock Portfolio (monthly VAR at 95% level)

		Covariance Matrix			
	Cash ($m)	GM	FORD	HWP	VAR($m)
VAR		14.01	13.41	15.68	
Beta		0.806	1.183	1.864	
Cov. Matrix					
Full					
GM	33.33	72.17	43.92	26.32	11.76
FORD	33.33	43.92	66.12	44.31	
HWP	33.33	26.32	44.31	90.41	
Diagonal					
GM	33.33	72.17	11.35	17.87	10.13
FORD	33.33	11.35	66.12	26.23	
HWP	33.33	17.87	26.23	90.41	
Beta					
GM	33.33	7.73	11.35	17.88	7.30
FORD	33.33	11.35	16.65	26.24	
HWP	33.33	17.88	26.24	41.32	
Undiversified					
GM	33.33	72.17	69.08	80.78	14.37
FORD	33.33	69.08	66.12	77.32	

VARs are $11.76, $10.13, $7.30, and $14.37. These numbers indicate that the diagonal model provides a good approximation of the actual portfolio VAR, although slightly on the low side. The beta model, in contrast, substantially underestimates the true VAR because it ignores residual risk.

Finally, the undiversified VAR is too conservative. The value of $14.37 is also obtained from a simple average of the VAR for the three assets, $1/3 \times (14.01 + 13.41 + 15.68) = \$14.37$. This measure of risk fails to recognize the diversification properties of portfolios.

As the number of stocks in the portfolio increases from three to hundreds, we would expect that the VAR from the diagonal model will provide an increasingly better approximation of the actual VAR. This is because the total portfolio risk decreases as the number of assets increases.

CHAPTER 12

Structured Monte Carlo

Deus ex machina.

Wall Street is often compared to a casino. The analogy is appropriate in one respect: securities firms commonly use simulation techniques, known as *Monte Carlo methods*, to value complex derivatives. The Monte Carlo method approximates the behavior of financial prices by using computer simulations to generate random price paths.

Numerical simulations were first used by atom bomb scientists at Los Alamos in 1942 to crack problems that could not be solved by conventional means. The name *Monte Carlo* was derived from the famous casino established in 1862 in the South of France (actually, in Monaco). What better way to evoke random draws, roulette, and games of chance?

Structured Monte Carlo (SMC) is used to simulate a variety of different scenarios for the portfolio value on the target date. The portfolio VAR can then be read off directly from the distribution of simulated portfolio values.

Because of its flexibility, Monte Carlo analysis is by far the most powerful method to compute value at risk. It can potentially account for a wide range of risks, including price risk, volatility risk, and credit risk. By using different models, it can even account for that most insidious form of risk, model risk. As such, SMC is the most comprehensive analytical method to measure financial risks. This approach, however, involves costly investments in intellectual and systems development.

This chapter shows how SMC can be used to uncover VAR. The first section focuses on a simple case with just one random variable. Market risk with many sources of risk is then discussed in Section 2.

1 SIMULATIONS WITH ONE RANDOM VARIABLE

The basic concept behind SMC is to simulate repeatedly a random process for the financial variable of interest, covering a wide range of possible situations. Thus simulations re-create the entire distribution of portfolio values. We first concentrate on a simple case with just one random variable.

1.1 Simulating a Price Path

The first, and most crucial, step in the simulation consists of choosing a particular stochastic model for the behavior of prices. A commonly used model is the *geometric Brownian motion* (GBM), which underlies much of option pricing theory. The model assumes that innovations in the asset price are uncorrelated over time and that small movements in prices can be described by

$$dS_t = \mu_t S_t dt + \sigma_t S_t dz, \qquad (12.1)$$

where dz is a random variable distributed normally with mean zero and variance dt. This variable drives the random shocks to the price and does not depend on past information. It is "Brownian" in the sense that its variance continuously decreases with the time interval, $V(dz) = dt$. This rules out processes with sudden jumps, for instance. The process is also "geometric" because all parameters are scaled by the current price S_t.

The parameters μ_t and σ_t represent the instantaneous drift and volatility at time t, which can evolve over time. For simplicity, we will assume in what follows that these parameters are constant over time. But, as μ_t and σ_t can be functions of past variables, it would be easy to simulate time variation in the variances as in a GARCH process, for example.

In practice, the process with an infinitesimally small increment dt is approximated by discrete moves of size Δt. As we have done before, define t as the present time, T as the target time, and $\tau = T - t$ as the horizon, or time to maturity. To generate a series of random variables S_{t+i} over the interval τ, we first chop up τ into n increments, with $\Delta t = \tau/n$.

Integrating dS/S over a finite interval, we have approximately

$$\Delta S_t = S_{t-1}(\mu\Delta t + \sigma\epsilon\sqrt{\Delta t}), \qquad (12.2)$$

where ϵ is now a standard normal random variable; that is, with mean zero and unit variance. We can verify that this process generates a mean $E[\Delta S/S] = \mu\Delta t$, which grows with time, as does the variance $V[\Delta S/S] = \sigma^2\Delta t$.

To simulate the price path for S, we start from S_t and generate a sequence of epsilons (ϵ) for $i = 1, 2, \ldots, n$. Then S_{t+1} is set at $S_{t+1} = S_t + S_t(\mu\Delta t + \sigma\epsilon_1\sqrt{\Delta t})$, S_{t+2} is similarly computed from $S_{t+1} + S_{t+1}(\mu\Delta t + \sigma\epsilon_2\sqrt{\Delta t})$, and so on for future values, until the target horizon is reached, at which point the price is $S_{t+n} = S_T$.

Table 12–1 illustrates a simulation of a process with a drift (μ) of zero and volatility (σ) of 10 percent over the total interval. The initial price is $100 and the interval is cut into 100 steps. Therefore, the local volatility is $0.10 \times \sqrt{1/100} = 0.01$.

The second column starts with the initial price. The next column displays the realization of a standard normal variable. With no drift, the increment in the following column is simply ($\epsilon \times 0.01$). Finally, the last column computes the current price from the previous price and the increment. The values at each point are conditional on the simulated values at the previous point. The process is repeated until the final price of $91.06 is reached at the 100th step.

Figure 12–1 presents two price paths, each leading to a different ending price. Given these assumptions, the ending price must follow a

TABLE 12–1

Simulating a Price Path

Step i	Previous Price S_{t+i-1}	Random Variable ϵ_i	Increment ΔS	Current Price S_{t+i}
1	100.00	0.199	0.00199	100.20
2	100.20	1.665	0.01665	101.87
3	101.87	−0.445	−0.00446	101.41
4	101.41	−0.667	−0.00668	100.74
. . .				
100	92.47	1.153	−0.01153	91.06

FIGURE 12–1

Simulating Price Paths

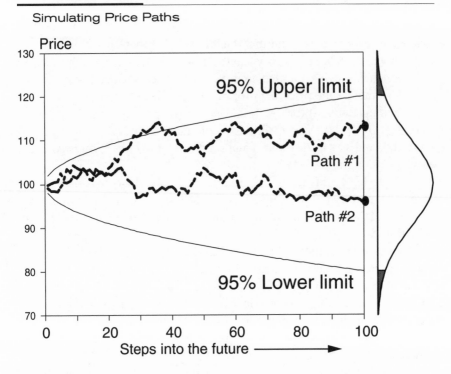

normal distribution with a mean of $100 and a standard deviation of $10.[1] This distribution is illustrated on the right side of the figure, along with 95 percent confidence bands, corresponding to two standard-deviation intervals.

The distribution also is known at any intermediate point. The figure displays 95 percent confidence bands, which increase with the square root of time until they reach $\pm 2 \times 10\%$. In this simple model, risk can be computed at any point up to the target horizon.

SMC, however, is prone to model risk. If the stochastic process chosen for the price is unrealistic, so will be the estimate of VAR. This is why the choice of the underlying process is particularly important. The geometric Brownian motion model in (12.1) adequately

---

1. In fact, the ending distribution is actually lognormal, as the price can never fall below 0.

describes the behavior of some financial variables, but certainly not that of short-term fixed-income securities. In the Brownian motion, shocks to the price are never reversed. This does not represent the price process for default-free bonds, which must converge to their face value at expiration.

Another approach is to model the dynamics of interest rates as

$$dr_t = \kappa(\theta - r_t)dt + \sigma\sqrt{r_t}dz \tag{12.3}$$

which was used by Cox, Ingersoll, and Ross (1985) to model the term structure in a general equilibrium environment.

This process is important because it provides a simple description of the stochastic nature of interest rates that is consistent with the empirical observation that interest rates tend to be mean reverting. Here, the parameter $\kappa < 1$ defines the speed of mean reversion toward the long-run value θ; situations where current interest rates are high, such as $r_t > \theta$, imply a negative drift $\kappa(\theta - r_t)$ until rates revert to θ. Conversely, low current rates are associated with positive expected drift. Also note that the variance of this process is proportional to the level of interest rates; as the interest rate moves toward 0, the variance decreases, so that r can never fall below 0.

Equation (12.3) describes a one-factor model of interest rates, which is driven by movements in short-term rates dr_t. In this model, movements in longer-term rates are perfectly correlated with movements in this short-term rate through dz. They may exhibit various trends, however. To avoid arbitrage, forward rates can be incorporated in expected returns μ_t across different maturities, as shown in equation (6.15). The Monte Carlo experiment consists of first simulating movements in short-term interest rates, then using the simulated term structure to price the securities at the target date.

The interest rate process can also be extended to a multicurrency environment, incorporating correlations across interest rates and exchange rates. For currencies, the drift can be based on short-term uncovered interest parity, which defines the expected return as the difference between the domestic and foreign interest rates. This creates a large system with interactions that provide realistic modeling of global fixed-income portfolios.

For more precision, additional factors can be added. Longstaff and Schwartz (1992), for example, extend the Cox, Ingersoll, and Ross (CIR) model to a two-factor model, using the short-term rate and its variance as sources of risk. They find that the two-factor model provides an acceptable description of the cross-section of bond prices, whereas the single-factor model is rejected by the data.

1.2 Creating Random Numbers

Monte Carlo simulations are based on random draws ϵ from a variable with the desired probability distribution. The numerical analysis usually proceeds in two steps.

The first building block for a random number generator is a uniform distribution over the interval [0,1], which produces a random variable x. More properly speaking, these numbers are "pseudo"-random, since they are generated from a algorithm using a deterministic rule. Starting from the same "seed" number, the sequence can be repeated at will.

The next step is to transform the uniform random number x into the desired distribution through the inverse cumulative probability distribution function (pdf). Take the normal distribution. By definition, the cumulative pdf $N(y)$ is always between 0 and 1. Therefore, to generate a normally distributed random variable, we compute y such that $x = N(y)$, or $y = N^{-1}(x)$.[2] More generally, any distribution function can be generated as long as the function $N(y)$ can be inverted.

At this point, an important caveat is in order. It seems easy to generate variables that are purely random, but in practice, it is quite difficult. A well-designed algorithm will generate draws that "appear" independent over time. Whether this sequence is truly random is a philosophical issue that we will not address. Good random-number generators must create series that pass all conventional tests of independence. Otherwise, the characteristics of the simulated price process will not obey the underlying model.

Most operating systems, unfortunately, provide a random number generator that is simple but inaccurate. All algorithms "cycle" after some iterations; that is, they repeat the same sequence of pseudo-random num-

---

2. Moro (1995) shows how to use approximations to the function N^{-1} to accelerate the speed of computation.

bers. Good algorithms cycle after billions of draws; bad ones may cycle after a few thousand only.

If the cycle is too short, dependencies will be introduced in the price process solely because of the random-number generator. As a result, the range of possible portfolio values may be incomplete, thus leading to incorrect measures of VAR. This is why it is important to investigate the qualities of the algorithm, which, after all, drive the entire results.

A final point should be made regarding the use of Monte Carlo methods. These methods are based on random points that "fill" an N-dimensional space, where N is the number of variables driving the price of securities. For complex financial instruments, such as mortgages, simulation methods are still relatively slow; that is, relative to fast-moving financial markets. Other methods exist, however.

Researchers now realize that the sequence of points $\{x\}$ does not have to be chosen randomly. It is possible to use a *deterministic* scheme that is constructed to provide a more consistent fill to the N space. The choice must account for the sample size, dimensionality of the problem, and possibly the shape of the function being integrated.

Paskov and Taub (1995), for example, find that, for a particular example of mortgage securities with high dimensionality, using simulations with predetermined sets of points provides a noticeable improvement in speed. As simulation methods become widely used to measure VAR, we can expect to see vast improvements in the delivery of results.

1.3 The Bootstrap

An alternative to generating random numbers from a hypothetical distribution is to sample from historical data with replacement. For example, suppose we observe a series of M returns $R = \Delta S/S$, $\{R\} = (R_1 \ldots R_M)$, which can be assumed to be iid random variables drawn from an unknown distribution. The historical-simulation method consists of using this series once to generate pseudo-returns. But this can be extended much further.

The bootstrap estimates this distribution by the empirical distribution of R, assigning equal probability to each realization. The method was initially proposed by Efron (1979) as a nonparametric randomization technique that draws from the observed distribution of the data to model the distribution of a statistic of interest.[3]

The procedure is carried out by sampling from $\{R\}$ with replacement, as many observations as necessary. For instance, assume that we want to generate 100 returns into the future, but we do not want to impose any assumption on the distribution of daily returns. We could project returns by randomly picking one return at a time from the sample over the past $M = 500$ days, with replacement. Define the index choice as $m(1)$, a number between 1 and 500. The selected return is then $R_{m(1)}$ and the simulated next day return will be $S_{t+1} = S_t(1 + R_{m(1)})$. Repeating the operation for a total of 100 draws yields a total of 100 pseudo-values $S_{t+1}, \ldots, S_{t+n}$.

An essential advantage of the bootstrap is that it can include fat tails, or jumps, or any departure from the normal distribution. For instance, one could include the return for the crash of October 19, 1987, which would never (or nearly never) occur under a normal distribution. The method also accounts for correlations across series, as one draw consists of the simultaneous returns for N series, such as stock, bonds, and currency prices.

The bootstrap approach, it should be noted, has limitations. For small sample sizes M, the bootstrapped distribution may be a poor approximation to the actual one. Therefore, it is important to have access to sufficient data points. The other drawback of the bootstrap is that is relies heavily on the assumption that returns are independent. By resampling at random, any pattern of time variation is broken.

The bootstrap, however, can also accommodate some time variation in parameters, as long as we are willing to take a stand on the model. For instance, the bootstrap can be applied to the normalized residuals of a GARCH process:

$$\epsilon_t = r_t/\sqrt{h_t},$$

where r_t is the actual return and h_t is the conditional variance from the estimated GARCH process. To re-create pseudo-returns, one would then first sample from the historical distribution of ϵ, then reconstruct the conditional variance and pseudo-returns.

---

3. The asymptotic properties of the bootstrap for commonly used statistics such as the mean, median, variance, and distribution quantiles have been studied by Bickel and Freedman (1981).

Overall, the advantages of the bootstrap far outweigh its disadvantages. Given that the purpose of VAR is to capture behavior in the tails and that historical data display fatter tails than in normal distributions, the bootstrap is ideally suited to VAR methods.

1.4 Computing VAR

Once a price path has been simulated, we can build the portfolio distribution at the end of the selected horizon. The simulation is carried out by the following steps:

1. Choose a stochastic process and parameters.
2. Generate a pseudo-sequence of variables $\epsilon_1, \epsilon_2, \ldots, \epsilon_n$, from which prices are computed as $S_{t+1}, S_{t+2}, \ldots, S_{t+n}$.
3. Calculate the value of the asset $F_{t+n} = F_T$ under this particular sequence of prices at the target horizon.
4. Repeat steps 2 and 3 as many times as necessary, say, 10,000, obtaining a distribution of values, $F_T^1, \ldots, F_T^{10,000}$, from which the VAR can be reported. At the selected significance level c, the VAR is the portfolio value exceeded in c times 10,000 replications.

The number of iterations should reflect the usual trade-off between accuracy and computation cost. There is always some error in simulation estimate due to sampling variability. As the number of replications increases, the estimate converges to the true value, usually at a speed proportional to $\sqrt{K}$, the square root of the number of replications. More replications lead to more precise estimates but take longer to estimate. In fast-moving markets, or with complex securities, speed may be more important than accuracy.

Figure 12–2 illustrates the convergence of the empirical distribution toward the true one. With 100 replications, the histogram representing the distribution of the ending price is quite irregular. The histogram becomes smoother with 1,000 replications, even more so with 10,000 replications, and should eventually converge to the continuous distribution in the right panel.

If the underlying process is normal, the empirical distribution must converge to a normal distribution. In this situation, Monte Carlo analysis should yield exactly the same result as the delta-normal method: The VAR estimated from the sample quantile must converge to the value of $\alpha\sigma$. Any deviation must be due to sampling variation.

FIGURE 12–2

Convergence to True Distribution

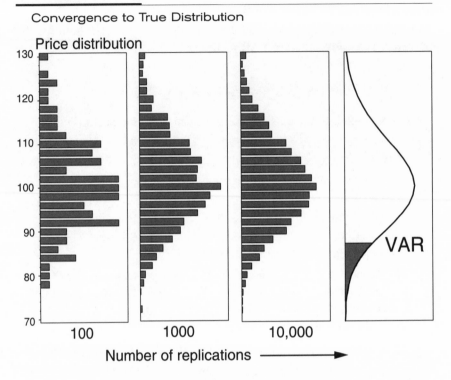

It is interesting to note that the Monte Carlo method was originally proposed in the context of option valuation.[4] Simulations are particularly useful to evaluate options that have no closed-form solution. Under the risk-neutral valuation method, Monte Carlo simulation consists of (1) simulating prices moving into the future using a drift equal to the risk-free rate, (2) evaluating the payoff of the derivative at expiration T, $F(S_T)$, and (3) discounting this payoff at the risk-free rate. The operation can be repeated as often as needed, and the current value of the derivative is obtained from averaging across all experiments:

$$f_t = E^*[e^{-r\tau}F(S_T)], \tag{12.4}$$

where the expectation indicates averaging and the asterisk is a reminder that the price paths are under risk neutrality; that is, changing both the ex-

---

4. See Boyle (1977).

pected return and the discount rate to the risk-free rate. In practice, with 10,000 replications, f_t is estimated as

$$f_t = (1/10,000)\sum_{k=1}^{10,000} e^{-r\tau} F_T^k.$$

This method is quite general and can be applied to options that have price-dependent paths (such as lookback options or average rate options) or strange payoffs at expiration (such as nonlinear functions of the ending price). Its main drawback is that it cannot price accurately options where the holder can exercise early. Also, the distribution of prices must be finely measured to price options with sharp discontinuities, such as binary options, which pay a fixed amount if the price ends above or below the strike price. With large "holes" in the price distributions, the payoffs on combinations of binary options could simply not appear in the final portfolio distribution. Thus, highly complex payoffs can be handled with increased precision.

Monte Carlo methods allow users to measure vega risk, or exposure to changes in volatility. All that is required is to repeat the simulation with the same sequence of ϵ values but with another value for σ. The change in the value of the asset due solely to the change in the volatility measures vega risk.

Simulations also handle well options that depend on more than one state variable. This is because the computation time increases linearly with N, while the time for other methods such as the binomial method or the finite difference method increases geometrically with N.

To summarize, computation of the VAR relies on the framework developed for the valuation of complex options, except that there is no discounting. Thus, the investment in intellectual and systems development for derivatives trading can be readily used for computing value at risk. No doubt this is why officials at the Fed have stated that derivatives "have had favorable spill-over effects on institutions' abilities to manage their total portfolios."

2 SIMULATIONS WITH MULTIPLE VARIABLES

In practice, portfolios contain more than one source of financial risk. Even simple securities such as corporate bonds depend on a combination of two or more financial variables. The simulation methodology can be easily extended to the more general multivariate case, which considers N sources of risk.

If the variables are uncorrelated, the randomization can be performed independently for each variable:

$$\Delta S_{j,t} = S_{j,t-1}\,(\mu_j \Delta t + \sigma_j \epsilon_{j,t}\sqrt{\Delta t}), \qquad\qquad (12.5)$$

where the ϵ values are independent across time period and series $j = 1,\ \ldots, N.$

But, generally, variables are correlated. To account for this correlation, we start with a set of independent variables η, which are then transformed into the ϵ. In a two-variable setting, we construct

$$\epsilon_1 = \eta_1$$
$$\epsilon_2 = \rho\eta_1 + (1 - \rho^2)^{1/2}\eta_2, \qquad\qquad (12.6)$$

where ρ is the correlation coefficient between the variables ϵ. First, we verify that the variance of ϵ_2 is unity

$$\text{Var}(\epsilon_2) = \rho^2\text{Var}(\eta_1) + [(1 - \rho^2)^{1/2}]^2\,\text{Var}(\eta_2) = \rho^2 + (1 - \rho^2) = 1.$$

Then we compute the covariance of the ϵ as

$$\text{Cov}(\epsilon_1, \epsilon_2) = \text{Cov}(\eta_1, \rho\eta_1 + (1 - \rho^2)^{1/2}\eta_2) = \rho\text{Cov}(\eta_1, \eta_1) = \rho.$$

This confirms that the values of ϵ have correlation of ρ. The question is, How was the transformation (12.6) chosen?

2.1 Cholesky Factorization

More generally, suppose that we have a vector of N values of ϵ, which we would like to display some correlation structure $V(\epsilon) = E(\epsilon\epsilon') = R$. As the matrix R is a symmetric real matrix, it can be decomposed into its *Cholesky* factors $R=TT'$, where T is a lower triangular matrix with zeros on the upper right corners.

Then start from an N vector η, which is composed of independent variables all with unit variances. In other words, $V(\eta) = I$ where I is the identity matrix with zeroes everywhere except on the diagonal. Next, construct the variable $\epsilon = T\eta$. Its covariance matrix is $V(\epsilon) = E(\epsilon\epsilon') = E(T\eta\eta'T') = TE(\eta\eta')T' = TIT' = TT' = R$. Thus, we confirmed that the values of ϵ have the desired correlations.

As an example, consider the two-variable case. The matrix can be decomposed into

$$\begin{bmatrix} 1 & \rho \\ \rho & 1 \end{bmatrix} = \begin{bmatrix} a_{11} & 0 \\ a_{12} & a_{22} \end{bmatrix} \begin{bmatrix} a_{11} & a_{12} \\ 0 & a_{22} \end{bmatrix} = \begin{bmatrix} a_{11}^2 & a_{11}a_{12} \\ a_{11}a_{12} & a_{12}^2 + a_{22}^2 \end{bmatrix}.$$

Because the Cholesky matrix is triangular, the factors can be found by successive substitution, by setting

$$a_{11}^2 = 1$$
$$a_{11}a_{12} = \rho$$
$$a_{12}^2 + a_{22}^2 = 1,$$

which yields

$$\begin{bmatrix} 1 & \rho \\ \rho & 1 \end{bmatrix} = \begin{bmatrix} 1 & 0 \\ \rho & (1-\rho^2)^{1/2} \end{bmatrix} \begin{bmatrix} 1 & \rho \\ 0 & (1-\rho^2)^{1/2} \end{bmatrix}.$$

And indeed, this is how (12.6) was obtained:

$$\begin{bmatrix} \epsilon_1 \\ \epsilon_2 \end{bmatrix} = \begin{bmatrix} 1 & 0 \\ \rho & (1-\rho^2)^{1/2} \end{bmatrix} \begin{bmatrix} \eta_1 \\ \eta_2 \end{bmatrix}.$$

This explains how a multivariate set of random variables can be created from simple building blocks consisting of iid variables. In addition to providing a method to generate correlated variables, this approach generates valuable insight into the random-number generation process.

2.2 Number of Independent Factors

For the decomposition to work, the matrix R must be positive definite. Otherwise, there is no way to transform N independent source of risks into N correlated variables of ϵ. For the matrix to be positive definite, the number of observations T must be at least as large as the number of factors N and the series cannot be linearly correlated, as discussed in Chapter 8.

When the matrix R is not positive definite, its *determinant* is 0. Intuitively speaking, the determinant d is a measure of the "volume" of a matrix. If d is 0, the dimension of the matrix is less than N. The determinant can be computed easily from the Cholesky decomposition into two matrices. Since the matrix T has zeros above its diagonal, its determinant reduces to the product of all diagonal coefficients, $d_T = \Pi_{i=1}^{N} a_{ii}$. The determinant of the covariance matrix R is then $d = d_T^2$.

In our two-factor example, the matrix is not positive definite if $\rho = 1$, which implies that the two factors are really the same. The Cholesky decomposition then yields $a_{11} = 1$, $a_{12} = 1$, and $a_{22} = 0$, and the determinant $d = (a_{11}a_{22})^2$ is 0. As a result, the second factor η_2 is never used, and ϵ_1 is always the same as ϵ_2. The second random variable is totally superfluous.

These conditions might seem academic but, unfortunately, soon become very real with simulations based on a large number of factors. As the size of the matrix increases, N can approach the number of time-series observations T and, with rounding errors, the matrix may turn out to be not positive definite. This is why the design of the experiment, including the number of variables to simulate, is critical. Oftentimes, a problem can be solved using a matrix of smaller dimensions, which also considerably speeds up the computation.

2.3 Computing VAR

To find the distribution of the portfolio value under a complex set of state variables, the simulation is first carried out as in the previous section.

For each experiment k, we calculate the value of all the assets $F_{i,T}^k$ in the portfolio. In general, the number of assets need not be the same as that of the random variables N. The portfolio value at the target horizon is then

$$P_T^k = \sum_{i=1}^{N} w_{i,t} F_{i,T}^k, \tag{12.7}$$

using current portfolio weights $w_{i,t}$.

Repeating the simulation for $K = 10,000$ times, for instance, we obtain the full distribution of the portfolio value on the target date P_T. The portfolio VAR can then be measured from the distribution of values at the target horizon.

Figure 12–3 displays the Monte Carlo distribution for a U.S. Government National Mortgage Association (GNMA) investment obtained by Bankers Trust's RAROC 2020 model. The market value of the investment

FIGURE 12–3

VAR for GNMA Investments

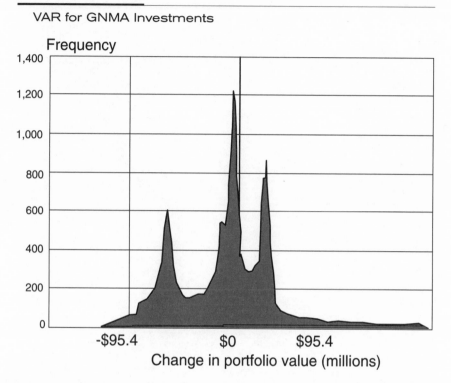

is $296 million. As these mortgages include complex option payoffs, they cannot be well approximated by a normal distribution. Indeed, the figure shows three modes, instead of one for a normal distribution. The estimated VAR over a year at the 99 percent level is $95.4 million.

CHAPTER 13

Credit Risk

Let them sing as long as they pay.

Jules Mazarin, chief minister to Louis XIV

Credit risk is becoming one of the key issues facing the derivatives industry in the 1990s. In the early 1980s, credit risk seemed to matter little as the market was enjoying rapid growth. Counterparties in the long-dated swap market, for example, were all initially top-rated credit risks, and defaults were few. As the market matured, greater volumes exposed participants to deteriorating credit risks. With tighter spreads, the emphasis turned to the precise measurement of credit risk. The issue is how to price and control potential losses from default.

Credit risk, one of the building blocks of the theory of particle finance, arises when counterparties are unwilling or unable to fulfill their contractual obligations. It encompasses both default risk and market risk. Default risk is the objective assessment of the likelihood that a counterparty will default; market risk measures the financial loss that will be experienced should the client default.

Credit risk in derivatives has two distinguishing characteristics. The first is the need to quantify exposure, or market risk. In traditional banking, the credit exposure is easily determined; for a bond or loan contract, it is measured as the outstanding principal plus any accrued interest. With derivatives, the exposure depends on whether the contract has positive or negative market value and on future changes in contract values. The second characteristic is the potential for diversification across counterparties and portfolios of instruments. As exposures tend to offset each other, the risk of the portfolio will be considerably less than the sum of each credit exposure. Institutions that can accurately quantify the credit risk of their portfolio will be able to price their products better, thereby gaining an advantage over the competition.

The theory of credit risk is relatively less developed than VAR-based models of market risk. Credit risk is also under intense research effort in both industry and academia. As a result, we should expect this area to evolve rapidly.

Section 1 provides a general overview of the nature of credit risk; credit risk is compared to VAR-based market risk measures. The market has developed a number of methods to mitigate credit risk, which are described in Section 2. These methods, as well as possible legal uncertainties about enforceability, must be taken into account when evaluating credit risk. Finally, Section 3 shows how to modify Monte Carlo methods to account for credit risk.

1 THE NATURE OF CREDIT RISK

The credit risk management function focuses on a set of issues that are quite different from those facing market risk managers. The two approaches are compared in Table 13–1. First, VAR focuses on market risk only, while credit risk deals with the combined effect of market risk and default risk. Second, risk limits apply to different units. For VAR, limits apply to levels of the trading organization (such as business units, trading desks, or portfolios); for credit risk, limits apply to the total exposure, gross or net, to each counterparty, a legally defined entity. Third, the time horizon is generally quite different, usually very short (days) in the case of VAR measures, but much longer (years) to account for potential default. Fourth, legal issues are very important for evaluating credit risk, while they are not applicable for market risk.

As a result of these additional factors, credit risk is much less amenable to precise measurement than market risk. Default probabilities and recovery rates are much more difficult to measure than dispersion in market movements. Because credit exposure covers long horizons, current positions may not adequately represent future risks if new transactions take place with the same counterparty. As there have been few defaults involving long-term swaps, the effects of bankruptcy rules and the enforceability of credit enhancement arrangements are still unclear; unfortunately, differences in legal interpretation can lead to dramatic changes in potential losses from default.

TABLE 13–1

Comparison of Value at Risk to Credit Risk

Item	Value at Risk	Credit Risk
Source of risk	Market risk	Market risk and default
Unit to which risk limits apply	Some level of trading organization	Legal entity of counterparty
Time horizon	Short (days)	Potentially long (years)
Legal issues	Not applicable	Very important

For default risk to create losses, two conditions must be satisfied. First, there must be a net claim against the counterparty and, second, that counterparty must default. The first condition is relevant when a party defaults on a derivatives contract, which can have either positive value (a net asset to the solvent party) or negative value (a liability of the solvent party).

In effect, the loss due to default is much like that of an option. Define V_t as the current, or replacement, value of the asset to the solvent party. Assuming no recovery in case of default, the loss is V_t, if positive,

$$\text{Loss}_t = \text{Max}(V_t, 0). \qquad (13.1)$$

If V_t represents the value of risky debt such as a corporate bond, then it must be positive. However, if V_t represents a derivative contract, it can be either positive or negative; positive-value contracts are usually called *in the money*.

This asymmetric treatment stems from the fact that if the counterparty defaults while the contract has negative value, the solvent party is typically not free to "walk away" from the contract, as shown in Box 13–1. In contrast, a loss may occur if the defaulting party goes bankrupt, in which case it may be "stayed" from making payments. Even if payment is effected, it is likely to be at less than the full current value of the contract as derivatives counterparties are likely to be ranked equally with unsecured senior creditors. Therefore, the *current* exposure from default has an asymmetric pattern, like an option.

Credit risk, however, should include not only the current replacement value but also the *potential* loss from default. Indeed, the G-30 report recommends that users "measure credit exposure in two ways: (1) current

BOX 13-1

WALK-AWAY FEATURES IN DREXEL'S COLLAPSE

The collapse of the Drexel Burnham Lambert Group (DBL Group) in 1990 provides an illustration of the asymmetry in payoffs when default occurs.[*]

DBL Group's bankruptcy placed its swap subsidiary, DBL Products in default. Most of DBL's swap agreements contained a walk-away clause that permitted the solvent party to cease payment even if it owed money to the defaulting party (the standard documentation for swaps has been changed since).

Even so, nearly all counterparties paid DBL Products the money they owed, for a number of reasons. DBL Products threatened to challenge the right to walk away through litigation. Counterparties settled to avoid expensive litigation, as there were unresolved legal issues as to the enforceability of these contracts. A number of counterparties also feared that other institutions would be less likely to do business with them if they took advantage of the walk-away clause with Drexel. As a result, DBL was paid 100 percent of what it was owed but negotiated to pay only about 70 percent of the value of the contracts that were in the money for the solvent parties.

---

[*]For more details, see the U.S. Congress (1993) hearings on derivatives.

---

exposure . . . and (2) potential exposure, which is an estimate of the future replacement cost of derivative transactions."

The *credit exposure* is often measured as

$$\text{Credit Exposure}_t = \text{Max } (V_t + \Delta V_\tau, 0), \tag{13.2}$$

where ΔV_τ represents the maximum increase in value over the life of the contract τ at a specified confidence level c. Credit risk is then measured as the credit exposure times the probability of default.

This approach has the merit of simplicity. Unfortunately, it is poorly adapted to portfolios of instruments, as the worst exposures can occur at different dates. Also, averaging over widely different contract durations makes little sense. More sophisticated approaches rely on the *potential exposure profile*, which describes the worst potential loss, measured at some confidence level, at a set of future dates (e.g., monthly intervals). The pattern of dynamic credit exposure can be combined with future default probabilities to create a credit risk profile.

This framework demonstrates that credit risk is related to market risk. But the relationship is even more complex for large portfolios. Sometimes credit risk is evaluated on a *transaction-by-transaction* basis, which essentially ignores portfolio effects. Portfolio diversification can occur across two dimensions: across transactions (market risk) and across counterparties.

Consider for instance a portfolio consisting of a long DM forward position and a short DM forward with two different counterparties. The portfolio is hedged as to market risk. The transaction-by-transaction approach would consider the effect of default on each position separately. A loss on the long position occurs if the DM appreciates and the first counterparty defaults; a loss on the short position occurs if the DM depreciates and the second counterparty defaults. In this approach, the potential losses from the two positions are added up.

As appreciation and depreciation of the DM are two mutually exclusive events, however, this method overstates the true potential loss from credit risk. Instead, a *portfolio approach* would take into account interactions between market movements and then determine the potential loss. In this case, assuming equal probability of appreciation/depreciation and of default by the two counterparties, the potential loss is only half of the previous measure. More generally, credit risk must account for portfolio diversification effects as well as the net benefit of credit enhancement arrangements, which are described next.

2 MITIGATING CREDIT RISK

Derivative contracts can be traded either on *organized exchanges* or over a decentralized network of financial institutions, typically called *over-the-counter* (OTC) *markets*. Each market has developed its own techniques to deal with credit risk. These methods must be formally modeled when assessing possible losses from default.

2.1 Organized Exchanges

Exchanges have implemented institutional arrangements that reduce counterparty risk, including margin requirements, daily marking to market, and an organized clearinghouse. Customers who wish to establish positions on U.S. exchanges must first open an account with a futures commission merchant (FCM). This firm performs a function similar to a brokerage house and is authorized to accept money to secure trades on organized exchanges. The FCM may or may not be a member of the *clearinghouse*. If not, all trades must be routed to a clearing FCM.

Margin Requirements

When a futures contract is initiated, it has no value. To guard against the possibility of customer defaults, initial margin must be posted as soon as the position is open. This margin serves as a performance bond, or collateral, to offset possible future losses should the customer default.

Margins are set at two levels. The clearinghouse sets margins that clearing members must maintain for all open positions, for both customer accounts and proprietary positions. Customer margins can be computed on the basis of either *net* or *gross* positions. A gross margin system requires the clearing member to post margins for each long and short position. With a net system, clearing members combine all customer contracts into a net position. In turn, each clearing member must require margins from customers that are at least as high as those required by the clearinghouse.

These margins are typically set in relation to price volatility and to the type of position, speculative or hedging. Some exchanges, for example, set margins at a level that covers the 95th percentile of absolute daily price changes, which is, in essence, a daily VAR system for credit risk.

Daily Marking to Market

Marking to market entails the daily settlement of gains and losses. When daily price movements create a loss, the customer is required to post additional margin. Should the customer default on the margin call, the FCM has the authority to liquidate the contract. This system maintains a dynamic cushion to cover losses from defaults.

Position Limits

Position limits can be applied to both traders and to clearing members. These serve to diversify further default risks.

Organized Clearinghouse

An important advantage of organized exchanges relative to OTC markets is the standardization of counterparty risk. After a trade on an exchange is confirmed, the *clearing corporation* interposes itself between all clearing members. This essentially eliminates the credit risk of the counterparty, which leads to more efficient transactions. As one observer put it, "Futures markets are designed to permit trading among strangers, as against other markets which permit only trading among friends."

Various levels of protection assure reliable operation of the exchange. The first level of guarantee is the customer's margin. The second is a guarantee given by brokerage houses; they answer for all their customers before a clearing member, who provides a third level of guarantee. Finally, if the clearing member defaults, the guarantee of last resort is the clearing fund, which is created by resources deposited by all members or backed by bank guarantees or both.

Margins, marking to market, and self-insurance arrangements ensure a superior credit rating for clearing corporations. As a result, there is very little credit risk on exchange-traded instruments. In over 120 years of futures trading in the United States, there has never been a clearinghouse default.

It should be noted, however, that the clearinghouse stands between clearing members only. This could not prevent customer margins to be used to cover the default of another customer at the same FCM. To illustrate, consider the case of Volume Investors, a FCM and clearing member of COMEX. In 1985, Volume defaulted because a large customer could not meet margin calls. As the clearinghouse margin call exceeded all of Volume's capital, the clearinghouse seized all of Volume's posted margin. This included the margins of nondefaulting customers, who effectively had substantial credit risk through their broker.[1] Thus the statement that the "clearinghouse becomes the legal counterparty to all trades," which is found in nearly all finance textbooks, is not strictly true.

Clearinghouses guarantee the net position only to clearing members, not all futures contracts. Therefore, customers still have to evaluate the financial integrity of their FCM.[2] Without this market incentive, we would fall back into the trap of the moral hazard, as with bank deposit insurance

---

1. For further details on this case and on the customer–broker relationship, see Jordan and Morgan (1990).
2. In the case of Volume's customers, the comment has been made that they were not innocent victims as they had chosen a low-commission broker in preference to more expensive but better capitalized brokers.

schemes. The moral of this story is that detailed knowledge of legal and institutional arrangements is essential to evaluating credit risk (as demonstrated in Box 13–2).

B O X   13–2

BARINGS'S COLLAPSE ON SIMEX

The Barings collapse focused the attention of traders on the creditworthiness of futures and options exchanges, supposedly among the safest places to trade.

Leeson had accumulated a position of 43,000 long Nikkei futures on the Singapore Monetary Exchange (SIMEX), which amounted to an astonishing 30 percent of all open interest in this contract. This was in excess of the theoretical limit of 1,000 contracts, but Barings had received an exemption as a clearing member.

Officials at U.S. futures exchanges have stated that such positions would have attracted their attention much sooner. In addition, on U.S. exchanges, customer funds deposited at the clearinghouse must be segregated from the broker's proprietary funds. In the event of default by the broker, customer funds cannot be used to pay for losses incurred by the broker (although the Volume Investors example has shown that commingled customer funds can be used to pay for other customer losses).

On SIMEX, in contrast, Barings had not maintained such segregation. On February 27, 1995, as Barings went into administration, SIMEX took over the futures positions and all customer accounts were frozen, including $350 million of U.S. customer funds. One customer who was locked into a large position as the market was falling had to establish an offsetting position with another broker as a hedge. For a while, it was not clear whether the clearinghouse would default. At that time, SIMEX's exchange reserve fund was only $5.5 million.

In the end, the situation was largely resolved when Internationale Nederlanden Group, a Dutch bank, assumed Barings's liabilities. Barings's funds were also sufficient to cover all the positions at SIMEX and the clearinghouse weathered the storm. As this crisis made clear, standards of creditworthiness do vary among clearinghouses. Assessing credit risk involves taking a hard look at safeguards against defaults.

2.2 OTC Markets

Over-the-counter participants mitigate credit risk by a variety of credit enhancement features, which can also be factored into simulations.

Netting Arrangements

Swap participants can reduce the potential impact of default by bilateral
closeout *netting agreements*. It is common nowadays for dealers that frequently engage in swaps with the same counterparties to use *master swap
agreements*. These agreements provide for the netting of payments
across a set of contracts. In case of default, a counterparty cannot stop
payments on contracts that have negative value while demanding payment on positively value contracts. Essentially, this system reduces the
exposure to the net payment for all the contracts covered by the netting
agreement.

Position Limits

OTC participants typically establish limits on the amount of exposure they
are willing to take with each counterparty. Information on transactions is
centralized in back-office systems that generate an "exposure profile" for
each counterparty. The exposure profile is then used to manage credit line
usage for several arbitrarily defined maturity buckets. Each proposed additional trade with the same counterparty is then examined for incremental effect on total exposure.

Here again, portfolio considerations are important. While counterparty limits may seem reasonable on an individual basis, they may amount
to excessive exposure to some sectors that are vulnerable to specific
shocks. Concentration of exposure to Japanese banks or the oil industry,
for instance, may not be advisable.

Margins and Collateral

Increasingly, participants in the swap markets now require margins to be
posted by their counterparties. These margins may be changed as the value
of the contract evolves over time or in relation to changes in the credit
rating of a counterpart. Determining the appropriate level of collateral is
critical—too little does not offer adequate protection, too high increases
the cost of using derivatives.

Recouponing

Recouponing consists of periodically changing the coupon to bring the transaction back to a zero mark-to-market value. This is achieved by making additional payments to the counterparty that is in the money.

Credit Triggers

Most long-term swaps contain credit triggers. These specify, for instance, that, if either counterparty falls below investment grade, the other party has the right to have the swap cash settled. These triggers offer protection in situations where the credit rating of a firm deteriorates slowly, as few firms go directly from investment-grade into bankruptcy. This protection, however, is a double-edged sword, as it could place substantial liquidity pressure on a counterparty precisely when its creditworthiness is weakening and its access to liquidity curtailed. In other words, these credit triggers can precipitate a crisis if used unwisely.

Derivative Product Companies (DPCs)

Credit rating is becoming a paramount concern for some corporations, which for regulatory or reputational reasons prefer to deal with top-rated counterparties only. To fulfill this need, a number of brokerage firms have established derivative product companies as separately capitalized subsidiaries. Typically, the creators of DPCs are OTC participants that have seen their market share decline as they have been unable to maintain top ratings. These firms are consolidating their presence in this credit-sensitive market by establishing AAA/Aaa-rated DPCs.[3] High credit-ratings are achieved providing a level of capital that is more than sufficient to guard against credit and market risks. Also, the parent guarantees the subsidiary, but full separation implies that the subsidiary does not guarantee the parent company.

It is important to note, however, that the protection offered by some of these arrangements may not be totally effective. There are still many unresolved issues as to how bankruptcy courts would treat margins and netting agreements.

As a result, two scenarios can be played out in simulations. In the first, the default value of all the contracts is determined and settled simul-

---

3. These DPCs can be defined with a termination structure, where all contracts are terminated in case of default by the DPC or its parent, or with a continuation structure, where a new manager takes over the portfolio and all contracts can continue to maturity.

taneously (the "freezing" scenario); all closeout netting agreements are enforced by the court at the time of freezing. In the second scenario, the bankruptcy court allows all contracts to run until maturity; settlement can then proceed sequentially, cherry-picking contracts that have positive value (the "cherry picking at settlement" scenario). The second scenario is much worse for the nondefaulting party since contracts that have negative value at time of default can be picked later as they turn in the money. To date sequential cherry picking has not been ordered by any bankruptcy court but it remains a possibility feared by many lawyers.

3 MODELING CREDIT RISK

Credit risk depends on a number of factors: the current fair value of the contracts, the potential future credit exposure, the extent to which netting arrangements and collateral can effectively reduce exposure, and the likelihood of default by the customer. The issue is how to model all of these factors into a quantitative measure of credit risk.

Structured Monte Carlo (SMC) methods presented in the previous chapter can be modified to account for credit risk. The procedure is the same as before, but now includes a probability of default at each step. We first illustrate credit risk when the asset must have positive value, such as a bond, and then continue to the case of derivatives, where contracts can have both positive and negative values.

3.1 Default on Bonds

The simplest example of a security with credit risk is that of a corporate bond. Default occurs when the company fails to make either a coupon payment or to repay the principal. In this case, the *credit exposure*, which is the replacement cost if the other party defaults, is simply the face value of the bond.

SMC can accommodate defaults as follows. The goal is to measure the value of the risky bond between the current time t and maturity T. As we have done before, we chop up the horizon $\tau = T - t$ into n increments $\Delta t = \tau/n$. First, we model the price of a risk-free asset P_t that is identical to the risky bond except for the possibility of default. In practice, this will be a government bond with the same maturity, whose price can be obtained using standard simulation models.

At each point in time, a default loss model creates random counterparty defaults. Define λ as the instantaneous rate of default; over a time interval Δt, default occurs with a probability of $\lambda \Delta t$. We also have to make an assumption about the value of the residual payment to investors (after legal expenses) if default occurs. Define f as a fraction representing the *recovery rate*, which can be modeled from historical experience.[4] The price of the risky bond, P_t^*, is derived from the probability of no default $(1 - \lambda \Delta t)$ and the probability of default $\lambda \Delta t$, is

$$P_t^* = (1 - \lambda \Delta t) \times P_t + \lambda \Delta t \times f P_t. \tag{13.3}$$

In general, the rate of default λ can vary over time. Default experience is typically correlated with the economic cycle. Default rates can also depend on the age of the bond, on corporate profitability indicators, on geographical and industry considerations, or on the state of the economy. The rate of default can be modeled as

$$d\lambda_t = \mu_t dt + \sigma_t dz, \tag{13.4}$$

where interactions with interest rate innovations can be introduced through correlation in the random terms.

Consider, for instance, a zero-coupon bond. If λ is constant, the cumulative probability of no default is given by $(1 - \lambda \Delta t)^n$, which tends to $e^{-\lambda \tau}$ as n increases. The expected price at expiration is

$$P_T^* = e^{-\lambda \tau} P_T + (1 - e^{-\lambda \tau}) f P_T = f P_T + (1 - f) e^{-\lambda \tau} P_T. \tag{13.5}$$

The price of the risky bond is given by two terms, the first involving a fractional default-free bond and the second the no-default probability times the loss.

Assuming no recovery, we can deduce the probability of default from the yield on the risky bond. If y is the default-free yield, the current price of the risky bond P_t^* is

$$P_t^* = e^{-\lambda \tau} P_t = e^{-\lambda \tau} e^{-y\tau} = e^{-(\lambda + y)\tau}. \tag{13.6}$$

As $P_t^* = e^{-y^* \tau}$, the yield on the risky bond y^* is equal to the risk-free rate plus the annual default rate $y^* = y + \lambda$. Here, the *credit spread*, $y^* - y$, represents an annualized default rate; more generally, it also accounts for partial recovery.

---

4. Moody's, the ratings agency, estimates that historical default rates for U.S. corporate bonds have typically been around 45 percent of principal, and recovery may take years. There is insufficient evidence on recovery rates for derivatives contracts, although their holders would probably be also treated as senior unsecured creditors.

Finally, the expected credit loss is measured by the drop in the value of the bond due to the possibility of default:

$$\text{Expected credit loss} = P_t(\text{risk-free}) - P_t^*(\text{risky}). \qquad (13.7)$$

Default probabilities can be estimated from close inspection of the counterparty; this includes financial statements, financial history, and historical default rates from similar credit risks.[5] Alternatively, the market's expectation of default can be directly recovered from credit spreads, which may depend on maturity. Sarig and Warga (1989) use zero-coupon corporate and Treasury bonds to recover the term structure of credit spreads. Figure 13–1 shows that the credit spread depends on the *quality* of the counterparty and the *tenor* of the loan.

This pattern of credit spreads provides support for Merton's (1974) view of risky debt. He models debt as the value of the firm minus the value of a call on the firm's assets issued to shareholders by debtholders. The value of risky debt is then affected by the same factors that determine the value of this option. For highly rated bonds (AAA), the term structure slopes upward, reflecting the fact that these companies have a low probability of defaulting in the near future, but that their fortune can deteriorate later. This behavior is opposite for low-rated bonds (B/C), for which default is more likely if debt must be repaid shortly, but less so for later payments. In between, BB-rated bonds display a humped shape, reflecting an increased possibility of defaulting in the medium term. Market prices therefore provide a rich source of information about the effects of default, which vary across credit ratings and maturities.

3.2 Default on Derivatives

Perhaps the most important reason for the growth of the swap market is the reduced exposure of swaps to defaults. The origins of swaps can be traced to parallel loans, which involve an exchange of payments in two currencies. The problem with parallel loans was that default by one party did not allow the other party to stop payment as well. In contrast, swaps provide a legal structure where the right of offset is firmly established.

In a fixed-to-floating interest rate swap, for instance, only the *net* interest payments are exchanged every period. Thus, exposure will be much less than the notional principal. Assuming a $100 million swap, a fixed

---

5. There is a considerable literature on the history of default on corporate bonds. See, for instance, Blume and Keim (1991). Gluck (1996) also reviews methods to assess default probabilities.

FIGURE 13–1

Term Structure of Credit Spreads

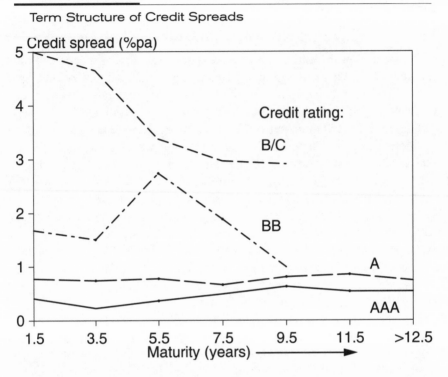

rate of 6 percent, and a current floating rate of 5 percent, the initial pay-ment involves only 1 percent annually, or $1 million.

The current exposure is limited to the *replacement value* of the swap. At initiation, the swap typically will be priced in such a way that the pre-sent value of the payments is 0. As time goes by, the value of the swap will wander away from 0. Thus we need to account for the potential exposure of the swap.

Figure 13–2 presents the average replacement value for a five-year interest rate swap with semiannual payments. Initially, the exposure is 0. After two years, it rises to about 1 percent of the notional. The exposure falls each time a payment is made. Eventually, the value of the swap con-verges to 0 at maturity. In contrast, the exposure on a long-term currency swap increases steadily with the passage of time, reaching 10–20 percent before maturity. This is because substantial exchange rate risk remains be-fore the exchange of principal in two currencies. This risk is nil for inter-est rate swaps.

FIGURE 13–2

Average Replacement Cost for 5-Year Interest Rate Swap

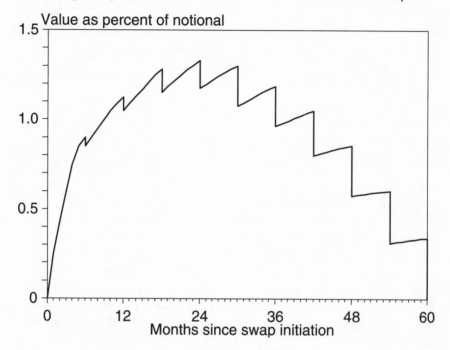

While the average exposure is only about 1 percent of notional for interest rate swaps, the maximum exposure can be much greater, at 10–15 percent of notional. The exposure also depends on the shape of the term structure. If the yield curve slopes upward, the "pay fixed" side will initially make greater payments to the counterparty and thus is more exposed to credit risk.

The 1988 Basle accord attempts to measure the dynamic credit exposure of derivatives by specifying an "add-on" to cover potential credit exposure. The total capital requirement is the sum of the current replacement value plus this add-on factor, shown in Table 13–2. The add-on increases with the maturity of the contract and with the volatility of the underlying instrument, like options. This explains why the add-on is greater for currency swaps than for interest rate instruments.

For instance, take the case of a $100 million interest rate swap with a domestic corporation. With a residual maturity of four years, the typical current market value of the swap is $1 million. Using the 0.5 percent

TABLE 13–2

Capital Ratios for Potential Credit Exposure (percent of notional)

Residual Maturity (tenor)	Contract			
	Interest Rate	Exchange Rate, Gold	Equity	Other Commodities
<1 year	0.0	1.0	6.0	10.0
1–5 years	0.5	5.0	8.0	12.0
>5 years	1.5	7.5	10.0	15.0

capital ratio, the total Basle credit exposure is $1m + $100m \times 0.5\% =$ $1.5m. This number must be multiplied by the risk weight and 8 percent to derive the minimum level of capital needed to support the swap.

In the Basle framework, credit risk is evaluated on a *transaction-by-transaction* basis. Default risk is indirectly taken into account through the risk weights, which are used to compute the minimum capital charge and vary across types of counterparties. The drawback of this approach is that it completely ignores the potential for diversification to reduce risk.

Although the Basle approach has the advantage of simplicity, the Monte Carlo approach provides a dynamic estimate of credit risk that is more accurate than these static add-ons. Simulations can account for diversification, varying levels of volatility, remaining maturities, expected default rates, and other features. Netting can be explicitly modeled. So can option components, which mitigate credit risk. If the swap contains an American option, the holder of an in-the-money swap may want to exercise early if the credit rating of its counterparty starts to deteriorate.

Credit loss is a function of credit exposure and default parameters. In the case of risky debt, credit exposure is the principal. With derivatives, credit exposure is much more complex, as it represents the positive value of a contract. To simplify, suppose that the payoff is normally distributed. The average credit exposure at any future date is then

$$\text{Average credit exposure} = \int_{-\infty}^{+\infty} \text{Max}(x, 0)f(x)dx, \qquad (13.8)$$

where $f(x)$ is the normal distribution function. After integration, the expected credit exposure is $\sigma/\sqrt{2\pi}$. But the distribution of credit exposure is also important. The worst credit exposure at the 95 percent level, for instance, is given by 1.65σ. These numbers can be combined with default and recovery rates to yield the expected and unexpected credit loss for each derivatives transaction. *Expected credit loss* can be used to compute a minimum bid-ask spread and a credit provision. *Unexpected credit loss* is used to establish the required capital needed to support the transaction.

To illustrate, consider a $100 million five-year interest rate swap. Our horizon is one year, over which the volatility of the market value of the swap is $4.5 million. The swap counterparty is rated Ba, for which Moody's estimated default rate is 1.7 percent over a year. The typical recovery rate is 45 percent. The average exposure is then $\sigma/\sqrt{2\pi} = \$1.8m$; at the 95 percent level, the worst exposure is $1.65\sigma = \$7.4m$. We can compute the expected default loss as $1.8 million times 0.017 (the probability of default) times 0.5 (the probability the swap will be in the money) times 0.55 (one minus the recovery rate), or $8,400. Similarly, at the 95 percent level, the worst-case default loss is $34,750. This number can be used to establish a provision against the credit risk of this swap.

Compared to corporate bonds, the potential loss is much less than the notional amount. Duffie and Huang (1995), for instance, develop a model where the probability of default is summarized by the credit spread. Their base case is a counterparty with a credit spread of 100 basis points for a five-year corporate bond. For a typical interest rate swap with the same counterparty, the credit spread is much lower, only 1 basis point. The spread on a currency swap of like maturity is slightly higher, about 9 basis points, reflecting the risk in exchange of principal.

3.3 Netting Arrangements

Swap participants can further reduce risks by netting agreements. Close-out netting is by now a standard provision in the legal documentation of OTC derivative contracts, including the widely used 1992 International Swap and Derivatives Association (ISDA) master agreement.

Bilateral closeout netting agreements cover a set of N derivatives contracts between two parties. In case of default, a counterparty cannot stop payments on contracts that have negative value while demanding payment on positively valued contracts. Essentially, these agreements stipulate that the net loss in case of default is the positive sum of the market value of all contracts in the agreement:

$$\text{Net loss} = \text{Max}(V, 0) = \text{Max}(\sum_{i=1}^{N} V_i, 0). \tag{13.9}$$

This applies to long and short positions in swaps and forward and futures contracts, as well as to long positions in options. No credit exposure is associated with written positions, as these represent obligations rather than assets when the option premium is paid up front.

In contrast, without a netting agreement, the potential loss is the sum of all positive value contracts

$$\text{Loss} = \sum_{i=1}^{N} \text{Max}(V_i, 0). \tag{13.10}$$

This is always greater than the loss under a netting agreement. At worst, the two calculations will be the same if all payoffs are perfectly correlated. For a given total notional, the benefit from the netting agreement depends on the number of contracts N, and the extent to which contract values covary with each other. The larger the N and the lower the correlation, the greater is the benefit from netting.

Without netting agreements or collateral, the derivatives-related *gross replacement value* (GRV) is the sum of the worst-case loss over all counterparties:

$$\text{GRV} = \sum_{k=1}^{K} \text{Loss}_k = \sum_{k=1}^{K} [\sum_{i=1}^{N_k} \text{Max}(V_i, 0)]. \tag{13.11}$$

With netting agreements, the potential exposure is defined as the *net replacement value* (NRV):

$$\text{NRV} = \sum_{k=1}^{K} \text{Net loss}_k = \sum_{k=1}^{K} \text{Max}(\sum_{i=1}^{N_k} V_i, 0). \tag{13.12}$$

Finally, default risk can be reduced even further by the collateral held and applied to positions that are in the money. This defines the total *credit at risk* (CAR):

$$\text{CAR} = \sum_{k=1}^{K} \text{Net loss}_k = \sum_{k=1}^{K} [\text{Max}(\sum_{i=1}^{N_k} V_i, 0) - \text{Collateral}_k]. \tag{13.13}$$

In July 1994, the Basle Committee explicitly recognized netting in the calculation of capital requirements for credit risks.[6] The credit exposure is the sum of the current exposure plus the potential exposure:

$$\text{Credit exposure} = \text{NRV} \tag{13.14}$$
$$+ \ [\text{Notional} \times \text{Capital ratio} \times (0.5 + 0.5 \times \text{NGR})],$$

where the capital ratio remains the same as in Table 13–2, and NGR is the *net-to-gross ratio* (NGR), or ratio of current net market value to gross market value, which is always between 0 and 1. Risk-weighted amounts are then obtained by applying counterparty risk weights to the credit exposure.

To illustrate the importance of netting, Table 13–3 compares derivatives information provided in annual reports for a group of major U.S. commercial banks. In line with the size of the derivatives market, the notional amounts in the first column are quite large, all in excess of a trillion dollars. A more appropriate measure of risk is the credit at risk, in the last column. This summarizes the potential loss if all counterparties defaulted at the same time, and it is computed in two steps.

First, the bank computes the gross replacement value of its derivatives position, which is the sum of the positive replacement costs of all items in the portfolio. This represents a worst-case scenario where every single counterparty against which derivatives are in the money would default. Positions where the bank has a negative position, or owes money to the other party, are not considered.

In the second step, the bank makes an allowance for master netting agreements and collateral. These netting agreements reduce the exposure to one party by collapsing a set of contracts with the same party into one agreement. Default then involves losing only the net replacement value minus any collateral held and applied, if positive. Typically, banks also break down information about the credit quality of counterparties and the maturity profile of the derivatives portfolio.

Whereas the CAR number measures the current credit risk of a bank's portfolio, some observers argue that the GRV is more useful to compare different banks, since it gives a better indication of the overall level of derivatives activity. As some institutions have more netting agreements in place than others, the CAR measure is not directly comparable across banks.

---

6. Only for contracts with no "walkaway" features, as discussed before.

TABLE 13-3

Derivatives Disclosure: 1994 ($ billions)

Bank	Notional	Gross Replacement Value	Credit at Risk
Chemical	3,182	18.0	17.9
Citibank	2,665	27.5	20.5
J. P. Morgan	2,472	31.1	19.5
Bankers Trust	1,982	26.7	10.9
Bank America	1,401	14.4	6.3
Chase	1,293	14.5	8.3

For Bankers, for instance, the notional portfolio is $1,982 billion, with a much smaller GRV of $26.7 billion. Typically, the ratio of the GRV to notional is only around 1–3 percent. The GRV is further reduced to a CAR of $10.9 billion. This worst-case measure still fails to capture credit risk properly as it ignores the probability of default, potential future exposure, and diversification effects.

The Basle risk-weighted amount for derivatives aggregated to $8.1 billion, for a total of $48.3 billion in risk-weighted assets for Bankers. With a total of $7.1 billion in capital, the corporation was enjoying a comfortable capital ratio of 14.77 percent, well above the regulatory guideline of 8 percent.

3.4 Portfolio Credit Risk

Once all component assets are modeled, portfolio risk can be measured by running a large-scale simulation, which can potentially account for all interactions between defaults and market risks. As in the case of VAR, the simulation creates a frequency distribution of potential losses at various future dates that can be used to assess the capital required to support credit and market risks.

The method is also uniquely flexible and can be tailored to the specifications of end users. The legal structure of transactions, for instance, can be modeled by assigning individual transactions to master netting agreements, master netting agreements to counterparties, and even counterparties to countries. Credit risk can then be assessed by modeling various default events using this structure.

This approach is superior to the simple Basle add-ons because it can fully account for portfolio diversification across transactions and counterparties. In particular, counterparty diversification benefits are driven by default correlations. As seen in Chapter 8, zero correlations quickly reduce portfolio risk as the number of counterparties increases. If correlations are greater, perhaps reflecting systemic risks, counterparty diversification will be less effective. Still, simulation methods appear to offer the most comprehensive and flexible approach to credit risks.

Unfortunately, these methods are expensive to implement in-house, which is why they are now used primarily by sophisticated users with large portfolios. With the growth of third-party developers, we should expect greater emphasis on Monte Carlo simulations to measure credit risks.

PART FOUR

Risk Management Systems

CHAPTER 14

Implementing Risk Management Systems

At the close of each business day, tell me what the market risks are across all businesses and locations.

Dennis Weatherstone, J. P. Morgan

In today's rapidly evolving financial markets, risk management systems offer essential protection against market risk. Value at risk is an important component of such systems, as it allows firms to measure and control their financial risks. VAR systems can even provide a competitive advantage, as firms can alter strategies to develop sectors where they add risk-adjusted value.

This chapter illustrates applications of VAR methods to financial risk management. For institutions that require centralized risk management, VAR is a must. Section 1 lists factors that create a need for global risk systems. VAR may prove particularly useful to institutions that engage in proprietary trading, but also for asset managers and nonfinancial corporations such as multinationals.

Institutions on the cutting edge of risk management have established global risk-management committees that report directly to senior management. These teams aggregate companywide risks into a single VAR measure that is easy to communicate to top management and shareholders. Because they operate independently of corporate business functions, risk managers can set and enforce position limits for traders and business units, which can now be evaluated in terms of their risk-adjusted performance. Thus, VAR can be used as an information reporting tool, as a resource allocation tool, and as a performance evaluation tool. These three functions are analyzed in Sections 2, 3, and 4, respectively.

Next, Section 5 discusses the information technology challenge created by the need for comprehensive risk-management systems. Measuring an institution's VAR requires integrating the front and back offices with a newly created "middle" office. In addition to risk measurement, this integration offers many side benefits. A central repository for trades, positions, and valuation models offers some protection against operational risks and rogue traders. Decent risk-management systems might have avoided many of the financial debacles of recent years. And in the end, centralized risk management need not be difficult to implement, as an army of software developers offers ready-made solutions to the measurement of value at risk. Section 6 provides such an example.

1 WHY GLOBAL RISK MANAGEMENT?

A recent trend is the race toward *centralized* risk management. For a number of years, financial institutions have maintained local risk-management units, especially around derivatives that need to be carefully controlled because of their leverage. But only recently have institutions started to measure risk on a global basis.

This trend to global risk management is motivated by two driving factors, exposure to new sources of risk and the greater volatility of new products. While 20 years ago, most securities traded by banks consisted of plain-vanilla bonds, nowadays products such as derivatives on 30-year municipal indices or exotic options are common. With the globalization of financial markets, investors are now exposed to new sources of risk such as foreign currency risk. Greater volatility is induced by greater risk in some underlying variables, such as exchange rates, or by the design of products that are more sensitive to financial variables.

For credit risk management, centralization has also become essential. The continued expansion of derivatives markets has created new entrants with lower credit ratings and greater exposure to counterparties. A financial institution may have a myriad of transactions with the same counterparty, in currencies, fixed-income, commodities, and so on. Even though all of the business units may have a reasonable exposure when considered on an individual basis, these exposures may add up to an unacceptable risk. Moreover, with netting agreements, the total exposure depends on the net current value of contracts covered by the agreements. All of which becomes intractable unless a global measurement system for credit risk is in place.

Financial institutions were the first to monitor on a centralized basis counterparty exposure, country and market risks across all products and geographical locations. But, as this section shows, asset managers and nonfinancial corporations would also benefit from global risk-management systems.

1.1 Proprietary Trading

The trend toward global risk management is explained by a number of factors. First, as financial institutions have become more global, their exposure to risk has widened from domestic interest-rate risk to a multitude of global business risks. This has made risk much more difficult to measure. Consider, for instance, a bank where traders are awaiting U.S. unemployment numbers. Currency traders might short the dollar; they bet on unexpectedly high figures, leading to a fall in U.S. interest rates that should push the dollar down. Bond traders might also expect joblessness to rise, and go long Treasury bonds. The fall in inflationary expectations might push commodity traders to short gold. Individually, these risks may be acceptable but as whole, they sum to a sizable bet on just one number. Global risk management provides a uniform picture of the bank's risk. It fully accounts for correlations across locations and across asset classes. It allows firms to understand their risk better and therefore to hedge and price their risk better.

Table 14–1 shows the global trading business of J. P. Morgan. Trading activities are grouped into seven business areas, each of them active in up to 14 locations. Altogether, the bank has 120 independent risk-taking units that handle over 20,000 transactions per day with a total volume exceeding $50 billion. Although decentralized trading appears very profitable, strong central risk controls are essential to understand the global risk exposure of the bank.

At the end of the day, all trading units report their estimated profit and loss for the day, their position in a standardized mapping format, and their estimated risk over the next 24 hours. Corporate risk management then aggregates the information with centrally administered volatilities and correlations. This leads to the global consolidated 4:15 PM report, which is discussed by business managers before being sent to the board's chair.

TABLE 14–1

J. P. Morgan's Trading Business

	Fixed Income	Currency	Commodity	Derivatives	Equities	Emerging Markets	Proprietary	Total
Number of active locations	14	12	5	11	8	7	11	14
Number of independent risk-taking units	30	21	8	16	14	11	19	120
Thousands of transactions/day	>5	>5	<1	<1	>5	<1	<1	>20
$ billions in daily trading volume	>10	>30	1	1	<1	1	8	>50

1.2 Asset Management

Asset managers such as pension funds and mutual funds are also embracing VAR as a method to control their risks (see Box 14–1). Although investment managers have long relied on quantitative techniques based on portfolio theory, it is only recently that dynamic risk measurement is being applied to the pension fund as a whole.

Generally, investment decisions for pension funds are implemented in two steps. In the first step, the board or a consultant provides a strategic, long-term, asset allocation study, usually based on mean–variance portfolio optimization. This study determines the amounts to be invested in various asset classes, domestic stocks, domestic bonds, foreign stocks, foreign bonds, and perhaps additional classes such as emerging markets, real estate, and venture capital. In the second step, the fund may delegate the actual management to a stable of outside managers, which are periodically reviewed for performance relative to their benchmark.

The problem with this approach is that it is relatively static. Because the assets of the fund are dispersed over a number of managers, it is difficult to create a current picture of the overall risk of the fund. During a quarter, for instance, many fund managers may have increased their exposure to one particular industry. Taken separately, these risks may be acceptable, but as a whole, they may amount to an unsuspected large bet on one source of risk.

BOX 14-1

VAR AND CURRENCY HEDGING

Bankers Trust recently provided its RAROC 2020 risk management system to the Chrysler pension fund.[a] The system provides measures of total and incremental VAR for the various asset classes in which the fund is invested. It can be used, among other things, to evaluate the effectiveness of hedging strategies. For example, the fund was considering adding a currency hedge to protect the currency risk of its foreign stock and bond positions.

The RAROC system showed that the risk of a $250 million currency position was $44 million at the 99 percent level over a year, which appears substantial. However, the pension fund realized that the incremental contribution to total risk of a passive currency-hedge program was only $3 million. Currency risk was already largely diversified in the current portfolio. The fund decided not to hedge its currency exposure, thereby saving hefty management fees.

This result parallels the discussion in the academic literature, where currency hedging has been initially advocated as a "free lunch"; that is, lower risk at no cost.[b] Indeed currency hedging reduces the volatility of individual asset returns, but this is not the relevant issue. Absent currency views, what matters is total portfolio risk. Empirically, total risk is generally affected little by currency hedging if the proportion of assets invested abroad is small.

The fund also considered implementing a $250 million equity hedge account. This had absolute risk of $38 million and incremental risk of $35 million. An equity hedge therefore was found to be much more effective than a currency hedge. Of course, this comes at a cost. The stock market returns a risk premium averaging 8 percent per annum, and therefore a short position in equity futures is expected to lose on average about 8 percent annually. The issue is whether this performance penalty is worth accepting in return for lower risk.

[a]*Risk* (October 1995).
[b]As in Pérold, and Schulman (1988). Jorion (1989), however, argues that the benefit of hedging must be viewed in the context of total portfolio risk.

In addition, money managers sometimes change their investment strategies, either deliberately or inadvertently. If so, the fund should be able to detect and correct such changes quickly. As in the case of bank trading-portfolios, the increased exposure of investment funds to more sources of risk and more complex instruments has created a need for better risk control.

This need was made more pressing by recent spectacular losses suffered by institutional investors. For instance, many investors were burnt when David Askin's $600 million "hedge" fund collapsed. Had the positions been known and marked to market on a frequent basis, investors would have been able to measure their risk. In response, some investors have now decided to aggregate all of their portfolio holdings with a single custodian. With a single global custodian, position reports give a consolidated picture of the total exposure of the fund. The custodian may also provide an important additional benefit, portfolio valuation reports independent of the manager.

Another source of concern is the "rogue trader" syndrome, described in Box 14–2. No doubt this is why pension funds are also moving toward centralized risk management. VAR systems provide a central repository for all positions. Independent reconciliation against manager positions makes fraud a lot more difficult. VAR systems also allow users to quickly catch deviations from stated policies.

In addition to providing better operational controls, VAR systems allow finer measurement of market risks. Pension funds, for instance, can use real-time measurements of deviations from the benchmark to assess investment parameters. Typically, managers receive ad hoc guidelines such as a maximum range for currency exposure or limits on cross-hedging of exchange rates. These guidelines presumably limit the downfall relative to the index. With a VAR system in place, pension funds can directly evaluate the cost or effectiveness of these guidelines. Or, they can specify that the forecast tracking error, based on an outside system such as RiskMetrics, cannot be more than 3 percent. Also, pension funds can consider changing allocations across money managers according to their VARs, rewarding, for instance, profitable managers with low VARs. Therefore, VAR systems are becoming indispensable tools for dynamic evaluation of portfolio risk.

1.3 Nonfinancial Corporations

Nonfinancial corporations are also now implementing risk management systems, especially when involved with derivatives. In a recent survey by *Institutional Investor*, a third of the chief financial officers polled said they use VAR to measure market risks; about half said they use some form of stress testing.

Consider for instance Mobil Corporation, a multinational with exposure to interest rates, exchange rates, and oil and gas prices. In its 1994 annual report, the company stated that "it has significant exposure to these risks," but that, "if Mobil did not use derivatives instruments, its exposure

B O X   14–2

RISK CONTROLS AT THE COMMON FUND

In 1995, the Common Fund, a nonprofit organization that manages about $20 billion on behalf of U.S. schools and universities, announced that it had lost $138 million due to unauthorized trading by one of its managers. Apparently, Kent Ahrens, a trader at First Capital Strategies, had deviated from what should have been a safe index-arbitrage strategy between stock index futures and underlying stocks. One day, he failed to complete the hedge and lost $250,000. He then tried to trade his way out of this loss but with little success. The growing loss was concealed for three years until Ahrens confessed in June 1995.

This loss was all the more disturbing in that, after the Barings affair, the Common Fund had specifically asked First Capital to demonstrate that a rogue trader could not do the same thing at First Capital. The firm answered that market neutrality was being verified daily. In this case, it seems that proper checks and balances were not in place.

To prevent such mishaps, the fund created the new position of chief investment officer. All managers now directly report to a function geared toward centralized risk management. The Common Fund still intends to use derivatives, which have long added value and are an integral part of the investment strategy.

to market risk would be higher." The total notional amount of the firm in derivatives was $11.9 billion as of year-end. The company reports that it uses simulations to measure the daily VAR of its debt and currency portfolio, which was $6 million at the 99.7 percent confidence level.

Thus, value-at-risk methods extend beyond trading or investment portfolios. Corporations with material operating exposure to financial risks often have in place hedging programs. If so, they will benefit from the discipline imposed by VAR. For corporations that already use derivatives, VAR is a must.

For corporations for which cash flows are difficult to measure or are uncertain, VAR is not so beneficial. The economic exposure of cash flows depends on the competitive environment in which the firm operates. Exporters, for instance, can have little exposure if they compete with domestic firms; if they compete with foreign firms, however, their exposure can be substantial. Even more difficult to assess is the effect of "strategic options" whereby firms can alter their marketing strategy (product or pricing) or production strategy (such as product sourcing or plant location) in response to movements in financial variables.

Corporate risk-management policies generally proceed in three steps. First, senior management defines the objective function, for instance cash flows over the next reporting period. Risk is then defined in terms of missing targets in the firm's business plan. Second, the firm measures its VAR, an estimate of how much could be lost over a period due to financial price risk. This information is essential for the third step, implementing an informed hedging decision.

Consider, for instance, Figure 14–1, which displays the distribution of cash flows over the reporting period. Without hedging, the 95 percent VAR is $145 million. This analysis is essential, as management can now assess the probability of a critical shortfall of funds. The firm can decide to self-insure by not hedging. If the firm decides to hedge with derivatives, VAR provides a consistent measure of the effect of hedging on total risk, including correlations. This is a significant improvement over traditional hedging programs, which typically focus on individual transactions only. Here, the hedging program accounts for interactions between various sources of risk.

Assume for instance that the firm has decided to hedge with linear contracts, such as forwards or swaps. As shown in Figure 14–1, hedging narrows the distribution of cash flows. After hedging, the VAR number is reduced to $70 million. Note that hedging reduces risk but does not change the mean of the distribution if the contracts are fairly priced. If the firm had decided to purchase options, the distribution would have a shorter left tail, but at the expense of a reduction in the mean cash-flows, reflecting the option premium.

In practice, there may be a number of reasons for firms to hedge; for instance, to avoid bankruptcy costs or to lower taxes.[1] Alternatively, external financing may be more costly than internal sources of funds. Without hedging, the company is exposed to unfavorable situations that require temporary external financing, such as bank borrowing. Or, the company may need to keep sufficient cash on hand to absorb shortfalls. Both approaches may be more costly than a policy where the firm hedges financial risks and makes full use of its assets. Therefore, the firm may decide to lay off its financial risks in the derivatives markets.

---

1. Smithson, Smith, and Wilford (1995) provide a good survey of why firms should hedge.

FIGURE 14–1

VAR and Corporate Hedging

Probability distribution

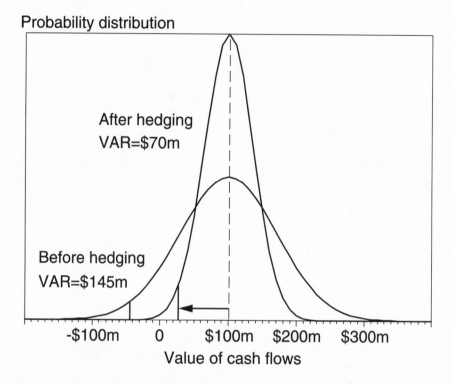

Value of cash flows

Overall, VAR provides essential information on market risk. To the extent that the exposure of operating cash flows can be measured, VAR reveals the effects of natural exposures to financial risks. If the corporation decides to hedge, VAR provides an integrated framework to evaluate the effectiveness of hedging policies.

1.4 Factors That Favor Global Risk Systems

Implementing a global risk-management system, however, is no small feat. It involves integrating systems, software, and database management, which can be very expensive. In addition, it requires substantial investment in intellectual and analytical expertise.

As such, it may not be appropriate for all institutions (see for instance Box 14–3). This is why it is useful to delineate circumstances that favor the development of such systems.

Diversity of Risk

Firms or institutions that are exposed to one principal source of risk, such as U.S. interest-rate risk, do not benefit much from diversification and hence may not require a global risk-management system. In contrast, corporations or investors with exposure to numerous interest rates, exchange rates, and commodity prices should have a global risk-management system in place. Interestingly, the diversity of exposure may reflect a deliberate policy to seek diversification benefits. Bankers Trust, for instance, has a general philosophy of taking moderate positions in many markets that are relatively uncorrelated. And these positions are monitored very closely.

Amount of Proprietary Trading

Firms that take aggressive proprietary positions would benefit from the discipline imposed by a global risk-management system. On the other hand, firms that routinely match all trades have less of a need for such a system. One such example is foreign exchange "brokers," who simply match buyers and sellers without ever taking positions.

BOX 14–3

MERRILL'S APPROACH

Merrill's approach to global risk management differs from other banks. A much smaller proportion of revenues is generated by position trading. Most of its profits come from customer orders, which are generally immediately hedged.

Merrill also takes the view that it has natural "business" exposure to volatility that offsets the exposure of its financial portfolio. When volatility increases, more customer orders flow in, which generate additional profits. These profits offset potential falls in the value of its inventory. The firm also keeps a positive vega (long volatility) position on its option books, just to be sure.

Complexity of Systems

A major benefit of a centralized risk-management system is that it provides a central repository for all trade processing, price quotes, and analytics. As the complexity of system has increased over time, this keeps traders honest and avoids arguments about appropriate valuation. Firms that deal with complex markets surely need the safety of a global risk-management system.

2 VAR AS AN INFORMATION REPORTING TOOL

VAR is rapidly becoming an essential tool to communicate to shareholders the financial risks of the company. Indeed, disclosure is improving rapidly. A 1995 report by banking and securities industry regulators finds that 18 banks and securities houses provided quantitative information on VAR in their 1994 annual reports, compared to only four firms in 1993.[2] The report strongly encourages financial institutions to improve disclosure, which

> can reinforce the efforts of supervisors to foster financial market stability in an environment of rapid innovation and growing complexity. If provided with meaningful information, investors, depositors, creditors and counterparties can impose strong market discipline on financial institutions to manage their trading and derivatives activities in a prudent fashion and in line with their stated business objectives.

Therefore, disclosure of quantitative information about market risk is viewed as providing stability to the financial system. Firms that fail to reveal this information may be susceptible to market rumors, possibly resulting in loss of business or funding difficulties.

Disclosure about trading and derivatives activity usually appears in two places in annual reports:

- **Management discussion and analysis** This section typically contains a narrative statement of the types of risks the firm is exposed to. More detailed information includes a qualitative description of risk-management procedures, objectives, and strategies for using derivatives, and quantitative information about market and credit risks.

---

2. The joint report was issued by the the the Basle Committee on Banking Supervision and the International Organisation of Securities Commissions (IOSCO).

TABLE 14–2

Disclosure of Market Risks: 1994

	Number of Institutions			
Country	Total Examined	Disclosed Daily Trading VAR	Disclosed Changes in Portf. Value	Disclosed Information on Trading Income
Belgium	3	0	0	3
Canada	6	0	0	2
France	8	5	1	7
Germany	7	1	0	7
Italy	8	0	0	8
Japan, banks	7	3	0	1
Japan, securities h.	2	0	0	0
Netherlands	3	0	0	3
Sweden	4	0	0	0
Switzerland	3	1	0	3
UK	8	0	0	8
US, banks	10	8	4	9
US, securities h.	10	0	0	8
Total	79	18	5	59

■ **Financial statements** This section describes the financial position of the firm and, depending on national accounting rules, can include information about derivatives positions in footnotes. Annual financial statements and footnotes are audited by independent accountants.

Table 14–2 provides a summary of disclosure of market risks. Out of the 79 banks and securities firms surveyed, 18 report a VAR measure but only 5 report the actual change in portfolio value corresponding to the reported VAR. This information is also important, because it enables users to assess the effectiveness of internal risk-management systems. More firms disclose information about trading income, although few bother to give details about line of activity.

The table also reveals wide discrepancies across national borders. While U.S. banks are in the vanguard of risk management practices, banks in most other countries provide no information on credit or information risks. It is fair to predict that the pressure will be on marginal players to improve disclosure.

Table 14–3 compares the information provided in annual reports for a group of major U.S. commercial banks that are reporting VAR measures.

TABLE 14–3

VAR Reporting by U.S. Banks: 1994

Bank	Reported VAR Confidence Level (%)	VAR ($ million)	Risk Adjustment Factor (σ)	99% Confidence VAR ($ million)
Chemical	97.5	12	2.24	12.5
J.P. Morgan	95	15	1.65	21.2
Bankers Trust	99	35	2.33	35.0
Bank America	97.5	8	2.24	8.3
Chase	97.5	17	2.24	17.7

The table shows daily VARs reported at various confidence levels. As disclosure is voluntary, standards vary. Assuming a normal distribution, however, translation into a common standard is straightforward.

Perhaps the most informative report is from Bankers Trust, which details the VAR for every day of the year and across functional areas. Other banks only report the year-end VAR or minimum and maximum values. In its qualitative discussion, Bankers states

> The Global Risk Management Department and the Global Credit Department monitor and develop management policies for the market and credit risk of the Corporation's businesses worldwide. These teams of risk management professionals are independent of the Corporation's business functions and report directly to senior management.

No doubt this is the direction of the financial industry. Corporations heavily involved with derivatives markets but that fail to reveal this essential information should be subject to economic pressures by shareholders. Not only does VAR provide otherwise difficult to assess information on market risk, it also reassures shareholders that a proper risk-management system is in place.

3 VAR AS A RESOURCE ALLOCATION TOOL

VAR is not only useful for reporting purposes but also for decision making. VAR models allow users to control risk and decide how to allocate limited resources. Bankers Trust, for instance, imposes a capital charge to traders based on risk-adjusted capital. This creates a natural incentive for traders to take a position only when they have strong views on markets. If they have no views, they will optimally abstain from investing.

Traders should also rationally adjust positions as risk changes through time. In the face of an increasingly volatile environment, for instance, a sensible response is to scale down positions. An example of this reaction is presented in Figure 14–2, which plots the evolution of the daily VAR at the 99 percent level for Bankers Trust's combined portfolio during 1994.

The figure shows that the bank's VAR started at about $70 million at the beginning of January 1994, then declined sharply during February to about $30 million and, except for minor fluctuations, remained at that level for the rest of the year.

Bankers explains this orderly withdrawal as follows:

> The year began with a sharp, global increase in interest rates.... The Corporation responded to this adverse and unsettled market environment

FIGURE 14–2

Bankers Trust VAR

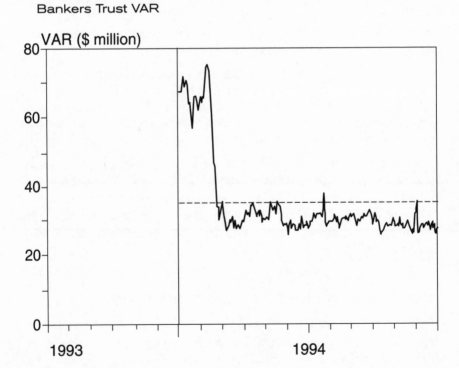

through an orderly withdrawal in the first quarter of 1994 from substantial market positions... The risk reduction that occurred during February 1994 reflected the Corporation's decision to reduce its exposure in its Trading and Positioning accounts due to fluctuations in interest rates... Also, interest-rate risk was the single largest source of market risk during the year with an average Daily Price of $29 million. In comparison, the Corporation's average Daily Price Volatility across all market risks was $35 million in 1994.

In other words, this withdrawal is rationalized by the increased volatility of the fixed-income market, which was a substantial contributor to the overall risk of the corporation in 1994. Figure 14–3 shows the level and expected volatility of short-term interest rates during the same period. As interest rates started to rise in February 1994, volatility also increased. In response, Bankers scaled down its positions substantially, by an amount that must have more than offset the increase in volatility. Thus, VAR can help as a guide to decide how much exposure to financial risks should be allowed.

At the business area or unit level, VAR can also be used to set position limits for traders and decide where to allocate limited capital resources. A great advantage of VAR is that it creates a common denominator with which to compare various risky activities.

Traditionally, position limits are set in terms of notional exposure. A trader, for instance, may have a limit of $10 million on overnight positions in five-year Treasuries. The same limit for 30-year Treasuries or T-bond futures, however, is substantially riskier. VAR provides a common denominator to compare various asset classes and can be used as a guide to set position limits for business units.

In addition, since VAR accounts for correlations, position limits can be set such that the risk limit at higher levels can be lower than the sum of risk limits for individual units. As Figure 14–4 shows, diversification allows the risk limit for business group A to be $60 million, which is less than the sum of $75 million for units A1, A2, and A3, because of diversification benefits.

4 VAR AS A PERFORMANCE EVALUATION TOOL

A third major use of VAR is performance evaluation. This applies to both investment performance and model performance.

FIGURE 14–3

Interest Rates: Level and Volatility

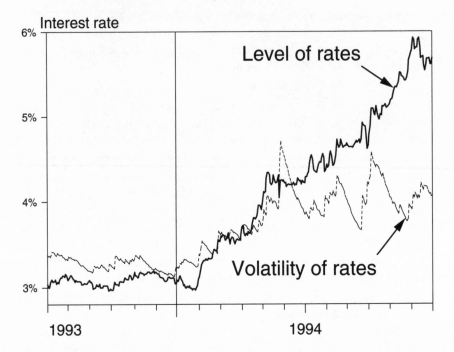

At the strategic level, risk-adjusted performance measures can be used to identify where shareholder value is being added throughout the corporation. Bankers Trust, for instance, expanded into businesses that provide a high RAROC, such as asset management and MBS processing, both of which produce stable income returns.

At the tactical level, these methods are essential to evaluate trader profits and model performance. First, VAR allows managers to adjust the profit performance of traders for the risk they are taking. Traders involved in different markets might produce very different profit numbers just because of the underlying volatility of the market in which they operate, not because of skill. The VAR approach offers a standardized base for comparing markets with different risk characteristics.

Furthermore, risk adjustment provides a solution to the *moral hazard* problem inherent in linking compensation to profits. Without controlling for risks, traders may have an incentive to take more ag-

FIGURE 14-4

Setting VAR Limits

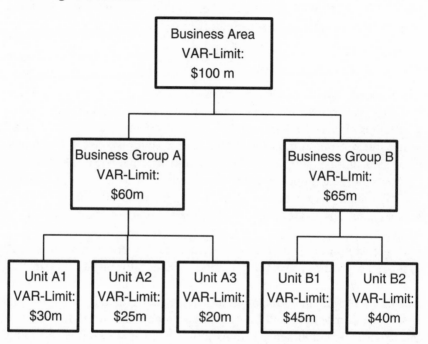

gressive positions. This is because traders are given the equivalent of an option: They receive a percentage of (or bonus based on) profits, which is much greater than their penalty for losses. As option values increase with volatility, traders have an incentive to increase the risk of their positions. Such behavior may be optimal for them, but not for the corporation. As with risk-based capital requirements for financial institutions, imposing an ex-ante penalty for higher risk attempts to curb this behavior.

Managers can evaluate performance using either expected risk or realized risk. In each case, risk-adjusted profits can be measured by one of two measures. First, the *Sharpe ratio* measures the ratio of average return, in excess of the risk-free rate, to the total volatility of returns:

$$S_i = \frac{\overline{R}_i - R_F}{\sigma(R_i)}. \qquad (14.1)$$

This concept can be translated into excess profit and its value at risk. Profits consist of revenues minus expenses and expected losses to cover possible credit risks. VAR represents the amount of capital economically required to support market and credit risks:

$$S_i = \frac{\text{Profit}_i}{\text{VAR}_i}. \tag{14.2}$$

More specifically, a trading business can be decomposed into various components such as customer execution, customer positioning, and house positioning. Each of these must be assigned revenues and costs. For instance, the revenue component of customer execution consists of commissions and bid-ask spreads; the cost component includes operating and clearance costs and operational risks.[3] The benefit of such detailed analysis is that it allows financial institutions to identify profitable and money-losing operations and to redirect efforts toward functions that add the most value.

A major complication arises because trading profits may be related to the risks of other departmental units. Consider, for instance, an institution with two units, a bond trading desk and a futures desk. If both departments go long in anticipation of a decrease in interest rates, the total risk to the corporation will be very large. In contrast, if the futures desk goes short, the combined positions might be nearly risk free. Applying VAR separately to each unit, however, overstates their combined risk.

This is why a second measure of performance is also useful. The *Treynor ratio* is the ratio of average return, in excess of the risk-free rate, to the contribution of this trader to the firms' total profits:

$$T_i = \frac{\overline{R}_i - R_F}{\beta_i}, \tag{14.3}$$

where β_i is the systematic risk of unit i relative to the total firm's portfolio p. In the chapter on portfolio risk, we have seen that the total VAR can be decomposed into $\text{VAR}(\Sigma_{i=1}^{N} w_i \beta_i)$ where w_i is the weight placed on unit i.

---

3. For further analysis of performance measurement in the trading room, see Bralver and Kuritzkes (1993).

The Treynor measure is

$$T_i = \frac{\text{Profit}_i}{(\text{VAR} \times w_i \beta_i)}.$$
(14.4)

As β is strictly valid only for small changes in positions, it is also useful to look at the total change in the portfolio VAR, especially if the portfolio has substantial option components. Defining ΔVAR_i as the change in total VAR due to unit i, the performance measure is

$$T_i = \frac{\text{Profit}_i}{(\Delta\text{VAR}_i)}.$$
(14.5)

The Sharpe ratio focuses on the volatility of a trader's position. If this position, however, has low correlation with the remainder of the bank's portfolio, it is more appropriate to focus on its systematic risk vis-à-vis the rest of the bank. In practice, this measure runs into difficulties if β is very low, which creates abnormally high measures of the Treynor ratio.

The other major function of VAR is model calibration. VAR should be used as a feedback mechanism to check the validity of the underlying valuation and risk models, as shown in Chapter 5. When the model is perfectly calibrated, about 5 percent of observations must fall outside VAR measures estimated at the 95 percent confidence level. Comparing actual profits and losses to their predicted distribution provides feedback to the risk manager. If substantially more than 5 percent of observations fall outside the theoretical 95 percent bands, the model underestimates risk. It should then be reexamined for faulty assumptions, wrong parameters, or inaccurate modeling.

Figure 14–5 displays the fit between actual and forecast daily-VAR for Bankers Trust. The diagram shows the absolute value of the daily profit and loss (P&L) against the price volatility. Observations that lie above the diagonal line indicate days when the absolute value of the P&L exceeded their VAR. According to the statistical model, only 2 percent of the observations should lie above the diagonal, which implies about five daily observations. As this is close to the actual number, the methodology appears to provide a reasonable picture of exposure to market risk.

More generally, deviations between realized and model risk should be tracked closely. The *risk efficiency ratio* measures the ratio of observed, ex-post risk to that predicted by the model

FIGURE 14–5

Model Evaluation: Bankers Trust

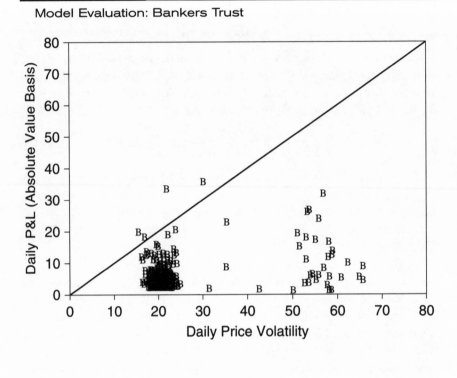

$$E_i = \frac{\sigma^{\text{Observed}}(R_i)}{\sigma^{\text{Predicted}}(R_i)}. \tag{14.6}$$

Systematic deviations from unity indicate that risk is consistently measured with error. If so, risk managers must go back to their model to examine what went wrong.

5 THE INFORMATION TECHNOLOGY CHALLENGE

In the quest to tame financial risks, institutions will have to make heavy investment in information technology (IT). The development of systems is
widely viewed as a necessary component of doing business and can even
provide a competitive edge.

   As the G–30 report points out: "Dealers that have integrated their derivatives risk management systems with their back-office systems have
found that the integration enhances operating efficiency and reliability."

5.1 Global Risk Systems

Implementing a global risk-management system, though, is a major technological challenge. Currently, the software programs that support trading at dealer banks fall into three areas:

- *Trading systems* (or front-office systems) used by traders to evaluate and make deals and to track current positions.
- *Back-office systems* used to settle transactions (i.e., validating trades and communicating accounts to be debited and credited) and account for new transactions into the bank's books.
- *Risk-management systems* (or middle-office systems) used by an independent risk-control unit to monitor traders and the global risk exposure of the firm.

These systems typically operate on different platforms, a legacy of disparate systems having grown out of widely different requirements. Front offices, which directly generate profits, have the most modern application systems installed on decentralized platforms, typically powerful PCs or workstations. Often, different risk-management systems are used to control different business units. In contrast, unglamorous back offices can suffer from antiquated equipment, usually mainframe based.

Back offices suffer from the perception that they do not directly contribute to the bottom line. This perception is seriously mistaken, as many institutions have suffered losses that could have been avoided by decent back-office support. The $1.1 billion loss incurred by Daiwa, for instance, has been partly blamed on an inadequate back-office system that prevented the bank from getting a complete overview of its position.

The challenge is to integrate these systems. Integration involves automating the flow of data for each transaction, sending it to the settlement and risk-management units for verification and bookkeeping. Integration is made easier by the rising capabilities of PCs and workstations, along with their falling costs.

Integration of systems provide many advantages. First, it allows banks to analyze their global risk exposure through a comprehensive system. Second, it enables banks to take full advantage of netting. Offsetting exposures to the same counterparty is possible only with a global reporting system. Third, integration imposes discipline on traders whose positions are evaluated in real time against limits, through trade capture systems. This can help avoid breakdowns in controls such as happened to Barings.

Finally, integration ensures that a single source is used for price quotes, which ideally should be completely independent from the trading desk. Independent prices and valuation models sharply reduce the likelihood of traders reporting fictitious profits.

Admittedly, comprehensive risk-management systems can never completely eliminate operational risks. Rogue traders can always feed false data or violate trading limits. However, redundant systems, double checks, and automation should reduce the chances of catastrophes. As Box 14–4 shows, the Barings's failure would most likely have been avoided by a simple separation of trading and back-office functions.

Additional types of safeguards can also be implemented. Another approach, decidedly low tech, is to provide incentives for employees to inform on colleagues who exceed trading limits. Such a system has been used by Bear Stearns with success. Although there is no foolproof system, risk-management policies provide much-needed safeguards against operational risks.

5.2 The Need for Integration

Unfortunately, integration is not a one-step process. It can be bogged down by existing equipment, which performs its function well in isolation but not across platforms. In addition, there may be organizational resistance to integration, as departmental rivalries may create conflicting objectives.

The trend to integration will be helped by two developments:

■ *Object-oriented tools* allow firms to develop new programs with parts of old ones. Chunks of application logic are constructed as separate "objects" with well-defined functions and interfaces. Programs are built by combining objects. Individual objects can be used in many programs or in the design of other objects, which speeds up development time. This approach is particularly important for derivatives, which evolve very fast and constantly require new software. The new software then can be constructed with pieces of existing programs that price simpler derivatives.

■ *Relational databases* are organized collections of items of data, like all databases, but information is organized into tables that enable users to sift through large amounts of data for specific information. They provide a centralized location for trade positions and live data-feed that can be accessed by a wide variety of programs. The interface with relational databases consists of a query language with one in particular, Structured Query Language (SQL), being a *de facto* standard, which allows easy transfers of data between different databases.

B O X   14-4

BARINGS'S RISK MISMANAGEMENT

The Barings failure is a case in point of lack of trader controls. A good risk-management system might have raised the alarm early and possibly avoided most of the $1.3 billion loss.

Barings had installed in London a credit risk-management system in the 1980s. The bank was installing a market risk-management system in its London offices. The system, developed by California-based Infinity Financial Technology, has the capability to price derivatives and to support VAR reports. Barings's technology, however, was far more advanced in London than in its foreign branches. Big systems are expensive to install and support for small operations, which is why the bank relied heavily on local management.

The damning factor in the Barings affair was Leeson's joint responsibility for front- and back-office functions, which allowed him to hide trading losses. In July 1992, he created a special "error" account, numbered 88888, which was hidden from the trade file, price file, and the London gross file. Losing trades and unmatched trades were parked in this account. Daily reports to Barings's Asset and Liability Committee showed Leeson's trading positions on the Nikkei 255 as fully matched. Reports to London therefore showed no risk. Had Barings used internal audits to provide independent checks on input, the company might have survived.

Flexibility is the essential requirement of such systems. With continuously evolving financial products, changes can be accommodated by rewriting specific modules instead of reconstructing entire systems. Flexibility also guarantees that further regulatory changes require only minor adjustments instead of the major overhauls now facing financial institutions installing VAR systems.

All of this will not come cheap. Financial corporations are among the heaviest users of IT. Just in 1994, $3 billion was spent on risk management technology, 60 percent of which was devoted to internal systems, the rest to external systems. Most of this was spent by U.S. and European banks. And this is just one segment of the $16 billion spent by U.S. banks on technology. Providers of financial services have come to realize that they are as much in the business of managing information as making money. Banks can gain a competitive advantage in financial services only if they make their products more relevant to customers.

Figure 14–6 describes the typical structure of a risk management system. It is composed of three parts. The "analytics" platform collects and filters market data. Market data can be pulled either from traditional data research services, such as Datastream or Data Resources Incorporated, or from on-line data sources, such as Reuters, Telerate, or Knight-Ridder, that now increasingly provide *digital feeds*, as opposed to analog, or video, feeds. With digital feeds, the data can be retrieved on-line in a computer-readable format for use in valuation models for securities and risk forecasts.

The "positions" platform serves as a global repository for all trades, which are received from the front office and transmitted to the back office. It then decomposes deals into component positions. This is a delicate process, as errors in position information will directly translate into errors in the measurement of risk. Simplifications of complicated positions are

FIGURE 14–6

Components of a Risk Management System

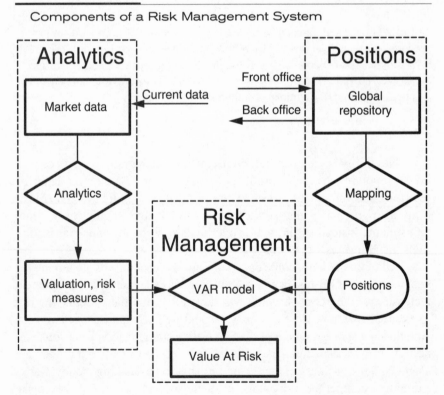

often necessary for manageability and consistency; risk measurement systems are generally not intended to be used as traders' pricing systems.

The third platform, "risk management," integrates analytics and positions with a VAR model to create a measure of market or credit risk or both.

After having decided to implement a risk management system, a major issue is whether to develop the system in-house or to purchase an off-the-shelf system provided by an outside vendor. This choice is crucial since it will determine operational costs as well as the level of competitive advantage. Generally, in-house systems offer more flexibility and integration with existing systems. However, they can be extremely expensive to develop; they require long development periods; and in the end, there is no guarantee the system will be completed. Outside packages, in contrast, offer immediate functionality at a lower cost. Generally, only large institutions that need a high level of customization require in-house systems.

By now, it should be clear that risk management cannot be implemented in a piecemeal approach. The required level of integration is such that it needs to be addressed at very high levels in the organization. In addition, it must be supported through the bank's culture and technology.

6 AN APPLICATION

As an example, we now illustrate the application of a global risk-management system. Sailfish Systems Ltd. is a vendor of firmwide risk-measurement and performance-analysis software. A major benefit of the system is that it implements support for all risk measurement methodologies in a single application. Users have the option of choosing one of the four VAR methods and, therefore, can assess whether the results are sensitive to the methodology.

Figure 14–7 displays the "risk grid" screen. The upper left corner displays a breakdown of the risk profile by asset class and by currency. The adjoining panel represents the net risk aggregated either by currency (below) or by asset class (to the right). For instance, the net risk due to the Australian dollar is $7.5 million; the net risk due to the currency position is $10.6 million. The right bottom panel describes the allocation of risk to client-defined classes, such as risk types (e.g., interest, currency), products (e.g., securities, derivatives), profit center, and counterparties. At the

F I G U R E   14–7

Sailfish System: Risk Grid

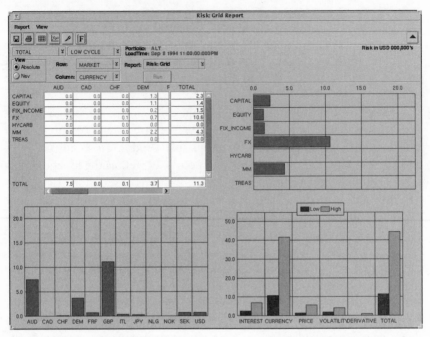

F I G U R E   14–8

Sailfish System: Distribution of Profits

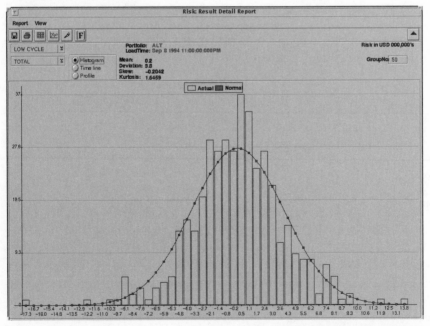

FIGURE 14–9

Sailfish System: Historical Simulation

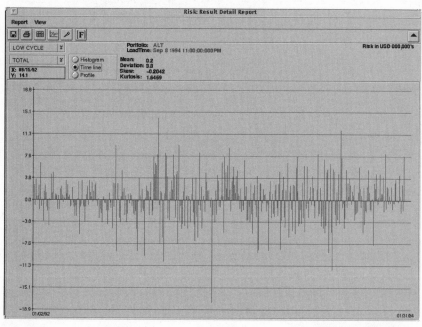

95 percent confidence level, the total portfolio risk is $11.3 million short term and $43 million long term.

This display is interactive, in the sense that users can click on various elements to run further reports. This encourages users to seek out more detailed information within a portfolio.

Figure 14–8 presents the entire distribution of profits, instead of just the 95 percent VAR number. The screen shows the empirical distribution, measured by the histogram, as well as the normal approximation that provides the best fit. The shape of the distribution can be compared to the normal approximation. With this information, the user can select a point risk-estimate based on a standard deviation or a sample quantile.

In this example, VAR is measured using the historical-simulation method. Figure 14–9 displays the time-series of simulated portfolio returns using about two years of data. This provides visual information about the volatility of the selected period. Users can expand or narrow the sample period as desired. In addition, the returns can be specialized to asset classes or to the events with the largest gains and losses. Based on this information, users can get a better sense of their risk exposure.

Such a centralized risk management system provides many benefits: information reporting, resource allocation, and performance evaluation. Without these tools, corporations are essentially flying blind in financial markets.

CHAPTER 15

Risk Management: Guidelines and Pitfalls

> Risk management is asking what might happen the other 1 percent of the time.
>
> *Richard Felix, chief credit officer at Morgan Stanley*

The string of derivatives disasters led to well-publicized threats of legislative actions against derivatives. In response, the private sector came up with recommendations for better control of derivatives. A landmark review was published by the Group of Thirty (G–30), an industry-funded association, in July 1993. But these recommendations cover much more than derivatives risks, and they have become a benchmark for prudent management of all financial risks. This chapter summarizes a set of good practices for risk management, in which VAR is just a building block—more properly, a cornerstone.

Section 1 reviews the G–30 best practices guidelines, of which implementation of the VAR system is only one component. Firms that ignore these guidelines expose themselves to potential losses and also reputational risks. Section 2 emphasizes the role of senior management. Section 3 discusses pitfalls in the interpretation of value at risk, and important risks, some of them quite subtle, of which users should beware. Finally, Section 4 serves as a reminder that, even with the best risk-management systems, corporations are still exposed to strategic risks.

1 "BEST PRACTICES" RECOMMENDATIONS FROM G-30

The G–30 study examines the risks associated with derivative products and concludes that "derivatives do not introduce risks of a greater scale than those already present in financial markets." The key words here are *already present*, meaning that derivatives do not create new risks. It also provides a set of 20 sound management practices, the most important of which are summarized as follows (using the original G–30 numbering method):

1. Role of Senior Management

Policies governing derivatives should be clearly defined at the highest level. Senior management should approve procedures and controls to implement these policies, which should be enforced at all levels. In other words, derivatives activities merit the attention of senior management, because they can generate large profits or losses. Senior management, the board of directors, or the board of trustees is the first point of responsibility.

2. Marking to Market

Derivative positions should be valued at market prices, at least on a daily basis. This is the only valuation technique that correctly measures the current value of assets and liabilities. Marking to market should be implemented regardless of the accounting method utilized. Even firms that use accrual accounting should establish a separate set of books to measure market risks.

5. Measuring Market Risk

Dealers should use a consistent measure to calculate daily the market risk of their positions, which is best measured with a *value at risk* approach. Once a method of risk measurement is in place, market-risk limits must be set based on factors such as tolerance for loss and capital resources.

6. Stress Simulations

Users should quantify market risk under adverse market conditions. Value at risk systems usually are based on normal market conditions, which may not reflect potential losses under extreme market environments. Stress simulations should reflect both historical events and estimates of future adverse moves.

8. Independent Market-Risk Management

Dealers should establish market-risk management functions to assist senior management in the formulation and implementation of risk control systems. These risk management units should be set up with clear independence from trading, and should have enforcement authority. They should establish risk-limit policies, measure value at risk, perform stress scenarios, and monitor whether actual portfolio volatility is in line with predictions.

10. Measuring Credit Exposure

Users should assess the credit risk arising from derivatives activities based on frequent measures of current and potential exposure. Current exposure is the market value, or replacement cost, of existing positions. Potential exposure measures probable future losses due to default over the remaining term of the transaction.

11. Aggregating Credit Exposure

Credit exposure to each counterparty should be aggregated taking into account netting arrangements. Credit risk can be reduced by broadening the use of multiproduct master agreements with closeout netting provisions.

12. Independent Credit-Risk Management

Users should establish oversight functions for credit risks with clear authority, independent of the dealing function. These units should set credit limits and monitor their uses.

16. Professional Expertise

Users should authorize only professionals with the requisite skills and experience to transact. These professionals include traders, supervisors, and those responsible for processing and controlling activities.

We should note that the G-30 recommendations are much more general than just for derivatives and can be applied to any investment portfolio. Indeed they can help to control the risk of any asset/liability portfolio.

2 THE ROLE OF SENIOR MANAGEMENT

The Barings failure highlighted the role of senior management, which came at the top of the G-30 recommendations. By one estimate, Barings had ignored half of these recommendations. On July 18, 1995, four months after Barings's demise, the Bank of England published a report on the circumstances of this affair.

2.1 Guidelines from the Bank of England

The Barings report mentioned for the first time *reputational risk*. This relates to the risk to earnings arising from negative public opinion. Reputational risk can expose an institution to litigation or financial loss due to the disruption of relationships. Concerns over the use of derivatives have appeared in corporate board rooms since 1994. No one likes to have the name of his or her company or pension fund quoted in relation to losses on instruments that one cannot quite explain nor understand.

While some introspective analysis of the use of derivatives is certainly beneficial, as recommended by the G-30, some companies have chosen to terminate their involvement in derivatives markets. One notable example is Kodak, which discontinued its highly successful managed futures program. Complete termination of all derivatives activity appears to be an extreme step.

This is especially true since derivatives can be used to hedge financial or operating risks. Ignoring them does not solve the problem, as companies have been sued for not using derivatives. In 1992, for instance, an Indiana grain co-op suffered losses when grain prices fell. The directors were sued and found liable for retaining a manager inexperienced in derivatives.

The Bank of England report concluded that the bank's collapse was due to unauthorized trading by Nick Leeson, which was made possible by an "absolute" collapse of controls and managerial confusion. A later report by the Singapore government went even further, blaming the collapse on "institutional incompetence."

The report also identified several lessons from this disaster. The first one is that front and back offices need to be clearly segregated, with distinct reporting lines. In addition, the report stated that

- Management teams have a duty to understand fully the businesses they manage.
- Responsibility for each business activity must be clearly established.
- Clear segregation of duties is fundamental to any effective risk control system.
- Relevant internal risk controls, including independent risk management, have to be established on all business activities.
- Top management must quickly resolve significant weaknesses.

All of these appear to be common-sense recommendations.

2.2 Organizational Guidelines

Senior managers bear a particular responsibility since they define objectives, procedures, and controls. They can also foster safe or unsafe environments, through the choice of organizational structure.

TABLE 15-1

Risk Management Practices

Stage of Development	Risk Policy Committees	Aggregation Level	VAR Analysis
Leaders	Yes—multiple	Companywide	Yes
Followers	Credit—yes Market—sometimes	Business unit level	Sometimes
Laggards	Credit risk only	None	No

Risk management practices vary widely. As described in Table 15–1, less-advanced companies may operate a credit risk committee only and generally aggregate their risks at the business level only. More-advanced institutions have global risk committees for credit and market risk and use quantitative measures of risk. Generally, banks in the United States appear to have the most developed risk management systems. U.S. commercial banks are actually ahead of U.S. investment banks in terms of global risk-management practices, somewhat perversely due to the imposition of strict capital requirements by regulators. Close behind come British banks, followed by German, Swiss, and Dutch institutions. Outside of these countries, banks typically manage only credit risks.

Japanese financial institutions are notably behind the times in terms of risk management. In the 1980s, Japanese banks grew through lending not securities trading, so there was little need for management of market risks. They were also shielded from competition through cartel arrangements orchestrated by the Ministry of Finance. These banks failed to adjust their oversight procedures to match their changing business.

Figure 15–1 describes one implementation of a control model. The key to this flowchart is that the risk management unit is independent of the trading unit. Risk managers should not report to anybody whose compensation is linked to the success of a trading unit but rather should report directly to top management. Also, the compensation of risk managers and auditors cannot be associated with how well traders perform. In this structure, each unit has segregated duties and no overlapping management at lower levels. This provides for a system of checks and balances.

FIGURE 15–1

Organizational Structure for Risk Management

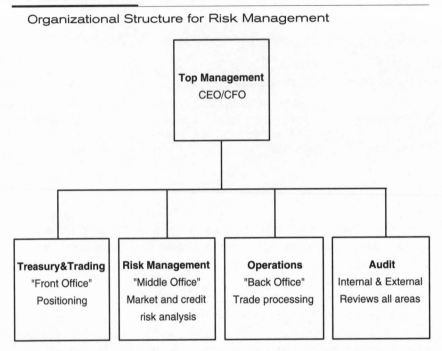

So far, the development of risk management systems has been slow, particularly outside the United States. In addition to the cost and intellectual development needed to develop the technological support for risk management, there is often a conflict of culture between the trading area and traditional bankers. Whereas most traders are typically well-versed in risk-measurement tools, traditional loan officers are often befuddled by these concepts. The challenge is to convince the whole organization of the benefits from better control and pricing of risks. Faster-moving financial markets, regulatory pressure, and lessons from recent financial disasters should all prod global banking into better management of financial risks.

2.3 Risk Managers

Unfortunately, there is a great temptation to cut corners on risk management and controls. Unlike traders, these units do not directly contribute to the bottom line of the firm. Jobs in back and middle offices are unglamorous. In particular, risk managers serve a function similar to selling an option: At best, nothing happens; at worst, they fail to detect a problem and may be out of a job. This is the opposite of traders, for whom the performance–bonus link is similar to buying an option.

Risk managers are a special breed. They must be thoroughly familiar with financial markets, with the intricacies of the trading process, and with financial and statistical modeling. They must be attentive to details, as they continuously put their reputations on the line. Yet they cannot receive huge bonuses as traders do.

The compensation of such risk managers is a delicate issue. Institutions that try to skimp on the remuneration of back- and middle-office personnel will fail to attract a qualified staff. A recent G-30 survey, for instance, finds that there is "some concern that the development of staff in support areas lags behind."

This is where senior management again plays an important role. Strong internal controls are in the best interests of the institution, since views of a counterparty's integrity are vital to the continuous flow of business. Effective oversight also reduces the likelihood that an institution will be exposed to litigation, financial loss, or reputational damage. The spectacular failures of institutions that lacked internal controls should serve as a powerful object lesson in the need for risk management.

3 PITFALLS IN THE INTERPRETATION OF VAR

Although VAR provides a first line of defense against financial risks, it is no panacea. Users must understand the limitations of VAR measures.

3.1 Event and Stability Risks

The main drawback of models based on historical data is that they assume that the recent past is a good projection of future randomness. Even if the data have been perfectly fitted, there is no guarantee that the future will not hide nasty surprises that did not occur in the past.

Surprises can take two forms, either one-time events (such as a devaluation or default) or structural changes (such as going from fixed to floating exchange-rates.) Situations where historical patterns change abruptly cause havoc with models based on historical data.

Stability risk can be addressed by stress testing, developed in Chapter 10, which aims at addressing the effect of drastic changes on portfolio risk. To some extent, structural changes can also be captured by models that allow risk to change through time or by volatility forecasts contained in options. An example of structural change is the 1994 devaluation of the Mexican peso, which is further detailed as follows.

VAR and the Peso's Collapse

In December 1994, the emerging-market ploy turned sour as Mexico devalued the peso by 40 percent. The devaluation was widely viewed as bungled by the government, and led to a collapsing Mexican stock market. Investors who had poured money into the developing economies of Latin America and Asia faced large losses as the Mexican devaluation led to a widespread decrease in emerging markets all over the world.

Figure 15–2 plots the peso/dollar exchange rate, which was fixed around 3.45 peso for most of 1994 and then jumped to 5.64 by mid-December.

FIGURE 15–2

Peso/Dollar Exchange Rate

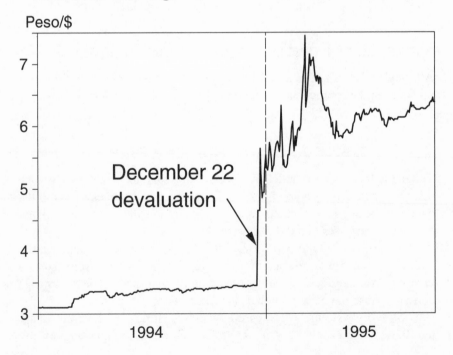

Apparently, the devaluation was widely unanticipated. This was in spite of a ballooning current-account deficit running at 10 percent of Mexico's GDP and a currency widely overvalued according to purchasing-power parity. A conventional VAR system would not have anticipated the magnitude of the devaluation. Based on an exponential volatility forecast, Figure 15–3 shows that the 35 percent devaluation was way outside the 95 percent confidence band. After December, the forecasts seem to capture reasonably well the turmoil that followed the devaluation. This was little solace for investors caught short by the devaluation.

This episode indicates that, especially when price controls are left in place for long periods, VAR models based on historical data cannot capture potential losses. These models must be augmented by an analysis of economic fundamentals and stress testing. Interestingly, shortly after the devaluation, the Mexican government authorized the creation of currency futures on the peso. It was argued that the existence of forward-looking prices for the peso would have provided market participants, as well as the

FIGURE 15–3

Peso/Dollar Volatility

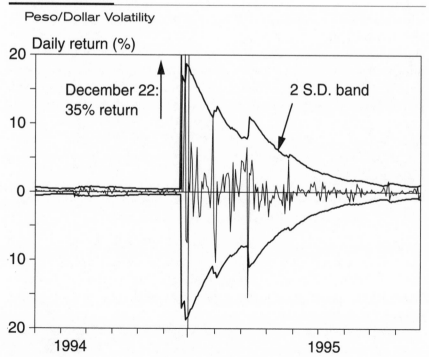

central bank, with an indication of market pressures. In any event, this disaster was not blamed on derivatives.

3.2 Transition Risk

Whenever there is a major change, a potential exists for errors. This applies, for instance, to organizational changes, expansion into new markets or products, implementation of a new system, or new regulations. Since existing controls deal with existing risks, they may be less effective in the transition.

Transition risk is difficult to deal with, because it cannot be explicitly modeled. The only safeguard is increased vigilance in times of transition.

3.3 Changing Positions

A similar problem of instability occurs when trying to extrapolate daily risk to a longer horizon, which is especially of concern to bank regulators. As we have seen in a previous chapter, the typical adjustment is by a square root of time factor, assuming constant positions. However, this adjustment ignores the fact that the trading position might very well change over time in response to changing market conditions. There is no simple way to assess the impact on the portfolio VAR, but it is likely that prudent risk-management systems will decrease risk relative to conventional VAR measures. For instance, the enforcement of loss limits will gradually decrease the exposure as losses accumulate. This dynamic trading pattern is similar to purchasing an option that has limited downside potential. It is also possible, however, as Barings has demonstrated, that traders who lose money increase their bets in the hope of recouping their losses.

3.4 Problem Positions

Problem positions are in a category similar to transition. All the analytical methods underlying VAR assume that some data are available to measure risks. For some securities, such as infrequently traded emerging-market stocks, private placements, or exotic currencies, meaningful market-clearing prices may not exist, however.

Without adequate price information, risk cannot be assessed from historical data (not to mention implied data). Yet, a position in these assets will create the potential for losses that is difficult to quantify. In the absence of good data, educated stress-testing appears as the only method to assess risks.

3.5 Model Risks

Most risk management systems use past history as a guide to future risks. Extrapolating from past data, however, can be hazardous. This is why it is essential to beware of the pitfalls from model risks.

Functional Form Risk

This is the purest form of model risk. Valuation errors can arise if the particular functional form chosen for valuing a security is incorrect.

The Black-Scholes model, for instance, relies on a rather restrictive set of assumptions (geometric Brownian motion, constant interest rates, and volatility). For conventional stock options, departures from these assumptions generally have few consequences. However, there are situations where the model is inappropriate, such as for short-term interest rate options.

Model risk also grows more dangerous as the instrument becomes more complicated. Pricing CMOs requires heavy investments in the development of models, which may prove inaccurate under some market conditions.

Parameter Risk

Also known as *estimation risk,* parameter risk stems from the imprecision in the measurement of parameters. Even in a perfectly stable environment, we do not observe the true expected returns and volatilities. Thus some random errors are bound to happen just because of sampling variation.

As shown in Chapter 5, one could formally assess the effect of estimation risk by replacing the sample estimates by values that are statistically "equivalent." An alternative method consists of sampling over different intervals. If the risk measures appear to be sensitive to the particular choice of the sample period, then estimation risk may be serious.

Estimation risk increases with the number of estimated parameters. The more parameters are estimated, the greater is the chance that errors will interact with each other and create a misleading picture of risk. Errors in correlations, in particular, are dangerous when they are associated with large "arbitrage" positions. Parsimony breeds robustness.

The problem of estimation risk is often ignored in VAR analyses. Users should realize the fundamental trade-off between using more data, which leads to more precise estimates, and focusing on more recent data, which may be safer if risk changes over time.

Unfortunately, the data may not be available for very long periods. Only very limited histories are available, for instance, for emerging markets or exotic currencies. All the more reason to remember that VAR numbers are just estimates.

Data Mining Risk

This is among the most insidious form of risk. It occurs when searching over various models and reporting only the one that gives good results. This is particularly a problem with nonlinear models (such as neural network or chaos models), which involve searching not only over parameter values but also over different functional forms.

Data mining also consists of analyzing the data until some significant relationship is found. Take for instance an investment manager who tries to find "calendar anomalies" in stock returns. The manager tries to see if stock returns systematically differ across months, weeks, days, and so on. So many different comparisons can be tried that, in 1 case out of 20, one would expect to find "significant" results at the usual 5 percent level. Of course, the results are significant only because of the search process, which discards nonsignificant models. Data mining risk manifests itself in overly optimistic simulation results based on historical data. Often, results break down outside the sample period because they are fallacious.

Data mining risks can be best addressed by running *paper portfolios*, where an objective observer records the decisions and checks how the investment process performs on actual data.

Survivorship Risk

Survivorship is an issue when an investment process only considers series, markets, stocks, bonds, or contracts that are still in existence. The problem is that assets that have fared badly are not observed. Analyses based on current data therefore tend to project an overly optimistic image or display certain characteristics.

Survivorship effects are akin to the "peso problem" in the foreign exchange market. Before the devaluation of 1982, the Mexican peso was selling at a large discount in the forward market (the forward price of the peso was well below the price for current delivery). This discount rationally anticipated a possible devaluation of the peso. An observer analyzing the discount before 1982 would have concluded that the market was inefficient. The failure, however, was not that of the market, but rather of the observer, who chose a sample period where the data did not reflect any probability of a devaluation.

More generally, unusual events with a low probability of occurrence but which have severe effects on prices, such as wars or nationalizations, are not likely to be well represented in samples, and may be totally omitted from survived series. Unfortunately, these unusual events are very difficult to capture with conventional risk models.[1]

4 STRATEGIC RISKS

As was explained in the first chapter of this book, VAR can help to measure and control financial risk. However, it is impotent in the face of strategic risks that also face corporations. *Strategic risks* are those resulting from fundamental shifts in the economy or political environment. One such example is the story of Bankers Trust (Box 15–1), which before 1994 was widely admired as a leader in risk management but became a victim of the backlash against derivatives.

The derivatives market has been subject to political and regulatory risks, which are part of the menagerie of strategic risks affecting corporations, either at the firm or industry level.

Political risks arise from actions taken by policy makers that significantly affect the way an organization runs its business. Although the 1994 Congress adjourned without taking action on derivatives, a flurry of bills have been proposed and may be revived in the future. These may impose limitations on the use of derivatives, thus negatively affecting the profitability of many firms involved in this market. It is perhaps in response to these threats that the private sector has come up with initiatives to address the issue of measuring market risks.

Regulatory risks are the result of changes in regulations or interpretation of existing regulations that can negatively affect a firm. For instance, as a result of the Bankers Trust case, the Commodities and Futures Trading Commission (CFTC), and Securities and Exchange Commission

---

1. Brown, Goetzmann, and Ross (1995) show that the time-series properties of survived series can be markedly different from the original series.

BOX 15–1

BANKERS TRUST'S STRATEGIC TRANSFORMATION

Charles Sanford transformed Bankers Trust from a sleepy commercial bank into a financial powerhouse using risk management as a competitive tool.

In 1994, however, the bank became embroiled with two lawsuits, one with Gibson Greetings and the other with Procter & Gamble. The first was settled out of court after tapes were discovered that revealed that Bankers's officers had misled Gibson about the size of its losses. The bank contested the case with P&G.

These affairs sullied the bank's reputation. The bank in addition had to navigate through a period during which derivatives came under intense scrutiny. Bankers Trust was particularly vulnerable since it relies more heavily than other banks on derivatives activity.

The bank also recognized that its profit-driven culture often placed the bank's profit before the client's interest. Focusing on financial risks only can become harmful if it detracts from the client relationship, which is still an important part of the banking business. Bankers later implemented changes in its compensation schemes to reward salespeople for improving relationships with customers. It also turned its risk management savvy into new products, such as its RAROC 2020 system.

(SEC) have extended their jurisdiction over market participants by declaring swaps to be "futures contracts" and "securities," respectively. This allowed the CFTC to classify Bankers Trust as a commodity trading advisor, which is subject to specific statutes. Another example are recent guidelines by federal bank regulators to prohibit the sale of types of structured notes to money-market mutual funds, small savings institutions, and community banks.

5 CONCLUSIONS

Derivatives have caused much anxiety in recent years. As corporations and institutional investors inevitably scan financial markets for the best risk-return trade-off, they will inevitably become exposed to derivatives. In response, institutions could completely shy away from derivatives, which may be very difficult to do given the pervasiveness of derivatives in financial instruments. Or, they could try to tame the "derivatives monster."

In fact, the large losses suffered by several players in financial markets can serve as powerful object lessons in risk management. Derivatives have shown the path toward better control of financial risks. Along this path lies the value-at-risk method, which represents a giant step away from unbridled risk taking.

CHAPTER 16

Conclusions

To allow investors to assess more easily overall market risk, the proposed amendments would . . . require disclosure . . . of quantitative market risk information for derivative financial instruments, other financial instruments, and derivative commodity instruments, to the extent it is material.

Securities and Exchange Commission

1 DERIVATIVES AND RISK MANAGEMENT

Merton Miller, who received the 1990 Nobel prize in economics for his path-breaking contributions to finance, has described the last 30 years in finance as nothing short of a "revolution." Among financial innovations during this period, Professor Miller views *financial futures* as the most significant. The first such contracts were futures on foreign currencies, launched in 1972 by the Chicago Mercantile Exchange. Shortly thereafter came options, along with the celebrated Black-Scholes model.

The subsequent growth of financial derivatives has been phenomenal. Derivatives grew in response to a need to hedge financial risks, along with its inevitable counterpart, a search for speculative profits. As risk management tools, derivatives provide a market for the reallocation of risks. They laid the foundation for a thriving financial engineering industry, which fostered a pool of knowledge for better risk management. As the derivatives market becomes more mainstream, this pool of knowledge is now applied to a wider variety of financial instruments. Risk management, which grew up on a desk-by-desk basis, is now applied at the level of the whole corporation.

On the downside, the technology behind the creation of evermore complex derivatives instruments seems at times to have advanced faster than our ability to control it. Also, a major problem affecting all trading activity is that agents often have incentives to engage in risk-taking activity that may not be in the best interest of the firm they work for. One of the lessons of many financial disasters is the fundamental asymmetry in pay-offs to traders. Absent fraud, a losing bet just means a lost job and some reputational damage. In contrast, a winning bet could mean lifetime wealth. Thus profit-based compensation (or government insurance schemes) create incentives to take on extra risk. No doubt this is why there is now such a great focus on controls and risk management systems.

2 VAR REVISITED

Recent financial disasters also explain why value at risk is now taking the financial industry by storm. VAR grew from a desire to control the market risks of derivative assets, which are highly leveraged instruments that need to be precisely controlled. Once the technical expertise is in place, the next step is to extend the measure of market risk to all assets, be they stocks, bonds, or commodities.

Admittedly, VAR is no panacea. There is no universally accepted method to measure VAR, and there can be some divergence of results across methods. VAR is also subject to "event risk" and must be aug-mented by stress testing, or subjective evaluations of the economic envi-ronment driving financial markets. It should be remembered that, even with a 99 percent confidence interval, unusual events happen, and they sometimes do so with a vengeance. To make things worse, liquidity can dry up during such situations; the only alternative is then to sit tight and wait for normalcy to occur. On the other hand, managing financial risks is the *raison d'être* of financial institutions. It is impossible and undesirable to achieve 100 percent coverage of all risks; the bank would then become a risk-free investment, with much lower returns.

Thus VAR should be considered only as a first-order approximation. The fact that the value is generated from a statistical method should not hide the fact that it is only an estimate. Users should not be lulled into a state of complacency but rather recognize the limitations of VAR, which have been amply documented in this book. As Steven Thieke, chairman of J. P. Morgan's risk management committee says, "There has to be a point where this stops being a risk measurement methodology and becomes a management issue—what is the level of experience of the people in this business, and the firm's tolerance for risk."

Appropriate use of VAR, however, may have avoided some of the spectacular debacles of recent years, where investors had, or claimed to have, no idea of their exposure to financial risks. In addition, the implementation of VAR forces integration of the front office (trading desk), the back office, and a newly created middle office, which performs a risk management function. This integration, although not necessarily easy in terms of logistics, has the side benefit that it makes it harder to falsify data, providing a partial protection against rogue traders. Therefore, the process of getting to VAR may be as important as the number itself.

3 THE FUTURE OF RISK MANAGEMENT

The steps leading us to VAR provide an interesting reflection on the evolution of modern financial management, as described in Figure 16–1.

VAR's antecedents can be traced to asset/liability management systems in place in the 1980s. At the time, banking institutions carried most of their financial assets and liabilities on the balance sheet using *accrual*

FIGURE 16–1

Modern Financial Management

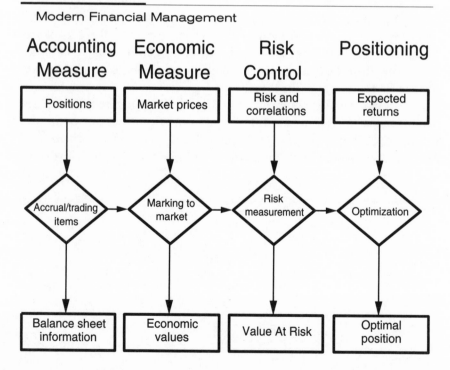

methods; that is, transactions were booked at historical costs with adjustments for accruals. Some items, such as those held for trading, were carried at market values.

The problem was that these accounting methods insulated the value of balance sheet items from their economic reality. Sometimes, forecasts of future rates were used to project income over long periods, in a manner somewhat similar to what we describe as "scenario analysis." Such accounting methods contributed to the great savings-and-loans debacle because it allowed institutions to present balance sheets that were in accordance with accounting rules but were hiding large losses.

Later, with the trend toward marking to market, balance sheets started to be reported at market values. Once market values are available, the next logical step is to assess risk. A simple method for computing VAR, for instance, consists of keeping track of the market value of all securities over a selected time interval, which gives an idea of the possible range of values for a trading portfolio. Thus the combination of positions, marking to market, and fluctuations in market values naturally leads to the concept of value at risk.

The final step, implemented only by leading institutions, consists of using the risk control system as a feedback mechanism to evaluate business units. VAR provides a framework to compare the profitability of various operations on a risk-adjusted basis. Firms can then make informed decisions about maintaining or expanding lines of business, or whether to hedge financial risks at the firm level.

More generally, optimization makes the best use of return forecasts, combined with risk measures, to find the set of portfolios or businesses that provide the best trade-off between risk and return. Thus, risk management is now poised to take full advantage of Markowitz's portfolio theory.

REFERENCES

Bair, S. and S. Milligan. "Voluntary Efforts to Provide Oversight of OTC Derivatives Activities." In *Derivatives Risk and Responsibility*, eds. R. Klein and J. Lederman. Chicago, IL.: Irwin, 1996.

Basle Committee on Banking Supervision. *An Internal Model-Based Approach to Market Risk Capital Requirements.* Basle, Switzerland: Basle Committee on Banking Supervision, 1995a.

Basle Committee on Banking Supervision. *Planned Supplement to the Capital Accord to Incorporate Market Risks.* Basle, Switzerland: Basle Committee on Banking Supervision, 1995b.

Bates, D. "Testing Option Pricing Models." NBER Working Paper 5129. Cambridge, Mass.: National Bureau of Economic Research, 1995.

Beckstrom, R. and A. Campbell, eds. *An Introduction to VAR.* Palo Alto, CA.: CATS Software, 1995.

Beder, T. "VAR: Seductive But Dangerous." *Financial Analysts Journal* 51 (1995), pp. 12–24.

Bickel, P., and D. Freedman. "Some Asymptotic Theory for the Bootstrap," *The Annals of Statistics* 9 (1981), pp. 1196–1271.

Black, F. "The Pricing of Commodity Options." *Journal of Financial Economics* 3 (1976), pp. 167–179.

Black, F., and M. Scholes. "The Pricing of Options and Corporate Liabilities." *Journal of Political Economy* 81 (1973), pp. 637–59.

Blume, M., and D. Keim. "Realized Returns and Defaults on Low-Grade Bonds: The Cohort of 1977 and 1978." *Financial Analysts Journal* 47 (1991), pp. 63–72.

Board of Governors of the Federal Reserve System. *Request for Comment on the Pre-Commitment Approach for Market Risks, Docket No. R–0886.* Washington, D.C.: Board of Governors of the Federal Reserve System, 1995.

Bollerslev, T. "Generalized Autoregressive Conditional Heteroskedasticity." *Journal of Econometrics* 31 (1986), pp. 307–327.

Bollerslev, T., R. Chou, and K. Kroner. "ARCH Modelling in Finance: A Review of the Theory and Empirical Evidence." *Journal of Econometrics* 52 (1992), pp. 5–59.

Boudoukh, J., M. Richardson, R. Stanton, and R. Whitelaw. "A New Strategy for Dynamically Hedging Mortgage-Backed Securities." *Journal of Derivatives* 2 (Summer 1995), pp. 60–77.

Boyle, P. "Options: A Monte Carlo Approach." *Journal of Financial Economics* 4 (1977), pp. 323–338.

Bralver, C. and A. Kuritzkes. "Risk Adjusted Performance Measurement in the Trading Room." *Journal of Applied Corporate Finance* 6 (1993), pp. 104–108.

Brown, S., W. Goetzmann, and S. Ross. "Survival." *Journal of Finance* 50 (1995), pp. 853–873.

Cox, J., S. Ross, and M. Rubinstein. "Option Pricing: A Simplified Approach." *Journal of Financial Economics* 7 (1979), pp. 229–263.

Cox, J., J. Ingersoll, and S. Ross. "A Theory of the Term Structure of Interest Rates." *Econometrica* (1985), pp. 385–407.

Culp, C., and J. Overdahl. "An Overview of Derivatives: Their Mechanics, Participants,

Scope of Activity, and Benefits." In *Financial Services 2000 A.D.: The Dissolving Barriers among Banks, Mutual Funds and Insurance Companies*, ed. C. Kirsch. Chicago, IL.: Irwin, 1996.

Culp, C. and M. Miller. "Metallgesellschaft and the Economics of Synthetic Storage." *Journal of Applied Corporate Finance* 7 (Winter 1995).

Derivatives Policy Group. *A Framework for Voluntary Oversight*. New York: Derivatives Policy Group, 1995.

Dimson, E., and P. Marsh. "Capital Requirements for Securities Firms." *Journal of Finance* 50 (1995), pp. 821–851.

Duan, J. "The GARCH Option Pricing Model." *Mathematical Finance* 5 (1995), pp. 13–32.

Duffie, D. and M. Huang. "Swap Rates and Credit Quality," mimeo, Stanford University, 1995.

Efron, B. "Bootstrap Methods: Another Look at the Jackknife." *The Annals of Statistics* 7 (1979), pp. 1–26.

Engle, R. "Autoregressive Conditional Heteroskedasticity with Estimates of the Variance of United Kingdom Inflation." *Econometrica* 50 (1982), pp. 987–1007.

Engle, R.; D. Lilien; and R. Robins. "Estimating Time-Varying Risk Premia in the Term Structure: The ARCH-M Model." *Econometrica* 55 (1987), pp. 391–407.

Estrella, A.; D. Hendricks; J. Kambhu; S. Shin; and S.Walter. "The Price Risk of Options Positions: Measurement and Capital Requirements." *Federal Reserve Bank of New York Quarterly Review* 19 (1994), pp. 27–43.

Finnerty, J. "Financial Engineering in Corporate Finance: An Overview." *Financial Management* 17 (1988), pp. 14–33.

Fisher, L. "An Algorithm for Finding Exact Rates of Return." *Journal of Business* 39 (1966), pp. 111–118.

Fisher, L. and R. Weil. "Coping with the Risk of Interest-Rate Fluctuations: Returns to Bondholders from Naive and Optimal Strategies." *Journal of Business* 44 (1971), pp. 408–431.

French, K.; W. Schwert; and R. Stambaugh. "Expected Stock Returns and Volatility." *Journal of Financial Economics* 19 (1987), pp. 3–29.

Garman, M., and S. Kohlhagen. "Foreign Currency Option Values." *Journal of International Money and Finance* 2 (1983), pp. 231–238.

General Accounting Office. *Financial Derivatives: Actions Needed to Protect the Financial System*. Washington D.C.: U.S. GAO, 1994.

Giovannini, A. and P. Jorion. "The Time-Variation of Risk and Return in the Foreign Exchange and Stock Markets." *Journal of Finance* 44 (1989), pp. 307–325.

Gluck, J. "Measuring and Controlling the Credit Risk of Derivatives." In *Derivatives Risk and Responsibility* eds. R. Klein and J. Lederman. Chicago, IL.: Irwin 1996.

Group of Thirty. *Derivatives: Practices and Principles*. New York: Group of Thirty, 1993.

Harlow, W. "Asset Allocation in a Downside Risk Framework." *Financial Analysts Journal* 47 (September 1991), pp. 28–40.

Hertsen, E. and P. Fields, eds. *Derivative Credit Risk*. London: Risk Publications, 1995.

Heston, S. "A Closed-Form Solution for Options with Stochastic Volatility with Applications to Bond and Currency Options." *The Review of Financial Studies* 6 (1993), pp. 327–343.

Hsieh, D. "The Statistical Properties of Daily Foreign Exchange Rates: 1974–1983." *Journal of International Economics* 24 (1988), pp. 129–145.

International Swap and Derivatives Association. *Public Disclosure and Risk Management Activities Including Derivatives.* New York: ISDA, 1995.

J. P. Morgan Bank. *RiskMetrics Technical Manual,* New York: J. P. Morgan Bank, 1995.

Jordan, J. and G. Morgan. "Default Risk in Futures Markets: The Customer-Broker Relationship." *Journal of Finance* 45 (1990), pp. 909–933.

Jorion, P. "Asset Allocation with Hedged and Unhedged Foreign Stocks and Bonds." *Journal of Portfolio Management* 15 (Summer 1989), pp. 49–54.

Jorion, P. "Predicting Volatility in the Foreign Exchange Market." *Journal of Finance* 50 (1995a), pp. 507–528.

Jorion, P. *Big Bets Gone Bad: Derivatives and Bankruptcy in Orange County.* San Diego: Academic Press 1995b.

Jorion, P. "Risk^2: Measuring the Risk in Value-At-Risk." *Financial Analysts Journal* (1996), in press.

Kendall, M. *Kendall's Advanced Theory of Statistics.* New York: Halsted Press 1994.

Klein, R. and J. Lederman, eds. *Derivatives Risk and Responsibility.* Chicago, IL.: Irwin, 1996.

Kupiec, P. "Techniques for Verifying the Accuracy of Risk Measurement Models." *Journal of Derivatives* 2 (December 1995), pp. 73–84.

Kupiec, P. and J. O'Brien. "A Pre-Commitment Approach to Capital Requirements for Market Risk." FEDS Working Paper No. 95–34. Washington, D.C.: Federal Reserve Board, 1995.

Longin, F. and B. Solnik. "Is the Correlation in International Equity Returns Constant: 1960–1990?" *Journal of International Money and Finance* 14 (1995), pp. 3–26.

Longstaff, F. and E. Schwartz. "Interest Rate Volatility and the Term Structure: A Two-Factor General Equilibrium Model." *Journal of Finance* 47 (1992), pp. 1259–1283.

Macaulay, F. *Some Technical Problems Suggested by the Movements of Interest Rates, Bond Yields and Stock Prices in the United States Since 1856.* New York: National Bureau of Economic Research, 1938.

Margrabe, W. "The Value of an Option to Exchange One Asset for Another." *Journal of Finance* 33 (1978), pp. 177–186.

Markowitz, H. *Portfolio Selection: Efficient Diversification of Investments.* New York: John Wiley, 1959.

McCulloch, H. "The Tax-Adjusted Yield Curve." *Journal of Finance* 30 (1975), pp. 811–829.

Merton, R. "Theory of Rational Option Pricing." *Bell Journal of Economics and Management Science* 4 (1973), pp. 141–83.

Merton, R. "On the Pricing of Corporate Debt: The Risky Structure of Interest Rates." *Journal of Finance* 29 (1974), pp. 449–470.

Merton, R. and P. Samuelson. "Fallacy of the Log-Normal Approximation to Portfolio Decision-Making over Many Periods." *Journal of Financial Economics* 1 (1974), pp. 67–94.

Miller, M. "Financial Innovations: The Last Twenty Years and the Next." *Journal of Financial and Quantitative Analysis* 21 (1986), pp. 459–471.

Moro, B. "The Full Monte." *Risk Magazine* 8 (February 1995), pp. 57–58.

Nelson, C. and A. Siegel. "Parsimonious Modeling of Yield Curves." *Journal of Business* 60 (1987), pp. 473–490.

Nelson, D. "ARCH Models as Diffusion Approximations." *Journal of Econometrics* 45 (1990), pp. 7–38.

Office of the Comptroller of the Currency. *Banking Circular BC–277: Risk Management of Financial Derivatives*. Washington, D.C.: Comptroller of the Currency, 1993.

Overdahl, J. and B. Schachter. "Derivatives Regulation and Financial Management: Lessons from Gibson Greetings." *Financial Management* 24 (1995), pp. 68–78.

Parkinson, M. "The Extreme Value Method for Estimating the Variance of the Rate of Return." *Journal of Business* 53 (1980), pp. 61–65.

Paskov, S. and J. Taub. "Faster Valuation of Financial Derivatives." *Journal of Portfolio Management* 22 (1995), pp. 113–120.

Pérold A. and E. Schulman. "The Free Lunch in Currency Hedging: Implications for Investment Policy and Performance Standards." *Financial Analysts Journal* 44 (May 1988), pp. 45–50.

Powers, M. "The Day the IMM Launched Financial Futures Trading." *Futures* (May 1992), pp. 52–58.

Rawnsley, J. *Total Risk : Nick Leeson and the Fall of Barings Bank*. New York: Harper, 1995.

Redington, F. "Review of the Principles of Life-Office Valuations." *Journal of the Institute of Actuaries* 78 (1952), pp. 286–340.

Sarig, O. and A. Warga. "The Risk Structure of Interest Rates." *Journal of Finance* 44 (1989), pp. 1351–1360.

Scott, D. *Multivariate Density Estimation: Theory, Practice and Visualization*. New York: John Wiley, 1992.

Sharpe, W. "Capital Asset Prices: A Theory of Market Equilibrium under Conditions of Risk." *Journal of Finance* 19 (1964), pp. 425–442

Shea, G. "Interest Rate Term Structure Estimation with Exponential Splines: A Note." *Journal of Finance* 40 (1985), pp. 319–325.

Shiller, R. and H. McCulloch. *The Term Structure of Interest Rates*. NBER Working Paper 2341. Cambridge, MA: NBER, 1987.

Silber, W. "Innovation, Competition and New Contract Design in Futures Markets." *Journal of Futures Markets* 1 (1981), pp. 123–156.

Smithson, C.; C. Smith; and S. Wilford. *Managing Financial Risk: A Guide to Derivative Products, Financial Engineering, and Value Maximization*. Chicago, IL: Irwin, 1995.

United States Congress. *Safety and Soundness Issues Related to Bank Derivatives Activities*. Washington, D.C.: U.S. Congress, 1993.

Vasicek, O. and G. Fong. "Term Structure Modeling Using Exponential Splines." *Journal of Finance* 37 (1982), pp. 339–348.

Wilson, T. "Debunking the Myths." *Risk* 7 (April 1994), pp. 67–72.

INDEX